Planning and Managing
School Facilities

D0169009

Planning and Managing School Facilities
SECOND EDITION

Theodore J. Kowalski

Bergin & Garvey
Westport, Connecticut • London

Library of Congress Cataloging-in-Publication Data

Kowalski, Theodore J.
    Planning and managing school facilities / Theodore J. Kowalski.—2nd ed.
        p. cm.
    Includes bibliographical references and index.
    ISBN 0–89789–770–6 (alk. paper)
    1. School facilities—United States—Planning.   2. School plant management—United
    States.   I. Title.
LB3218.A1K638   2002
371.6'8'0973—dc21   2001037652

British Library Cataloguing in Publication Data is available.

Library of Congress Catalog Card Number: 2001037652
ISBN: 0–89789–770–6

First published in 2002

Bergin & Garvey, 88 Post Road West, Westport, CT 06881
An imprint of Greenwood Publishing Group, Inc.
www.greenwood.com

Printed in the United States of America

∞™

The paper used in this book complies with the
Permanent Paper Standard issued by the National
Information Standards Organization (Z39.48–1984).

10 9 8 7 6 5 4 3 2 1

Contents

Part III: Completing a Facility Project

Part IV: Focused Issues

Preface

Planning and managing school facilities remains one of the most neglected areas of school administration. Yet, some practitioners have never even completed a separate course of study on these critical topics. This fact is astonishing in light of these facts:

- School buildings constitute multimillion dollar investments of public funds. New high schools in some parts of the country now have price tags exceeding $70 million.

- Administrators are expected to have the requisite knowledge and skills to facilitate planning and to manage buildings once they are constructed. And this knowledge base is getting larger each year.

- Many existing buildings are inadequate in light of changing curricula, instructional methods, and building codes. Decades of neglect, poor planning, cost-cutting, and deferred maintenance have contributed to the current crisis. Approximately half of America's school buildings need to be renovated or replaced. This problem extends from kindergarten to graduate and professional schools at some of the nation's most prestigious universities.

- There is substantial uncertainty regarding the nature of educational programming in just 15 or 20 years. Improperly planned schools could become obsolete well before their intended life spans.

Because of these and other evolving conditions, learning to plan and manage facilities on the job through trial and error has become a most precarious practice.

Over the next few decades, district and school administrators must shoulder three critical responsibilities if this nation's facility crisis is to be eradicated. First, these leaders must inform the public about the importance of educational facilities, especially in light of America's transition into an age of information. Second, they must facilitate planning processes that identify real needs and lead to sound decisions. Third, they must effectively communicate a rationale for recommended projects to the entire community to ensure economic and political support. These tasks require considerable knowledge regarding designing, funding, and operating large complex buildings. Unfortunately, when confronted with their first facility project, some superintendents have discovered, painfully, that they were not prepared adequately to assume these responsibilities.

This book addresses both planning and management. The intent is to provide a knowledge base for both educators and others involved in facility projects. The content is especially important for aspiring and practicing administrators. Planning is discussed from the perspective of individual facility projects as well as more comprehensive efforts, such as district-wide strategic planning. The concept of facility adequacy is defined within a systems framework; the various inputs, treatments, and outputs of the system are discussed. Particular attention is given to community-based planning, alternative planning paradigms, and the interface of district conditions and planning models.

The management of existing facilities is a topic that has been ignored even more than planning in the professional literature. This book addresses the responsibilities associated with managing school buildings from two perspectives: the district program and the individual school program. Practical examples are provided to help both superintendents and principals develop effective maintenance and custodial programs.

This edition includes several new chapters. One of them (Chapter 7) addresses public opinion polling. As school facility planning becomes increasingly political, this activity is being used to ascertain taxpayer sentiments. Professor Thomas Glass from the University of Memphis provided guidance for the development of this chapter. Another new chapter (Chapter 12), written by Professor T.C. Chan, examines administrator relationships with state and local government agencies during facility planning. This chapter provides many useful insights about being prepared to seek necessary approvals and to take advantage of available government resources.

Appreciation is expressed to Tina Strasburger, my office assistant, and to Rochonda Nenonene, my doctoral assistant. Both of them provided a great deal of help in preparing this edition. I also thank my partner in K & M Planning Consultants, Dr. Alex C. Moody, and the many fine administrators who have shared their valuable experiences with me over the years.

PART I

Historical and Contemporary Perspectives

CHAPTER 1

Importance of School Facilities

Beginning in the late 1980s, several national reports warned policy makers, educators, and the public of the fact that approximately half of the elementary and secondary schools in American needed to be replaced or renovated. Studies, such as *Wolves at the Schoolhouse Door* (Lewis, 1989), *Schoolhouse in the Red* (American Association of School Administrators, 1991), and *School Facilities: America's Schools Report Differing Conditions* (General Accounting Office, 1996), initially received considerable media attention. In addition to providing relevant statistics, these reports suggested that education reform would be stalled if problems with outdated, unsafe, and inflexible instructional environments were not addressed. The school facility crisis exists at a time when changing economic, political, social, and technological conditions make instructional environments more essential than ever. Even sound, relatively new buildings often require some reshaping to accommodate emerging instructional paradigms and modern communication systems. As a result, responsibility of planning and managing school facilities has become an even more important element of effective practice for both district-level and school-level administrators.

This book focuses on school administrator responsibilities associated with school buildings. These duties extend beyond the obvious functions of planning a new school to include other tasks such as political leadership, economic planning, and sound management. This introductory chapter traces how school facility administration has evolved over time. While early schools were merely intended to be shelters, today's buildings are expected to be modern, accessible, inviting, flexible, durable, and efficient. Consequently, new schools are expensive, and gaining necessary political and economic support can be one of the most difficult challenges an administrator will ever face. The stakes also are high for the community, because these structures reflect a community's priorities and commitments to future generations (Boyer, 1989). Given this importance, this chapter also examines the scope of responsibilities facing contemporary practitioners.

EVOLUTION OF SCHOOL FACILITIES

The design and size of school buildings have evolved over time. Many of the improvements reflected advancements in pedagogy, technology, and knowledge about environmental effects on learning. In ancient times, education was a much more informal activity than it is today and the physical setting for education was not considered important. Instruction usually occurred in open spaces or in structures designed for purposes other than teaching and learning. In Greece, for example, instruction was often conducted in open-air classrooms and in temples. The Romans also conducted school in unadorned environments, such as the veranda—essentially an outdoor shelter—and the taberna—a simple lean-to located off a street (Brubaker, 1947).

The earliest schools in this country indicate that Americans also believed that the setting in which education occurred was of little consequence. This philosophy was visible in both school buildings and their locations. The structures were typically plain, constructed from wood, and intended to protect their occupants from the elements. They were usually built on wasteland or dusty crossroads that were not desirable for farming. Describing these earliest schools, Brubaker (1947) wrote, "Ceilings were low; ventilation bad; lighting unsatisfactory; heating uneven; and sanitary arrangements often unmentionable" (p. 594).

Very few architects were available to assist with the planning and construction of schools in the early settlements. And even if they had been present, the educational philosophy of the colonials suggests that their services would not have been used. Most American settlers were self-governing adventurers not prone to seeking advice for tasks they believed could be mastered independently (Brooks, Conrad, & Griffith, 1980). In addition, many of the earliest schools were private institutions not subjected to the scrutiny of public officials. Known as one-room schoolhouses, many of these structures located in rural areas remained in use prior to World War II. At the beginning of the 20th century, however, larger and more complex schools started to be built. The evolution of the American schoolhouse over the past 100 years—from simple shelter to multimillion dollar structures—was shaped by many conditions.

FACTORS AFFECTING THE SIZE AND DESIGN OF
SCHOOL BUILDINGS

The movement from one-room schoolhouses to multimillion dollar high schools was incremental. Changes occurred for at least 125 years, and the more relevant factors contributing to more sophisticated instructional environments are summarized here.

Urbanization

Circa 1900, industrialization contributed to the development of large cities. The creation of manufacturing jobs prompted people to relocate from rural areas and it encouraged millions of immigrants to seek a better life in this country. As more and more families located in and around major cities, enrollment in elementary and secondary education in those communities surged. Two important organizational concepts for public education emerged from this rapid growth. One was the separation of elementary and secondary schools; the other was the configuration of school districts.

With large numbers of students to educate and prompted by the goal of efficiency, schools in big cities were divided into grammar schools (up to 8th grade) and high schools (grades 9 to 12). This division of students by age permitted a level of instructional specialization not previously possible in the one-room schoolhouse. It also permitted school buildings to be more responsive to the physical and educational needs of the student population being served. Over time, grammar school and high school buildings became distinctively different. For example, high schools were typically larger and provided more special instructional areas.

Having multiple schools in a local district presented new challenges. School boards rather than township trustees governed city districts, and this arrangement encouraged the creation of the position of school superintendent. As the school systems became larger, additional administrators were employed to assist superintendents with district-wide duties. This staffing pattern permitted and encouraged administrators to specialize in areas such as curriculum planning, supervision, and business management. Central office administrators often played pivotal roles in facility decisions. Their responsibilities in this area included:

- Identifying needs
- Analyzing possible solutions and making recommendations to the school board
- Detailing how facilities would be used
- Providing maintenance

By the 1920s, several of the large city school systems became the lighthouses of public education, and their school buildings became the trendsetters of their day. School officials across the country tried to emulate the practices that were emerging in these districts.

State Regulation

State departments of education also played a critical role in developing a new posture toward educational settings. Prior to the 20th Century these agencies exercised little control over local schools. But the passage of compulsory attendance laws and curriculum mandates (laws or state policies requiring that certain subjects be taught) created a need for both regulation and coordination. These requirements were used to advance the common school concept. The intent was to provide students in a state with a uniform set of educational experiences (Spring, 1994). In order to accomplish this goal, the state would have to oversee the instructional activities taking place in local districts.

With respect to school facilities, the involvement of state departments of education was gradual and less than uniform. Prevalent functions included providing technical assistance to local districts and developing rules or guidelines for school construction (e.g., site size and the size of instructional spaces). Tensions between state control and local autonomy were often heightened by state interventions into school construction. Local officials often resented state officials mandating specifications, especially in situations in which the state assumed none of the fiscal burden for school construction. But despite such objections, many (but not all) state departments of education eventually exercised substantial authority with regard to regulating school building designs and construction. In addition, state departments of education often were able to influence the policy positions of governors and legislators.

State government also became involved with school construction more generally by virtue of health and safety codes. The passage of state hygiene laws, for example, had a profound effect on school building design in the early 1900s (Teeple, 1993). Today, projects proposed by school officials must meet a myriad of state and federal standards ranging from fire safety to air quality to access for the disabled.

The extent of state control over school facility projects varies across the 50 states. Differences in state constitutions and differences in educational philosophy are responsible. The latter is commonly expressed politically, as state policy makers and voters place varying levels of importance on three national values: adequacy, liberty, and equality (see Figure 1–1). In relation to school facilities, adequacy addresses the issue of acceptable minimum standards for educational environments. States neither define adequacy nor evaluate whether districts achieve it uniformly. This is because adequacy can be defined and measured in three essential ways:

- Using inputs (for example, ensuring adequacy by requiring minimum classroom sizes)

- Using process (for example, judging adequacy by the degree to which a facility accommodates the curriculum)

Figure 1–1
National Values Influencing the Evolution of School Facilities

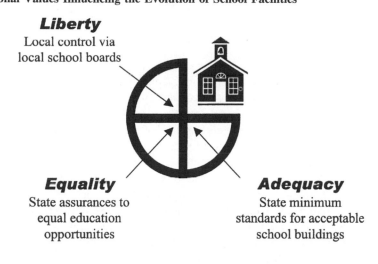

Liberty
Local control via
local school boards

Equality
State assurances to
equal education
opportunities

Adequacy
State minimum
standards for acceptable
school buildings

- Using outputs (for example, judging the adequacy of a building by student achievement scores)

Critics who continue to argue that school buildings are relatively unimportant to the overall educational process often use selected output data to defend their position.

While liberty encourages local-district autonomy, equality encourages state intervention in an effort to neutralize differences in local-district needs (e.g., number of students requiring special education) and wealth (e.g., differences in property tax values). Thus, these two values are basically incompatible. The states differ substantially in their treatment of them, and this variability is most visible in state funding plans for capital outlay. For example, seven states provide no fiscal support for local-district construction. They tend to be predominantly rural and have large numbers of small local districts—conditions that favor liberty over equality. At the other end of the spectrum, some states provide substantial support in an effort to nullify wealth-based disparities among local districts (i.e., differences in the amount of taxable property supporting each student enrolled). Two states, Arizona and Hawaii, actually provide 100 percent state funding for school construction (Kowalski & Schmielau, 2001). Chapter 14 provides more complete data showing how states differ in their treatment of liberty and equality regarding school finance.

In summary, state governments have played an important role in shaping the condition of school buildings. However, the extent to which the contributions have been positive varies from state to state. Discrepancies in the adequacy of school buildings are often rooted in philosophical dispositions that drive political decisions within a state. Thus, some states have high adequacy standards and contribute to equal educational opportunities by providing state assistance for construction—especially to low-wealth districts. Other states have low adequacy standards and provide no equalization for school construction.

Educational Philosophy

During the Industrial Revolution, public education policy was influenced by the widespread application of bureaucratic theory in manufacturing companies— a development that had a profound affect on the designs of school buildings. Many of the leading superintendents during that period embraced the principles of scientific management in an effort to achieve efficiency. Historian Raymond Callahan (1962) attributed their behavior to vulnerability; that is, he believed that superintendents during these formative years were politically helpless. Thus, board members, many of whom were captains of industry and influential patrons, were able to manipulate them. H. Warren Button (1991), however, argued that self-interests and not political weakness prompted administrators to impose bureaucratic theory on schools. And Spencer Maxcy (2000) has offered yet another perspective indicating that ideas of technical efficiency were embedded in American values long before the Industrial Revolution. While these scholars differ in their explanations of when and why scientific management became a part of school administration, they uniformly acknowledge that administrators commonly pursued the rational and efficient organization.

In the early 1900s, the prototype urban school was a two- or three-story building with dozens of identical classrooms lined on both sides of the corridors. In many ways, the structures looked like factories, and these structures were often called "egg crates." Although they were certainly safer and more diverse than wooden one-room structures, little attention was given to aesthetics and congruence between form and function.

A more positive shift in educational philosophy emanated from a combination of pragmatic considerations and professional inquiry. In the early 1900s, elementary and secondary education was affected by a rapidly expanding knowledge base. Observing the acceleration of change around them, forward-thinking educators during the early 1900s concluded that a student's fundamental education would have to go beyond the traditional three "Rs." They proposed that other subjects, such as health education and physical education, should become staples of the common public-school curriculum. Trade and industrial education also were emphasized, and this led to the development of vocational education. High schools, in particular, increased in size and special spaces for instruction were added; science laboratories, shop areas for industrial and vocational education, and music and art rooms are prime examples.

Research in disciplines such as educational psychology and sociology eventually revealed a linkage between the instructional environment and learning. The inclusion of these findings in professional journals prompted educators to promote schools that could accommodate specific teaching tasks and ensure that design features were congruent with the physical stature of the children. In fact, research provides considerable evidence that the physical environment affects student achievement and behavior (e.g., Bowers & Burkett, 1989; Burkhalter, 1983; Chan, 1988; Earthman & Lemasters, 1996; Greenwald, Hedges, & Laine, 1996). However, the idea that environmental factors (e.g., color scheme, lighting, and the like) influenced learning, was not accepted immediately. Historical depictions verify that until approximately 1950, the school building was given little consideration as a potential facilitator of effective teaching. After World War II and during the early 1960s, however, a nexus between environment and learning received wider acceptance. During that era, Leu (1965) wrote, "Recent school buildings reflect an increasing concern with the environmental effects of the physical space on teaching and learning. School buildings are being scaled to the ages, interests, and behavioral traits of children" (p. 5). Although educational practitioners now readily accept the importance of physical space, many taxpayers remain skeptical (Kowalski & Schmielau, 2001). Some modern-day remonstrators continue to view design features addressing the psychological, social, and emotional needs of students as frills.

Federal Government Intervention

The role of the federal government in the evolution of school facility planning has been limited but noteworthy. Politically, many Americans have resisted federal intervention in public elementary and secondary education for two reasons: there is no constitutional basis for federal involvement in public education and many believe that federal involvement will result in federal control. Resistance to federal intrusion continues as evidenced by Congress's rejection of President Clinton's proposal for massive school construction funding in the 1990s.

Significant federal involvement in school construction first occurred during a national economic crisis. During the great economic depression, the Public Works Administration played a direct role in funding school construction (Butts & Cremin, 1953). In an effort to create jobs during that troubled time, millions of federal dollars were made available for public school construction. These structures, some still standing today, were larger and sturdier than the one-room schoolhouses they replaced. Many included special-use areas, such as libraries, and special instructional areas, such as laboratories—spaces often omitted when local property taxes were the revenue source.

More recently, the federal government has influenced the design of schools through various laws establishing design requirements for public buildings. Access laws, such as Section 504 of the 1973 Rehabilitation Act, the 1990 Americans with Disabilities Act (ADA), the Individuals with Disabilities Education Act (IDEA), are prime examples. Such laws not only require school officials to ensure that new facilities are in compliance, but they also have required extensive modifications and improvements to older buildings.

School District Reorganization

One of the truly interesting evolutionary stages of school facilities occurred as a result of school district reorganization. In 1940, there were over 223,000 elementary and secondary schools in the United States. By 1977, this figure had fallen to 106,000 (Hentschke, 1986) and by 1998 the figure dropped even more to approximately 90,000 (*Digest of Education Statistics*, 1999). Reorganization resulted in mergers between very small, often single-township school districts in rural areas. A need for broader secondary school curricula, and the conviction that larger school districts would operate more efficiently, influenced the reorganization movement. The possibility for further consolidation still exists: During the 1997–1998 school year, over 1,700 of the nation's districts enrolled fewer than 150 students and almost half of the districts had fewer than 1,000 students (*Digest of Education Statistics*, 1999).

The union of small school systems gave birth to the need for larger and more modern school facilities, especially at the high school level. Post-reorganization, small, meager buildings were usually replaced by larger and more complex structures. These new schools could accommodate larger enrollments, and they allowed a more diversified curriculum to be implemented. In addition, many of the schools had to be designed to comply with recently developed state standards. In essence, reorganization affected rural schools much in the same way that urbanization and rapid growth affected city districts previously (Kowalski, 1999).

In many parts of the country, reorganization remains a controversial topic. In the past, some taxpayers resisted the movement because they viewed it as a loss of liberty; others argued that bigger schools would be less effective and would breed discipline problems. Even today, the debate continues relative to whether bigger is better. In this vein, Allen Ornstein (1989) wrote:

One can make a case for either large or small school districts. I do think, however, more people who attended small schools, if surveyed, would prefer to repeat their experiences as opposed to people who attended large schools. (pp. 42–43)

The purpose here is not to argue the merits of large schools, but rather to point out that school reorganization influences the size of schools, the scope of educational programming, and, ultimately, the design of buildings.

Several rural states, such as Nebraska, continue to operate hundreds of local districts with fewer than 500 pupils. The lack of reorganization in a state is often reflected in the types of school buildings that remain in use. Reorganized districts are larger, and, therefore, they almost always serve more diverse populations. Hence, differences of opinions about the importance of education, the need for a broad curriculum, and the importance of physical learning environments are more diverse—a condition that circuitously attenuates arguments for keeping outdated, small school buildings.

Inclusion of School Facility Planning and Management

As the need to improve the quantity and quality of school buildings increased, professors of school administration paid increasing attention to preparing their students for this important management task. Some preparation programs treated the responsibility as an extension of business management; others developed an entirely new course devoted to facility-related topics. Perhaps most important, graduate programs in school administration encouraged faculty and students to pursue research in this area; and the products of these efforts have contributed to the quality of schoolhouses.

Currently, the endeavors of both professors and practitioners in the area of school facility planning are evident through several national associations. The American Association of School Administrators (AASA), for example, includes an architectural exhibit and selected programs on school buildings at its annual convention. The Association of School Business Officials (ASBO) regularly publishes articles and research on this topic in its publications. The Council of Educational Facility Planners International (CEFPI) is an organization devoted entirely to improving the quality of school buildings throughout the world. It brings together educators and other professionals interested in this vital task.

Both through academic programs and through professional associations, the recognition of school facility planning as an essential element of school administration has had a positive effect on improving learning conditions for students in this country. Many school districts now retain professors who specialize in this area to conduct feasibility studies and performance specifications for proposed projects.

Involvement of Architects

One of the most significant variables responsible for changing values related to school design was the inclusion of architects in the planning process. These professionals contributed both scientific knowledge and artistic talent. In particular, they educated school administrators about the value of aesthetics, functionality, and flexibility. In addition, architects often influenced legislation concerning school buildings: laws and policies in areas such as building codes, safety standards, and site size.

The professional stature of architects was especially meaningful in removing two traditional barriers to effective school buildings. One was ignorance about the importance of a physical environment on human behavior; the other was an obsession with frugality. Their involvement had the effect of raising debates on design issues above the level of petty politics. Self-centered taxpayers, who boasted that they knew more about construction than did school administrators, often were reluctant to challenge the knowledge of architects in the same way. Today, school design is a specialized area of practice, and the American Institute of Architects (AIA) maintains a separate committee to address this task.

Technology

The rapid development of technology after World War II also contributed to a changing attitude about school buildings. The effects of technology on the evolution of school facilities have been most visible in two areas. First, technology was responsible for the development of better and safer building materials; for example, brick and mortar eventually replaced wood as the customary building material for schools. Modern school buildings are now equipped with highly sophisticated monitoring systems that contribute to safety, energy efficiency, and long-term maintenance.

Second, technology revolutionized instruction in most schools. Beginning as early as the 1950s, forward-thinking designers included audiovisual areas in schools to accommodate the storage of movie projectors and tape recorders. Later, the traditional school library was reconceptualized as a media center. Clearly, the introduction of audiovisual equipment was a discernable step toward closer ties between school design and instructional practices. And the influence of technology on how schools are built and used is accelerating. Prior to 1980, the personal computer was rarely found in schools; today, hundreds of them are scattered across classrooms, laboratories, and offices. Other new technologies, such as fax machines, visual information systems, and electronic classrooms, also required new design approaches for lighting, electricity, and security.

The Courts

State supreme courts have become another critical variable in the evolution of school facilities over the past few decades. Until the mid-1980s, school finance litigation largely ignored disparities in school buildings. However, a 1984 West Virginia case, *Pauley v. Bailey*, broadened judicial interpretations of equal educational opportunity to intentionally include facilities (Thompson, Wood, & Honeyman, 1994). More recently, three other state supreme courts have found inequities in school facilities to be relevant factors in determining the constitutionality of finance statutes—Tennessee: *Tennessee Small School Systems v. McWerter* (1993); Arizona: *Roosevelt Elementary School District 66 v. Bishop* (1994); and Ohio: *DeRolph v. State* (1997).

Litigation is likely to have a profound effect on school facilities in many states. By stressing equalization, the courts make it more likely that state government will become involved in funding and controlling construction projects. In addition, decisions in these lawsuits serve to clarify definitions of adequacy. In light of the nation's critical need to address thousands of facility projects, the proclivity of the courts to intervene in equality issues pertaining to school buildings may well prove to be one of the most critical variables determining the scope and quality of school construction in the 21st century.

WHY STUDY SCHOOL FACILITY PLANNING AND MANAGEMENT?

Over the past two decades, there has been a trend toward treating leadership and administration as if they were synonymous. More precisely, both leadership and management are essential components of administration. The former relates to decisions about what should be done and the mobilization of individuals and groups toward successful implementation; the latter pertains to how things should get done to ensure compliance and efficiency (Kowalski & Reitzug, 1993). An administrator's responsibilities in the area of school facilities include both functions. For example, a superintendent should play a pivotal role in identifying and recommending the need for a new school or a renovation project (a leadership function). The superintendent also is responsible for the proper maintenance and operation of facilities (a management function).

Compared to other elements of administrative practice—areas such as law, finance, and community relations—schoolhouse planning has generally received limited attention. For instance, some states do not require study in this area as a prerequisite for an administrative license, and some departments of educational administration generally ignore this responsibility in their curricula. The notion was principals and superintendents would learn how to manage facilities through on-the-job experience. Today, this idea is indefensible. Without foundational knowledge, an administrator is not likely to benefit from experience.

When school boards are asked to commit millions of dollars to construction projects, the potential for conflict and even legal problems are considerable. Essentially because school buildings have become larger, more complex, and more costly over the past 100 years, administrators commonly discover that they must devote considerable time to this single responsibility. Often a superintendent's reputation, if not career, has been affected by the outcomes of a facility project.

As noted earlier, administrative responsibilities in the area of school facilities are broad. Basically they can be summarized in five areas: data management, planning, problem solving, political and economic decisions, and evaluation (see Figure 1–2). These duties involve both assessment and evaluation; they require both leadership and management; and they necessitate both professional and political skills. Also noteworthy is the fact that the context for performing these duties has changed in most districts. The practice of the school board and superintendent making decisions about buildings in secrecy has basically disappeared. In a political environment emphasizing decentralization and shared governance, administrators must often inform and influence large, diverse committees. The good news is that these expanded expectations come at a time when technology permits practitioners to access and use information and to communicate quickly and easily.

The scope of knowledge and skills in school facility planning and manage-

Figure 1–2
Administrator Responsibilities in Modern Practice

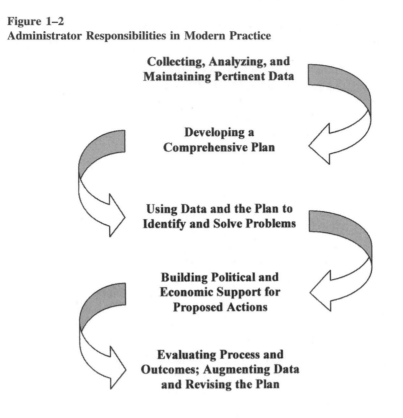

Collecting, Analyzing, and
Maintaining Pertinent Data

Developing a
Comprehensive Plan

Using Data and the Plan to
Identify and Solve Problems

Building Political and
Economic Support for
Proposed Actions

Evaluating Process and
Outcomes; Augmenting Data
and Revising the Plan

ment also can be viewed through six frames of practice. These frames, shown in Figure 1–3, include:

- *A Professional Domain.* The administrator is expected to infuse pedagogy into decisions about the size and nature of spaces provided for education. Knowledge about teaching and learning is fundamental.

- *An Economic Domain.* The administrator is expected to provide recommendations about the allocation of scarce resources and the efficient maintenance of those investments. Knowledge about public-sector economy, debt management, and construction costs is fundamental.

- *A Political Domain.* The administrator is expected to provide leadership and conflict-management skills in relation to competition for scarce resources. Knowledge about political behavior, coalition building, and compromise is fundamental.

- *A Cultural Domain.* The administrator is expected to provide leadership that expresses the values and beliefs of the community and the profession. Knowledge about organizational culture and symbolic behavior is fundamental.

- *A Social Domain.* The administrator is expected to make decisions that are beneficial to community and student development. Issues such as the location of schools and

Figure 1–3
Frames of Administrator Involvement in Facility Planning and Management

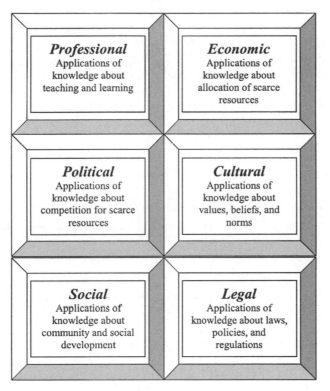

Professional Applications of knowledge about teaching and learning	*Economic* Applications of knowledge about allocation of scarce resources
Political Applications of knowledge about competition for scarce resources	*Cultural* Applications of knowledge about values, beliefs, and norms
Social Applications of knowledge about community and social development	*Legal* Applications of knowledge about laws, policies, and regulations

community access to schools relate to this frame. Knowledge about social behavior, communities, and social development is fundamental.

- *A Legal Domain.* The administrator is expected to make decisions that comply with laws and policies governing the construction of public buildings. Knowledge of pertinent laws, policies, and regulations is fundamental.

Collectively, these domains demonstrate the complexity and importance of the responsibility.

CHAPTER SUMMARY

The modern elementary or secondary school is a far cry from the bleak and unadorned one-room schoolhouse. This chapter examined variables that contributed to that evolution. They include the development of school districts in large cities, the involvement of state government, changes in educational philosophy, federal interventions, school-district reorganization, the study of facilities within educational administration, and the influence of architects, technology, and litigation. In addition, the need to study school facility planning was addressed in the context of the responsibility's growing complexity.

This book is intended to provide foundational knowledge in school facility planning and management. The remaining two chapters in Part I address variables currently shaping decisions about school buildings and the attributes of an effective school. Part II is devoted to assessing needs and initiating planning. Part III focuses on responsibilities associated with completing a facility project, including a summary of space needs for elementary and secondary schools. Part IV addresses focused issues such as technology and building maintenance.

ISSUES FOR DISCUSSION

1. In what ways were the earliest schools in this country different from those that now exist?

2. How did urbanization affect the evolution of school buildings?

3. What role does the Department of Education in your state play in school facility planning and management? Do you think this role is appropriate and sufficient?

4. What is meant by "equal access to educational opportunities?" Why should states be concerned with this concept? How do school facilities relate to this concept?

5. Some critics of education continue to argue that schools should operate as businesses. How has this argument affected the design of school buildings during the past century?

6. To what extent has school construction been a political issue in your school district? What are some possible reasons why some communities support school construction while others do not?

7. School buildings vary in size and quality. What are some possible reasons for variance within a state? What are some possible reasons for variance among states?

8. In what ways are school administrators expected to be politically effective when dealing with school facility issues?

9. How has school district reorganization affected the evolution of school facility designs?

10. In your state, what variables appear to have been most influential in determining the adequacy of educational facilities?

11. Why are the values of liberty and equality usually incompatible?

REFERENCES

American Association of School Administrators. (1991). *Schoolhouse in the red: A national study of school facilities and energy use.* Arlington, VA: Author.

Bowers, J., & Burkett, C. (1989). Effects of physical and school environment on students and faculty. *Educational Facility Planner, 27*(1), 28–29.

Boyer, E. (1989). Buildings reflect our priorities. *Educational Record, 70*(1), 24–27.

Brooks, K., Conrad, M., & Griffith, W. (1980). *From program to educational facilities.*

Lexington: Center for Professional Development, College of Education, University of Kentucky.

Brubaker, J. (1947). *A history of the problems of education.* New York: McGraw-Hill.

Burkhalter, B.B. (1983). Impact of physical environment on academic achievement of high school youth. *CEFP Journal, 21*(2), 21–23.

Button, H.W. (1991). Vulnerability: A concept reconsidered. *Educational Administration Quarterly, 27*(3), 378–391.

Butts, R. & Cremin, L. (1953). *A history of education in America.* New York: Henry Holt. and Company.

Callahan, R. (1962). *Education and the cult of efficiency.* Chicago: University of Chicago Press.

Chan, T.C. (1988). The aesthetic environment and student learning. *School Business Affairs, 54*(1), 26–27.

DeRolph v. State, 78 Ohio St. 3d 193 (Oh. 1997).

Digest of education statistics. (1999). Washington, DC: National Center for Education Statistics, U.S. Department of Education.

Earthman, G., & Lemasters, L. (1996, October). *Review of research on the relationship between school buildings, student achievement, and student behavior.* Paper presented at the annual meeting of the Council of Educational Facilities Planners, International, Tarpon Springs, FL.

General Accounting Office. (1996). *School facilities: America's schools report differing conditions.* Washington, DC: U.S. Government Printing Office.

Greenwald, R., Hedges, L.V., & Laine, R.D. (1996). The effect of school resources on student achievement. *Review of Educational Research, 66*(3), 361–396.

Hentschke, G. (1986). *School business administration: A comparative perspective.* Berkeley, CA: McCutchan.

Kowalski, T.J. (1999). *The school superintendent: Theory, practice, and cases.* Upper Saddle River, NJ: Merrill, Prentice-Hall.

Kowalski, T.J., & Reitzug, U.C. (1993). *Contemporary school administration: An introduction.* New York: Longman.

Kowalski, T.J. & Schmielau, R.E. (2001). Liberty provisions in state policies for financing school construction. *School Business Affairs, 67*(4), 32–37.

Leu, D. (1965). *Planning educational facilities.* New York: Center for Applied Research in Education.

Lewis, A. (1989). *Wolves at the schoolhouse door: An investigation of the condition of public school buildings.* Washington, DC: American Education Writers Association.

Maxcy, S.J. (2000, April). *Leadership clones, copies, and mutations: Scientific management and leadership philosophy in educational administration.* Paper presented at the annual conference of the American Educational Research Association, New Orleans, LA.

Ornstein, A. (1989). Controversy over size continues. *The School Administrator, 46*(4), 42–43.

Pauley v. Bailey, 324 S.E. 2d 128 (W. Va. 1984).

Roosevelt Elementary School District 66 v. Bishop, 179 Ariz. 233, 877 P. 2d 806 (Ariz. 1994).

Spring, J. (1994). *American education* (6th ed.). New York: McGraw-Hill.

Teeple, L.J. (1993). *Historical development of selected design amenities in central In-*

diana rural school buildings, 1875–1915. Unpublished master's thesis, Ball State University, Muncie, IN.

Tennessee Small School Systems v. McWerter. 851 S.W. 2d 139 (Tenn. 1993).

Thompson, D.C., Wood, R.C., & Honeyman, D.S. (1994). *Fiscal leadership for schools: Concepts and practices*. New York: Longman.

CHAPTER 2

Contemporary Issues

School administration is a profession guided by a professional knowledge base and accumulated wisdom shared among practitioners. In this vein, it is similar to other recognized professions such as law and medicine. Superintendents, business managers, and principals, however, apply their professional knowledge and skills in political contexts (especially those who are public school employees), and this condition makes their work rather unique when compared to other professionals (Wirt & Kirst, 1997). For example, when educational leaders get involved with facility projects, they must intertwine their professional knowledge with economic and political realities (see Figure 2–1). These conditions might include dealing with factions holding opposing views on tax increases or seeking approval for a badly needed construction project in a district that already has a high tax rate.

This chapter examines the condition of school facilities in the United States and the context in which administrators are expected to provide effective facility planning and management. Together, the information discussed in relation to these two topics provides insights into two recurring queries: Why is there a need to improve or replace nearly half of the nation's schools? Why is it often extremely difficult to gain support for school facility projects?

CURRENT CONDITION OF AMERICA'S PUBLIC SCHOOLS

The obvious reasons for America's current school facility crisis are outdated, poorly constructed, and poorly maintained buildings. As noted in the previous chapter, several national studies have documented the extent to which many

Figure 2–1
Elements of Facility Decisions

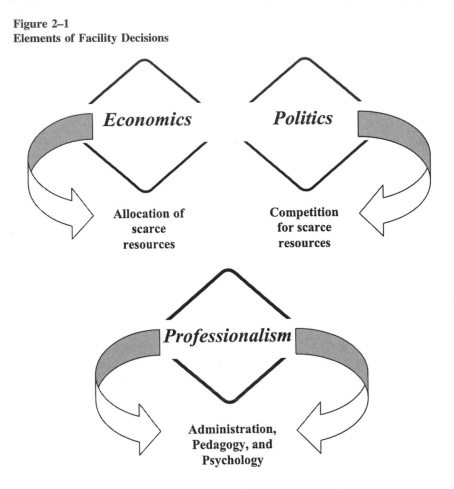

schoolhouses have become unsafe and ineffectual. The first of these, *Wolves at the Schoolhouse Door* (Lewis, 1989) included these primary findings:

- One-fourth of the nation's school buildings was inadequate; they were shoddy places for learning because they lacked sufficient space, suitability, safety, and maintenance for their occupants.

- Among the inadequate buildings, 43 percent were obsolete, 42 percent had environmental hazards, 25 percent were overcrowded, and 13 percent were structurally unsound.

- One in three school buildings were only marginally adequate and they were expected to become inadequate if problems associated with deferred maintenance were not addressed.

This study also reported that 61 percent of the nation's schools had been constructed during the 1950s and 1960s—"generally a time of rapid and cheap construction" (Lewis, 1989, p. 2).

A few years later two other national studies confirmed the findings reported in *Wolves at the Schoolhouse Door*. The first, sponsored by the American Association of School Administrators (AASA; 1991), indicated that one in eight buildings nationwide failed to provide an environment conducive for learning; and in rural areas, the figure was estimated to be as high as one in four. The second, sponsored by the General Accounting Office (GAO; 1996), found that (a) one-third of all students received instruction in buildings in need of extensive repair or outright replacement and (b) almost 60 percent of the schools reported at least one major building feature that required extensive repair or replacement. The estimated cost for addressing these problems (in 1995 dollars) was approximately $112 billion.

Reports about the poor conditions of America's school buildings are not surprising in light of the age of existing schoolhouses. Consider the following statistics reported by the U.S. Department of Education (1996):

- The average age of a school building in this country in 1995 was about 42 years.
- Nearly one-third of the schools was constructed prior to 1950; almost half were built between 1950 and 1969; and only 10 percent have been built since 1985.
- The oldest schools are most likely to be found in districts with high concentrations of students living in poverty.
- Nearly three-fourths of the schools have had at least one major renovation.

In his 1997 State of the Union Address, President Clinton proposed that Congress approve massive federal spending to assist states and local districts in addressing their facility needs. His proposal included $1.3 billion for loans and grant programs and $24.8 billion for new construction and renovation. Many legislators rejected his proposal on the grounds that the federal government had no legitimate responsibility to fund school construction. While strong political differences continue to cast a cloud over federal funding for school construction, the mere suggestion of massive federal intervention serves to frame the severity of this problem.

The types of deficiencies found in school buildings range from structural problems to poor air quality to inadequate size to an inability to accommodate instructional programs. Often, the typical taxpayer evaluates a facility very narrowly—usually on the basis of its external appearance. When the outer shell of a building is the sole criterion, many schools are wrongly categorized as being adequate. Narrow perspectives of adequacy partially explain why the general public is often skeptical when district administrators claim that there is a need for construction projects.

CURRENT CLIMATE OF FACILITY DECISIONS

A mixture of contextual variables is shaping public policy on education and the future direction of school facility planning. These variables include social change, political tensions, educational reform, technology, legal issues, economic issues, and uncertainty. A review of these variables reveals the reasons why groups and individuals may express different and frequently opposing positions with respect to school construction projects.

Social Change

Demographic analysis (population studies) is one of the most important variables in school facility planning. After World War II, many new schools were built to accommodate a rapidly growing student population—a group often referred to as "baby boomers." The upward enrollment trend peaked in 1971 when 51.5 million students were enrolled in elementary and secondary schools (National Center for Educational Statistics, 1997). In addition to growing numbers of students, population shifts among and within states, caused by the development of suburbs or the relocation of industries, created challenges for school officials from approximately 1950 to 1980.

Current projections indicate that enrollment in elementary and secondary schools is expected to increase well into the 21st century. In 1995, 36.8 million students were enrolled in elementary and secondary schools, and this figure is expected to reach 54.3 by 2007 (National Center for Educational Statistics, 1997). This projection suggests that many schools will have to be built in the next two decades just to accommodate enrollment growth. Equally important, much of the current population growth is occurring among minority groups. Thus, schools not only need to be designed to serve more students, they also need to be designed to serve a more diverse student population. Consider these evolving conditions that are certain to affect education policy in the next three or four decades:

- Approximately one-third of those attending school in the first quarter of the 21st century will be a racial or ethnic minority student.
- Approximately 20 percent of American children under the age of 18 already live in poverty, and the percentage is increasing.
- Approximately 60 percent of all African-American students live in one-parent families (National Center for Educational Statistics, 1997).
- Teen pregnancies, crime rates, and problems with illegal drug usage remain pervasive concerns.
- Many Hispanic children do not speak English, and large urban districts commonly face the challenge of having 40 to 50 different languages spoken by their students and parents (Glass, 2000).

• School districts within a state are often economically segregated causing substantial inequities among them in taxable wealth (Kowalski & Schmiclau, 2000).

The needs created by these conditions will make competition for scarce resources even more intense; and in states where all or most of the funding for school facilities must be generated from local taxes, the ability to fund school construction may well be diminished.

Another social issue affecting public education is school safety. Tragic shootings during the 1990s in cities such as Columbine, Colorado; Paducah, Kentucky; Flint, Michigan; Jonesboro, Arkansas; and Lake Worth, Florida, shocked America and brought to light a painful truth: Some school environments are dangerous. More than ever before educators and parents are asking: Can we have safer schools? While the actual influence of design on safety is still being debated, school facility experts agree that design is important to public perceptions of safety (Biehle, 2000). Consequently, school officials should expect to be questioned about environmental safety and crisis prevention in relation to proposed building projects. In many districts, adequate safety may require expensive and possibly distasteful features such as video surveillance systems and electronic access control systems. In all likelihood, security and safety will further increase the cost of improving and replacing school buildings.

The changing profile of America's population is another noteworthy social issue with facility planning implications. Most people do not realize that while school enrollment is increasing, so too is the average age of the country's population. These two trends are cogent for at least two reasons. First, districts in many communities need to build more schools at the same time that taxpayers are expecting broader community services. For example, most districts anticipate that demands for adult education, recreation programs, and services for the elderly (e.g., providing meal programs) will continue to escalate during the first quarter of the 21st century. Second, a high percentage of taxpayers—as high as 90 percent in some districts—do not have children enrolled in the public schools. As school officials struggle to improve facilities, many non-parents will be reluctant to provide either political or economic support.

Political Tensions

In a democratic society, individuals commonly affiliate with groups in an effort to advance ideas and personal interests. Such political alignments are forged to influence all aspects of government, but they are especially prevalent at the local level. This is because public education remains one of society's most democratic institutions. School board members and district administrators are neighbors and friends, and unlike state or federal officials, they are accessible to most citizens. On the one hand, their availability in the local community is an asset because citizens have an opportunity to be heard. On the other hand,

Figure 2–2
Values Guiding Education Policy

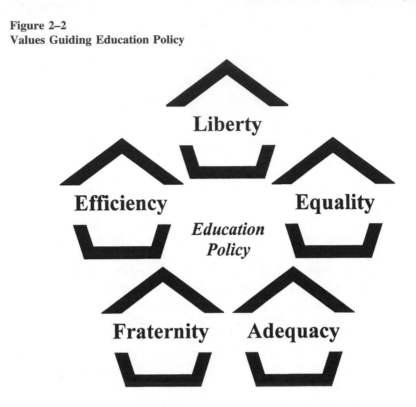

their availability encourages political action and spawns conflict as competing ideas and values surface.

Historically, education policy in the United States has been guided by five primary values (see Figure 2–2). *Liberty* is a deeply rooted principle in American society that basically refers to "the right to act as one chooses" (Swanson, 1989, p. 274). The centrality of this value is evidenced by the concept of local school boards, an organizational pattern for public education that is unique to the United States. With respect to school construction, liberty may be expressed in several ways:

- Allowing local school boards to determine the nature and scope of construction projects
- Allowing taxpayers to block a proposed project (e.g., remonstrance process)
- Requiring taxpayer approval of proposed projects (e.g., referenda)

Liberty, however, does not grant unrestricted powers to local districts. Typically, district-level decisions are subject to state review, especially when state government partially funds the cost of facility decisions.

Equality may be defined politically as the equal right to participate in a political system and economically to mean equal wealth (Fowler, 2000). In public education, the concept has been analyzed most often as equal opportunity. Crampton and Whitney (1996) concluded that if equality were defined as a fair and just method of distributing resources among public school students, it could be measured by variations in revenue and spending across local districts. In essence, an equitable state system would produce low or moderate variation in spending among local districts and minimal variations in the quality of school buildings.

Adequacy is a complex value that has two dimensions: setting state minimum standards and providing local districts the opportunity and incentives to exceed those standards. Policy makers and the courts have not uniformly treated one dimension as being more important than the other. In addition, judgments of adequacy have been based on varying criteria. Consider a legal judgment regarding the adequacy of a district's school buildings. As noted in the previous chapter, the decision could be based on any of the following:

- *Input Criteria.* Are the buildings adequate as evidenced by their cost and quality?
- *Process Criteria.* Are the buildings adequate as evidenced by the quantity and quality of the day-to-day experiences students have in them?
- *Output Criteria.* Are the buildings adequate as evidenced by learning gains after students have been educated in them?

These competing perspectives of adequacy increase conflict, because elements of the school community do not use uniform criteria to measure adequacy.

Efficiency pertains to the relationship between inputs and outputs. Typically, it is achieved in one of two ways: increasing outputs while holding inputs constant or holding outputs constant while decreasing inputs. In education, efficiency often is addressed through the concept of accountability (Swanson & King, 1997). In the case of school construction, taxpayers express their views about efficiency in different ways. For instance, some demand that taxes not be used to pay for frills, such as graphics in the hallways of an elementary school or a swimming pool in a middle school. Others argue that there is no evidence that high-cost facilities produce learning gains; hence, they believe that buildings should be low-cost structures or they demand that a building be used well beyond its intended life span. Others may have nearly opposite views; for example, they may define efficiency as an intricate mixture of learning opportunities and life-cycle costs.

Fraternity addresses the goal of developing a sense of community in a diverse society. Programs such as multicultural education are expressions of this value. Some aspects of facility decisions, such as drawing school boundaries, locating a school, or establishing the size of a school, often have fraternity implications. In this vein, the value of fraternity can play a pivotal role in facility planning and management.

While each of these values continues to guide educational policy, they are not necessarily compatible. As a result, administrators frequently face the persistent dilemma of trying to balance seemingly conflicting beliefs (Cuban, 1988). For example, liberty promotes local decision making; however, excessive liberty almost always leads to serious inequities among local districts. This is because affluent communities are usually more willing and able to generate and spend local tax dollars (Kowalski & Schmielau, 2000). Philosophical differences create political tensions as illustrated by the following additional examples.

- The General Assembly in a midwestern state recently enacted new laws governing school facility projects costing $2 million or more. All previous design regulations (e.g., minimum size for classrooms) were reduced to guidelines, and the property taxpayers were given the power to derail proposed projects via a petition process. Since the local tax generates about 90 percent of the needed revenue for school construction in this state, the new law is expected to widen inequities in the adequacy of school facilities across the state.

- Plans for a new urban high school came under attack because the specifications were based on a traditional curriculum that ignored many of the social, economic, and psychological problems faced by inner-city adolescents. The teachers' union charged that the school board and superintendent were controlled by pressure groups who opposed property tax increases and were indifferent to ensuring equal educational opportunities.

- Over the objections of the superintendent and principal, a rural school board eliminated the art room, the music room, and a science laboratory from a proposed elementary school. A group of angry farmers thought the cost of the proposed project was expensive; they threatened to oppose incumbent board members in the upcoming election unless the project's budget was reduced.

Resolving philosophically based conflict is often very difficult because people usually resist compromises that affect deeply held convictions.

As previously mentioned, fewer than 20 percent of the voters in many local districts have children enrolled in the public schools. Many senior citizens live on fixed incomes, own property, and express the view that students (and their parents) are the sole beneficiaries of public education. These beliefs have made it more difficult for school officials to gain broad-based support for initiatives requiring tax increases (Bauman, 1996). But opposition to raising taxes for school construction is by no means limited to senior citizens. Voters in all age and income brackets may oppose proposed construction projects for one or more of the following reasons.

- They simply act out of self-interest. If they believe that public education does not provide them with any benefits, they oppose tax increases.

- They believe that school buildings are inconsequential with respect to teaching and learning.

- They oppose certain aspects of proposed projects (e.g., the location of the building, the grade levels included in the building).
- They are misinformed or insufficiently informed about the need to improve facilities.

The potential for opposition exists in every district, and, therefore, superintendents should never assume that a proposed project would be approved without controversy. Accurately determining levels of support and opposition usually requires conscious efforts to scan the general community (e.g., conducting public opinion polls).

Educational Reform

Since the early 1980s, citizens representing every political persuasion have blamed public education for placing America at risk of losing its status as the world's most powerful nation. This is because most Americans continue to believe that there is a nexus between educational effectiveness and the condition of the country (Tyack & Cuban, 1995). But while critics agree that schools must improve, they disagree about the means for accomplishing this goal. Essentially, calls for reform have moved in two very different directions. One agenda has emphasized equality, postulating that all students must have a reasonable opportunity for success to compensate for a variety of social ills such as poverty, abuse, and dysfunctional homes. This position's advocates have had a greater influence on what actually occurs in schools. Included are most professional educators who commonly seek increased governmental support for public schools. The nearly opposite reform agenda postulates that schools are inefficient and insufficiently attentive to academic standards. This position's advocates have commonly included non-educators who are dominant in policy-making arenas (e.g., corporate executives and elected officials). These would-be reformers believe that public schools should be moved toward the market economy where "real" competition exists; hence, they call for alternative funding strategies such as vouchers, tax credits, and charter schools (Kowalski, 1999).

Ironically, critics at both ends of the political spectrum have generally supported the idea of improving schools through greater decentralization. That is, they believe that the authority to make certain decisions should be gradually shifted to individual schools. Concepts such as site-based management and school councils are reflective of this strategy. Decentralization is believed to produce three essential improvements: increasing organizational flexibility, using human resources more effectively, and making decisions closest to those affected (Certo, 1989). Although most reformers generally support the decentralization strategy, they disagree over its primary objectives. Those focusing on equal opportunities view local decision making as a way to respond more directly to students' needs; those focusing on greater efficiency view local decision making as a way to ensure greater accountability. As decentralization becomes more pervasive, new environmental requirements for schools can be expected.

As an example, greater policy independence for schools increases the need for highly flexible buildings, ensuring that the physical environment can accommodate sudden and dramatic program changes. In addition, policy-making activities at the school level require space. Many elementary schools, for instance, have not been designed with sufficient accommodations for such activities.

School reform also is broadening and revising traditional curricula and instructional practices. Consider the following examples:

- School buildings are increasingly being used during the summer months because of longer school years, remedial classes, and expanded community usage. As a result, specifications for climate control, even in northern states, are changing.

- Due to revised graduation requirements, many high schools are experiencing enrollment shifts, such as declines in home economics and art and increases in science and mathematics.

- In many high schools, industrial education has been transformed into industrial technology. This curriculum shift, reflective of America's movement into an information age, has made traditional shops (e.g., metal and wood shops) obsolete. At the same time, a need for new instructional areas, such as electronics labs, has been created.

Within the professional frame, theory and practice in educational administration and architecture also influence administrative decisions. Thought is given to the relationships between environment and learning, and effort is made to ensure that form is a product of intended function. Administrators also have a responsibility to provide a healthy environment, and in this regard, they consider issues such as air quality, hazardous materials (e.g., asbestos, radon), fire and disaster safety, and traffic patterns. The cultural dimensions of schooling are equally important. Here the administrator provides leadership to inform the school board and community about the symbolic nature of schools as expressions of community values and philosophy.

Technology

One of the most evident variables influencing facility decisions is technology. In less than 25 years, the personal computer has altered the way in which most teachers teach. Historically, teachers assumed a rather simple and direct role: They accumulated information and were expected to transmit that information to their students. This "bucket-filling" approach to education had two obvious imperfections. First, the amount of knowledge possessed by teachers was always limited if not outdated; second, teachers found it virtually impossible to keep updating their knowledge base. Largely because of computers and the Internet, the act of teaching is being revised. While teachers continue to provide content knowledge and to help students build basic skills, they also are focusing on the process of accessing and using information to identify and solve problems. For example, students studying social studies learn to use the Internet as a means for understanding state and local government agencies. As technology improves and becomes even more pervasive, teacher roles are expected to change even more. In the future, teachers may function largely as facilitators and evaluators. That is, they will direct students to learning resources, counsel them as they engage in independent learning, and evaluate learning outcomes.

Information-management systems and new communication technologies have already raised the threshold for school-building standards. For example, modern schools should have the capacity to send and receive programs via satellite or cable television for activities such as distance learning. Equipment such as fax machines and electronic mail are considered essential. And modern schools have systems that integrate voice, video, and data and deliver the products into all instructional areas. Design features, such as placing several computers in every instructional area and using raised floors to accommodate wires and cables, are now common (DeStefano, Van Hook, & Draht, 2000).

Legal Issues

The two most visible legal issues influencing school facility planning are challenges to state finance systems and federal and state legislation affecting the design of public buildings. In the past 30 years, lawsuits have helped to make the public more aware of inadequate and unequal facility conditions. As noted in the previous chapter, legal challenges to state finance programs for public education generally ignored the condition of school buildings. This changed, however, in 1984 when a West Virginia case, *Pauley v. Bailey*, served to broaden the judicial interpretation of equal educational opportunity to intentionally include facilities (Thompson, Wood, & Honeyman, 1994). Subsequently, three other state supreme courts also ruled that inequities in school facilities were relevant to determining the constitutionality of finance statutes—Tennessee: *Tennessee Small School Systems v. McWerter* (1993); Arizona: *Roosevelt Elementary School District 66 v. Bishop* (1994); and Ohio: *DeRolph v. State* (1997). Clearly, the fact that so many of the nation's schoolhouses are inadequate weighed on the minds of judges who ruled in these cases.

Much of the burden for resolving the nation's school facility crisis rests with state policy makers who ultimately have the responsibility to define adequacy and ensure equal access to educational opportunities (Kowalski, 1995). In many states, parents and educators are growing impatient as they are forced to live with the negative consequences of inadequate school buildings. For example, a unique lawsuit involving the adequacy and equality of school facilities was filed at the beginning of the new millennium in California. Plaintiffs charged that students in low-property-wealth districts often were forced to attend unclean and unsafe schools—a condition that restricted their educational opportunities. The plaintiffs further charged that the problem existed because California officials had not sufficiently compensated for disparities in local-district wealth (i.e., differences in taxable property). Many states actually lag behind California in dealing with issues of facility adequacy and equality (Kowalski & Schmielau, 2000), and, therefore, similar litigation is likely in other states unless poor schoolhouses are eradicated.

Federal and state statutes also influence decisions about school buildings. Starting with the Rehabilitation Act of 1973, several federal laws have addressed the civil rights of disabled citizens. Collectively, they specify that public buildings must be free of barriers that would deny access to disabled individuals. The most recent of these laws, the Americans with Disabilities Act (ADA), was enacted in 1990; it stipulates that students with disabilities will have the same access to transportation, school buildings, school experiences, and telecommunications as other students. Educational institutions fall under Title I, II, and III of the act (Otten, 1996). School districts not in compliance may be found to be violating the civil rights of covered individuals. All construction projects, including renovations, must be in compliance with the law; however, a school district is not required to make its existing facilities totally accessible if other steps can be taken to achieve compliance (Grubb, 1997).

The concept of a barrier-free environment pertains to the entire setting in which school programming occurs. All interior and exterior features of schoolhouses and support buildings (e.g., storage buildings) are included. Accordingly, sidewalks, parking lots, and playgrounds are as much a part of the school environment as is a classroom. To be in compliance, a school building must not have either architectural barriers (e.g., design or construction features) or equipment barriers (e.g., lab tables). Estimates suggest that ADA covers 10 to 12 percent of the population. Because of their implications for design and cost, requirements for barrier-free environments contribute to the political debates surrounding facility projects.

Economic Issues

In his insightful book, *Megatrends*, futurist John Naisbitt (1982) described the implications of America moving into an information age and global economy. At the time of the book's publication in the early 1980s, some new schools were still being designed without computer laboratories or provisions for using computers in classrooms. A year later, the National Commission on Excellence in Education (1983) published *A Nation at Risk*, a stinging report that argued that the poor quality of public education had jeopardized America's position as the world's economic leader. These publications reminded administrators that decisions for public education also should be guided by the goal of economic growth. That is, schools are expected to prepare individuals to be productive members of the workforce so that their collective efforts ensure the nation's economic growth (Swanson & King, 1997).

Although support for the educational goal of economic growth is wide, it has not produced a groundswell to improve the nation's school buildings. Why? Many citizens judge that proposed tax increases are either not necessary or not fair. The former is a philosophical issue predicated on the belief that school buildings have little effect on positive learning outcomes; the latter is an economic issue related to how individual taxpayers feel they are being treated. Two concerns are especially important with respect to perceptions of unfair treatment.

- From an economic perspective, capital development costs should have been shared by several generations of taxpayers so that no single generation assumed all or most of the burden. In some communities, however, large expenditures for school construction have been avoided for 30 or more years. In these situations, the last generation of taxpayers selfishly avoided paying for public education's infrastructure; and in so doing, they created an unfair burden for the current generation of taxpayers.

- In approximately 40 percent of the states, all or most of the revenues for financing capital outlay must be generated from the local property tax (Burrup, Brimley, & Garfield, 1999). Ever since the well publicized *Proposition 13* in California in the late 1970s, opposition to this unpopular tax has mounted. Large landowners, such as farmers, have generally argued that the economic burden for increased governmental services should be placed on income and sales and not wealth; tax reforms in Michigan during the 1990s reflect these sentiments. Administrators often find that there is a thin and indiscernible line between opposition to school construction and opposition to property taxes.

Uncertainty

Uncertainty is one of the greatest challenges for facility planners. No one can accurately predict how education will be delivered over the next 25 to 50 years because the rate change in American society and the world is accelerating. As noted, science and its applications (technology) already have had a profound effect on the work of teachers and on student experiences in schools. Since new school buildings are expected to last well over 50 years, how do educational administrators and architects deal with an unknown future?

There are two dimensions to dealing with uncertainty. Professionally, architects and school administrators approach this challenge by ensuring that buildings are both flexible and adaptable. These design attributes permit facilities to be reconfigured as new educational paradigms evolve. The second and more difficult dimension of coping with uncertainty involves an unwillingness to support school construction. Opponents of such projects often argue that uncertainty is a sufficient reason to avoid or delay needed construction; that is, they suggest that school officials should wait until future needs and programming are clearly known. This argument is predicated on the misguided assumption that complete and perfect information will be available at some time in the future. In truth, information will never be sufficiently comprehensive to guarantee foolproof decisions. Deferring needed construction almost always affects both educational programs and taxpayer costs negatively. Despite this fact, some opponents to school construction continue to use uncertainty as a powerful tool to advance their interests.

CHAPTER SUMMARY

Challenges facing the contemporary facility planner are framed by two conditions. The first is the current state of school facilities; nearly half of America's elementary and secondary schools either need to be replaced or renovated. Many of these inadequate buildings, constructed in the 1950s and 1960s, have been described as low-cost, low-life-expectancy buildings. As administrators seek to deal with unsafe and ineffective school buildings, their decisions are tempered by the contextual variables discussed in this chapter.

Recommendations made by administrators and decisions made by school boards often come under intense public scrutiny. This is especially so when millions of dollars are involved. Therefore, superintendents need to have an understanding of the possible reasons underlying taxpayer opposition to proposed construction projects. These reasons vary from district to district; and even when most taxpayers overwhelmingly support the need for a project, they may express different opinions regarding the project's scope and design.

ISSUES FOR DISCUSSION

1. What social issues are affecting the need for improved school facilities in America?
2. How has technology affected the delivery of education and the adequacy of school buildings?
3. What factors have contributed to the poor condition of many existing school buildings?
4. Why does excessive liberty often result in inequalities among local districts?
5. Do current reform strategies have any relevance for school facilities?
6. Some citizens see school buildings as being relatively unimportant. What factors contribute to this perception?
7. Since the mid-1990s, there have been several tragic shootings in schools. How have these incidents affected the need for improved facilities?
8. Administrators provide leadership for both planning and managing school buildings. How are these responsibilities affected by an increasingly uncertain future?
9. Over the past two decades, school finance litigation in several states has resulted in facilities becoming an equity issue. What is the importance of this legal trend?
10. What is the value of fraternity? How might this value affect policy decisions pertaining to school facility development?

REFERENCES

American Association of School Administrators. (1991). *Schoolhouse in the red: A national study of school facilities and energy use.* Arlington, VA: Author.

Bauman, P.C. (1996). *Governing education: Public sector reform or privatization.* Boston: Allyn and Bacon.

Biehle, J.T. (2000). Designing safer schools. *American School and University, 72*(8), 46–47.

Burrup, P., Brimley, V., & Garfield, R. (1999). *Financing education in a climate of change.* (7th ed.) Needham Heights, MA: Allyn and Bacon.

Certo, S.C. (1989). *Principles of modern management: Functions and systems* (4th ed.). Boston: Allyn and Bacon.

Crampton, F., & Whitney, T. (1996). *The search for equity in school funding. NCSL Education Partners Project.* Denver, CO: National Conference of State Legislatures.

Cuban, L. (1988). Why do some reforms persist? *Educational Administration Quarterly, 24*(3), 329–335.

DeRolph v. State. 78 Ohio St. 3d 193 (Oh. 1997).

DeStafano, J.R., Van Hook, M., & Draht, S. (2000). The future connection. *American School and University, 72*(5), 24–25.

Fowler, F.C. (2000). *Policy studies for educational leaders: An introduction.* Upper Saddle River, NJ: Merrill, Prentice-Hall.

General Accounting Office. (1996). *School facilities: America's schools report differing conditions.* Washington, DC: U.S. Government Printing Office.

Glass, T. (2000). Changes in society and schools. In T.J. Kowalski (Ed.), *Public relations in schools* (2nd ed.) (pp. 30–45). Upper Saddle River, NJ: Merrill, Prentice-Hall.

Grubb, D. (1997). Meeting disabled students' needs without breaking the bank. *School Planning and Management, 36*(5), 26.

Kowalski, T.J. (1995). Chasing the wolves from the schoolhouse door. *Phi Delta Kappan, 76,* 486–489.

Kowalski, T.J. (1999). *The school superintendent: Theory, practice, and cases.* Upper Saddle River, NJ: Merrill, Prentice-Hall.

Kowalski, T.J., & Schmielau, R. (2000, April). *Liberty and equality provisions in state funding policies for school construction.* Paper presented at the annual conference of the American Educational Research Association, New Orleans, LA.

Lewis, A. (1989). *Wolves at the schoolhouse door: An investigation of the condition of public school buildings.* Washington, DC: American Education Writers Association.

Naisbitt, J. (1982). *Megatrends.* New York: Warner Books.

National Center for Education Statistics. (1997). *The condition of education: 1997.* Washington, DC: U.S. Department of Education.

National Commission on Excellence in Education. (1983, April). *A nation at risk: The imperative of school reform.* Washington, DC: U.S. Government Printing Office.

Otten, K. (1996). Opening doors to compliance. *American School and University, 68*(8), 28–30.

Pauley v. Bailey, 324 S.E. 2d 128 (W. Va. 1984).

Roosevelt Elementary School District 66 v. Bishop, 179 Ariz. 233, 877 P. 2d 806 (Ariz. 1994).

Swanson, A.D. (1989). Restructuring educational governance: A challenge of the 1990s. *Educational Administration Quarterly, 25,* 268–293.

Swanson, A.D., & King, R.A. (1997). *School finance: Its economics and politics* (2nd ed.). New York: Longman.

Tennessee Small School Systems v. McWerter. 851 S.W. 2d 139 (Tenn. 1993).

Thompson, D.C., Wood, R.C., & Honeyman, D.S. (1994). *Fiscal leadership for schools: Concepts and practices*. New York: Longman.

Tyack, D., & Cuban, L. (1995). *Tinkering toward utopia: A century of public school reform*. Cambridge, MA: Harvard University Press.

U.S. Department of Education. (1996). *Survey on advanced telecommunications in U.S. public schools*. Washington, DC: Author.

Wirt, F.M., & Kirst, M.W. (1997). *The political dynamics of American education*. Berkeley, CA: McCutchan.

CHAPTER 3

Systems Perspective for Defining Adequacy

When school officials and taxpayers ponder the question of improving or replacing education facilities, they usually are guided by the value of adequacy; that is, they try to determine whether the building in question is adequate. Unfortunately, most of the literature on this topic never defines this key value. Instead, writers have usually prescribed assessment procedures for evaluating facilities; but even the best of these procedures are rather purposeless without a definition of adequacy. The failure to determine the parameters of this value has constituted a major barrier to effective facility planning.

Therefore, as a prelude to examining alternative planning paradigms, this chapter examines the concept of facility adequacy. First, the importance of this term is discussed. Then concept of systems theory is introduced, and then adequacy is defined in terms of the three components of systems analysis: inputs, throughputs (treatments), and outputs.

IMPORTANCE OF ADEQUACY

What constitutes an adequate school building? Some state officials have tried to answer this question normatively. For example, they ranked all buildings in a state from the best to the worst and those that were at or above the median were deemed adequate. This approach is pointless for at least two reasons. First, such rankings are often highly subjective and rarely criterion-referenced. Second, and even more important, such rankings ignore the possibility that relatively few school buildings in a given state may actually be adequate or inadequate.

Most often, determinations of adequacy in education are based on standards of sufficiency (Swanson & King, 1996). This method requires the development of minimal standards of adequacy to achieve predetermined goals. Using this perspective, adequate buildings may be defined as those that meet or exceed these minimal standards for achieving prescribed educational programs or their outcomes. Most often, however, minimal standards are expressed without being tied to educational objectives. In Arizona, for example, a school building is deemed adequate if it:

- Has sufficient and appropriate space and equipment to comply with the minimum school facility guidelines,

- Complies with applicable federal, state, and local building and fire codes and laws,

- Has integral systems that are in working order and capable of being properly maintained,

- Is structurally sound (Arizona School Boards Association, 1998).

Adequacy also can be studied from two separate perspectives: construction adequacy and program adequacy. A building could meet minimal construction standards and still not be large enough to support programs deemed essential by the community. Design, size, common work areas, and storage all have an impact on how usable a building is for teaching and learning (Lewis, 1989).

Although legal interpretations of adequacy developed in relation to school funding (including facility funding) have focused largely on outputs, the value may be defined in terms of inputs, treatments, and outcomes (Berne & Stiefel, 1999). In the case of school buildings, definitions are especially difficult because both the present and the future need to be considered; that is, a more complete understanding of adequacy is achieved when definitions include the extent to which a building effectively supports *and will continue to support* a school's intended program. In this book, a facility is deemed adequate when *minimal construction and program standards for achieving predetermined goals are currently met and are likely to be met in the future.*

When administrators fail to define adequacy properly, policy makers and other people in the community construct their own definitions. In many instances, these definitions are highly subjective, reflecting primarily self-interests, biases, and personal opinions. In other words, many individuals will define adequate simply as "good enough" in relation to what they believe to be appropriate educational goals. And when these individuals embrace different education goals—a condition that is becoming increasingly common as communities become more diverse—agreement regarding the adequacy of school facilities is unlikely. At the very least, the differing perspectives of a sufficient school building reduce the quality of planning decisions because compromises become necessary. This reality is demonstrated by the following dilemma that occurred in a rural school district.

The board and superintendent appointed a 12-member planning team consisting of eight non educators, a principal, and three teachers. Neither the superintendent nor the architect defined adequacy for the committee members. In the absence of such a definition, the committee members immediately began to argue over the size of the project budget. Ten committee members, none of them educators, voted to set a maximum project budget before any other decisions were made. In addition, the same group of committee members insisted that the school board approve the maximum figure before any other planning occurred. Not wanting to jeopardize the project, the school board did so, and neither the superintendent nor the architect raised objections. Consequently, the budget for the new high school was set before educational programs were even considered. This premature decision was responsible for obvious deficiencies once construction was completed and the school opened. For example, instructional spaces were inflexible; no provisions were made for future expansion; the quantity and quality of the science labs were insufficient; and no auxiliary gym was provided, causing serious scheduling problems for physical education and athletic programs.

The problem expressed in this example was created by a failure to define adequacy in a manner that linked minimal standards to program and learning expectations. As a result, a majority of the committee was able to restrict the planning process without being challenged.

Administrators must be prepared to deal with subjectivity because facility planning is never a totally rational and objective process. School officials and other planning participants inevitably inject their personal values and beliefs into the process. In addition, the competing interests and goals of subgroups ensure political influence will play some part in decision making. Given these realities, the planning challenge facing administrators is not the elimination of subjectivity, but rather the tempering of subjectivity through the infusion of objectivity. An appropriate understanding of adequacy is the most powerful tool for accomplishing this goal.

SYSTEMS THEORY

A system is essentially a set of units with the capacity to interact within the scope of their environment to achieve certain goals. Scholars in many disciplines have used systems theory to describe both living and nonliving phenomena. In medicine, for instance, systems analysis focuses on the arrangement of and relations between body parts (e.g., cells and organs) that connect them into a whole (the human body). This knowledge is essential to medical diagnosis and treatment. Unless a physician understands the body as a system, he or she would be unable to determine how a problem in one part of the body gets manifested in another, especially when there is no direct connection between the two body parts.

Although buildings are neither living organisms nor social entities, they are systems. Like mechanical systems, such as automobiles, they are organized assemblies of units that have a definable relationship and are intended to serve specific purposes. Thus, systems theory can be applied to facility planning as a means for assessing adequacy. The concept provides a mechanism for administrators to identify and understand inputs, to analyze the treatment of inputs, and to evaluate outputs. Both the concept of subsystems and the concept of multiple causation are central to systems theory (Owens, 2001). In the case of school buildings, the former indicates that a facility is composed of interrelated parts such as climate controls and spatial arrangements; the latter indicates that no single part typically determines if a building is functional. Guthrie and Reed (1991) pointed out that two other concepts also were fundamental: the boundaries (characteristics of a building that differentiate it from its broader environment) and homeostasis (equilibrium between the building and environmental resources). A state of disequilibria exists when a building is unable to use available environmental resources. For example, a school cannot house a computer lab even though the hardware is available if there is insufficient space. Adequate building design depends on how the components of a building interact with each other and how the building interacts with its broader environment.

Systems analysis is a technique based on systems theory. It provides a way to systematically investigate a planned or existing facility to determine its parts and functions and the interrelationships of those parts. Subsystems are viewed in terms of inputs (purposes or intentions), specifications (interpretations of purposes or intentions), and outputs (the degree to which purposes or intentions were achieved). The relationships among these components are shown in Figure 3–1. Outputs, the product of inputs and throughputs, reflect the degree to which a facility is adequate.

INPUTS FOR FACILITY SYSTEMS ANALYSIS

Without proper guidance and knowledge, people tend to evaluate the adequacy of school buildings too narrowly. For example, judgments may be based primarily on the external appearance of a building or on personal beliefs that adequacy only requires a building to protect its occupants from the elements. Considering a building in relation to its intended purposes or in relation to universally accepted criteria for modern schools is a complex process that entails both community-specific ideas and universal standards (see Figure 3–2).

Community-Specific Ideas

Community-specific ideas refer to thoughts generated by individuals who reside within the district. Three primary conditions frame the nexus between these ideas and determinations of adequacy.

• Public schools have a special relationship to the communities in which they exist; they are expressions of the community's disposition toward education.

• In many states, school facilities remain primarily a local matter, dependent on the

Figure 3–1
Elements of Systems Analysis

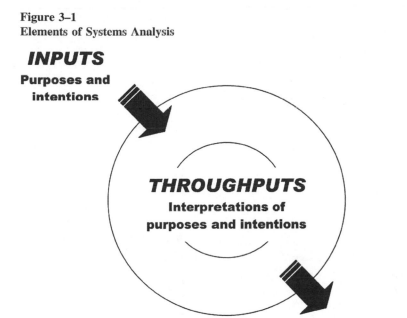

INPUTS
Purposes and
intentions

THROUGHPUTS
Interpretations of
purposes and intentions

OUTPUTS
Degree to which
purposes and intentions
were achieved

ability and willingness of local taxpayers to fund them. Thus, citizens often have vested economic and political interests in facility projects (Kowalski & Schmielau, 2000).

• Real needs are not constant across all districts; thus, minimum standards for meeting real needs are not constant.

Community-specific ideas are forged by two factors: values and beliefs (philosophy) expressed by the community and real needs determined through an analysis of existing conditions.

Philosophy. Philosophical dispositions enter the planning process as expressions of values and beliefs. Values have three dimensions: (a) an affective domain encompassing emotions attached to an idea, (b) a behavioral domain focusing on overt and/or covert actions, and (c) a cognitive domain integrating situations, objects, or people (Worell & Stilwell, 1981). Consider the following example.

Members of a school board are convinced that a new school has the potential for improving teaching and learning (an *emotion*). They approve a project that is grounded in a solid educational plan (an *action*). Their beliefs and actions subsequently shape their

Figure 3–2
Inputs for Systems Analysis

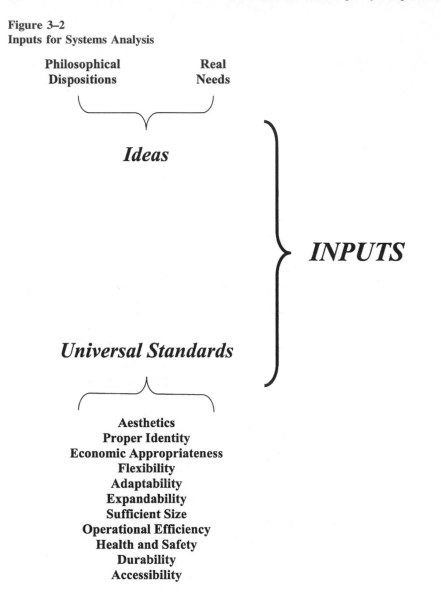

decisions about curriculum, faculty selection, and equipping the building (*cognitive mediation*).

Values may be expressed at any or all of these three levels during planning.

Values and beliefs may reflect community standards, the culture of the school district, or the sentiments of groups and individuals. They may be positive or negative as demonstrated by the examples presented in Table 3–1. Philosophical

Table 3–1
Examples of Values and Beliefs That May Affect Facility Planning

Origin	Value or Belief	Effect
Community	Education contributes to the quality of community life	Positive
	School buildings are relatively unimportant to educational outcomes	Negative
District Culture	School buildings should serve the entire community	Positive
	Community usage of school buildings results in problems	Negative
Individual/Group	Everyone benefits from having excellent school facilities	Positive
	Taxpayers without children in school should not pay for construction	Negative

inputs are basically subjective judgments that reflect community, district, group, and individual sentiments.

Needs. Needs represent gaps between what is and what is needed. Many needs are obvious even without formal assessment. For example, teachers and administrators usually recognize when additional classrooms are needed in an elementary school because they are directly affected by space deficiencies; placing 30 or more students in classrooms designed to accommodate no more than 25 students requires programmatic and human adjustments. Parents may be told to limit what their children bring to school because there is insufficient space to store personal belongings; teachers may not be able to integrate computers into instruction because there is insufficient space for the necessary equipment. These are the types of adjustments that typically make space needs apparent.

But relying solely on informal assessments to determine needs is precarious because the evaluators often suffer from tunnel vision; that is, they only see and respond to what is obvious and personally relevant; as a result, they are likely to overlook equally important but less discernible needs. For this reason, a comprehensive, formal needs assessment is a much more reliable option for planning a facility. When administrators fail to validate needs, individuals will draw their own conclusions and the result is likely to be conflicting opinions about what is needed and what is wanted. Whereas philosophical inputs are largely subjective, needs inputs should be highly objective. This is one reason why many school districts retain consultants to conduct a needs assessment.

Idea Formation. Ideas emerge when philosophical and needs inputs are considered together. In essence, subjective criteria (philosophy) are melded with objective criteria (real needs). Consider the following example from a district in which the superintendent was trying to replace a 77-year-old high school with a new building.

The planning process produced several philosophical dispositions held by a majority of the community. They included a belief that the high school should provide a safe and healthful environment and the belief that there was no need to add frills in order to ensure a safe and healthful environment. Many citizens initially felt that the high school could be made adequate if it were simply renovated. A facility assessment conducted by

Table 3–2
Congruence of Philosophy and Needs and Potential Effects on Ideas, Conflict, and Need Satisfaction

Level of Congruence Between Philosophy and Needs	Level of Difficulty Developing Input Ideas	Potential for Serious Conflict	Likelihood of Satisfying Existing Needs
High	Low	Low	High
Moderate	Moderate	Moderate	Moderate
Low	High	High	Low

architects, however, produced three noteworthy findings about the high school building: the facility was inflexible; the classrooms were too small; and the total space in the building was woefully inadequate. The superintendent tried to form ideas by combining these subjective and objective data.

When philosophy and real needs are not considered simultaneously, it is likely that dominant community factions will have sufficient political power to attenuate recommendations made by the administrative staff.

Obviously, the ideal is to have congruence between philosophies and needs. In most school districts, however, this does not occur without skillful facilitation from the superintendent or other administrators. Tensions between subjective and objective inputs rarely resolve themselves, and the extent to which the two factors are incongruous determines the amount of difficulty school officials will face in trying to form input ideas (see Table 3–2).

When school officials are unable to reconcile differences between philosophy and needs, one of two problems is likely to occur. One is that subjective judgments will override real needs. When this happens, needed construction is either ignored or addressed insufficiently. The other is that philosophical opposition to real needs will be ignored. If this happens, either the project will never materialize (e.g., because a tax referendum is defeated) or the project will generate serious political problems for those who approved it without public support (e.g., the eventual dismissal of a superintendent or turnover on the school board).

Universal Criteria

Adequacy also is determined by the degree to which a facility possesses generic qualities deemed essential for all modern schoolhouses. While some of these qualities (e.g., health and safety) have always existed, others have been spawned by uncertainty. For instance, adaptability and flexibility have become more important as the future nature of the educational process has become increasingly uncertain. Each of the criteria for a modern school building is discussed separately.

Aesthetics. A school is aesthetically pleasing when it has a pleasurable and inspiring effect on users and viewers. Thus, school buildings should exude warmth and beauty. Ensuring that a school meets this standard requires attention both in the original design and in provisions for maintenance. The aesthetic features of a schoolhouse symbolically transmit messages about the love of children and about the value placed on their education (Chan, 1988). Students in unattractive and poorly maintained schools often feel diminished. Some scholars (e.g., Uline, 1997) have recommended that facility planners give greater attention to the issue of aesthetics to avoid such problems. Unfortunately, the variable of aesthetics is often dismissed as being unimportant—especially when providing warmth and beauty increase the cost of a project. For example, planners may radically reduce the amount of natural lighting in a facility in order to achieve cost savings without properly weighing the potential negative effects on the teaching and learning process.

Proper Identity. Imagine that a photographer took pictures of 100 schools and then eliminated artifacts that reveal the building's purpose (e.g., exterior signs and playgrounds). Would individuals unfamiliar with the structures be able to identify the structures as schools? This question gets to the heart of proper identity criterion. A school that has proper identity would not be mistaken for a warehouse or an office building. A school with a positive identity symbolically sends the message, that "this community cares about children, youth, adults, and learning."

Economic Appropriateness. A school is economically appropriate when the cost of the project is in line with the community's fiscal ability and existing needs. Fiscal ability is a measure of a district's relative wealth, and the most common statistic used for this purpose is assessed valuation per pupil (i.e., the total assessed valuation divided by the district enrollment). Too often, the scope and cost of a project is determined solely by the wealth of a local district and not by real educational needs. This is especially true in the approximately 20 states where local districts are still required to pay for all or most of the facility costs. Because states vary considerably in the amount of support they provide to local districts for facility development, economic appropriateness is often difficult to measure. In general, however, a project's cost should neither drain the community of its resources nor should the cost be incongruent with real needs and the community's ability to provide an effective educational environment.

Flexibility. Flexibility refers to serving changing program purposes without altering the structural system of a building. For example, a school is flexible if it can be modified from a traditional design to an open space design without altering load-bearing walls. This criterion has become increasingly important because the scope and delivery of educational programming over the next 25 to 50 years are basically unknown. Movement into an age of information and the mass infusion of technology into American society exemplify changes that have already altered traditional instructional activities. The importance of flexibility is illustrated in the restructuring of industrial education and home economics in secondary schools over the past two decades. In the case of the former subject

Table 3–3
Selected Examples of Factors Requiring Expandability

Factor	Example	Consequence
Demographics	Enrollment increase	More space is added to a school
	Enrollment decrease	Two schools consolidate; one is closed and the other is made larger
Economics	Insufficient operating funds	The number of attendance centers are reduced; one or more surviving buildings must be larger
Curricular Revision	New courses are required	Additional instructional areas must be added
Instruction Revision	Teaming, block scheduling	Additional space is needed for small group instruction and faculty planning
Philosophy	Community school concept	Space for adult education and a broader range of student services are needed
New Programs	Title IX	Additional athletic facilities are needed because of increased programs for girls

area, hands-on programs in woods and metals have been transposed into high-technology curricula (e.g., electronics). In the case of the latter, more stringent graduation requirements and evolving opportunities for women have reduced enrollment significantly. Schools housed in flexible facilities were able to make transitions more quickly and economically.

Adaptability. Adaptability and flexibility are often confused, but they are separate attributes. Adaptability is measured by the extent to which spaces in a school can serve varying purposes; unlike flexibility, it does not entail redesign. For example, classrooms are adaptable if they can serve different instructional paradigms (e.g., small-group work, lecture, and hands-on activities) by simply rearranging or adding furniture. The criterion of adaptability is important because both curricula and modes of instruction are likely to change several times during the life span of a building.

Expandability. Expandability simply means that a building can be made larger at a later time if necessary. Often school officials make the mistake of believing that enrollment increases are the only possible reason for future expansion. In reality, curricular changes, new instructional paradigms, new programs, economic conditions, and philosophical shifts also may increase space requirements. Table 3–3 includes examples of factors creating the need for facility expansion.

Because new schools are intended to last at least 50 years, a decision to ignore expandability is certainly precarious. In the 1950s, for instance, few superintendents and school board members envisioned how consolidation and curriculum expansion would affect their facilities. Being prepared to expand a school facility is especially important because local district officials do not initiate many of the actions that make additional space necessary. Most often, the impetus for change has come from educational trends, state laws, state policy, or legal judgments. Consider two elementary schools constructed in 1981. Neither has computer laboratories; however, only one of the facilities was designed to accommodate expansion. While both may be able to respond to the need for infusing computers, the one with expandability is in a more favorable position.

Sufficient Size. Many states set minimums for site and building size; however, the adequacy of these standards depends on the scope of programming offered in a particular district. In addition, some states routinely grant waivers to their minimums. For example, a school district recently built a new four-section-per-grade-level elementary school on a site of just under two acres. While such a decision may be necessary in urban settings, it certainly is not warranted in other locations. Administrators should always ask educational planners and architects to provide reasonable standards for site and building size. Assume that a proposed new high school to accommodate 1,300 pupils is to be built on a 20-acre site and is to contain 200 square feet per pupil. Are the site and building adequate? The answer should be based on three factors: state requirements, the scope and nature of the proposed program, and emerging practices within a state.

Operational Efficiency. There are two primary economic decisions facing administrators in facility projects: the cost of constructing the school and the cost of operating the school once it is constructed. Although the two decisions are clearly connected, administrators and architects have often treated them as though they were unrelated. Perhaps the most common example of this error pertains to the quality of building materials. Frequently, less expensive materials are selected to hold down the initial cost of construction without regard to long-term operating costs. Operational efficiency means that a school can function as intended within a school district's financial capacity. To ensure this outcome, school officials must project the parameters for operating costs and determine if proposed designs will fall within those limits. In general, administrators should insist that the architects design a reasonably maintenance-free and energy-efficient environment.

Health and Safety. Far more attention is now being given to health and safety in schools for two primary reasons. The first is a heightened awareness of hazardous materials such as asbestos and radon. The Asbestos Hazard Emergency Response Act enacted in 1986, for instance, created new levels of health and safety standards. The other reason is mounting concerns about violence, accidents, and natural disasters. Dimensions of the health and safety criterion are vast and include services such as climate control, sanitary conditions, visual control, sound control, proper storage facilities, traffic flows, alarm systems, public address systems, driveways, sidewalks, playgrounds, and even surveillance equipment. Prevention of potential hazards begins early in planning, because inputs affect design. Surveys of elementary schools, for example, have

found that problems on playgrounds contributing to accidents and injuries could
have been eliminated by proper design decisions (Lewis, 1989).

Durability. Durability relates to structural design, building materials, and
equipment. Historically, school buildings in the United States have been used
for 50 to 60 years (Ehrenkrantz & Eckstut, 1995). Most modern school buildings
are expected to remain in use for even longer periods. In addition, they are
expected to absorb wear and tear during their life span without requiring substantial maintenance. Initial costs are a major issue with respect to durability.
As noted, equipment that is inexpensive initially is usually not cost-effective
over the life span of the facility. Consider two middle schools of identical size
built in the same county in the same year. One cost $20 million the other cost
$30 million. The cost difference is attributable to the quality of building mate-
rials. The $20 million school remains functional for 35 years; the other remains
functional for 60 years because it is more durable. In addition, the more durable
school has substantially lower annual operating costs. So despite its higher initial
price tag, it had the better cost-benefit ratio over its life span.

Accessibility. This attribute relates to making a building accessible to all potential occupants. Special attention is given to provisions for disabled individuals. Unlike some of the other criteria that may be ignored by school officials,
both federal and state laws mandate accessibility.

THROUGHPUTS FOR FACILITY SYSTEMS ANALYSIS

Throughputs pertain to process; that is, they involve the treatment of inputs.
In facility planning, refined inputs are called specifications. In a systems model
for school facilities, inputs are enhanced in three separate documents. They are
educational specifications, control specifications, and construction specifications.
These documents provide detail determining how the basic systems components
of a building will be treated (see Figure 3–3).

Educational Specifications

Educational specifications (also referred to as program specifications) provide
qualitative and quantitative statements detailing the programs and activities that
will occur in the facility. They also include decisions relative to the number,
type, size, layout, association, location, and content of spaces. Two problems
should be avoided when developing educational specifications. The first is a
lack of control over inputs that could lead to an unrealistic wish list. This occurs
when persons responsible for writing the specifications simply include every
request without evaluating necessity, practicality, and cost. For example, elementary school teachers may want to have separate restrooms placed in every
classroom. While this feature is common in kindergarten and first grade rooms,
costs usually prohibit providing it in every classroom.

The second problem results from providing design specifications in the edu-

Figure 3–3
Relationship between Inputs and Throughputs

Inputs
Ideas
Standards

Component Decisions
Spatial
Sonic
Visual
Thermal
Services
Hygiene
Safety & Security
Equipment
Structural

Specification Documents
Educational Specifications
Control Specifications
Construction Specifications

cational program statement. Educational specifications provide design architects with information about how the building will be used—not with information about actual designs. Sometimes planners go well beyond describing functions and include construction specifications (e.g., the height of wainscots or the U-values of windows) (Affleck & Fuller, 1988).

Several approaches are used to develop educational specifications. The three most common are:

• *Retaining an educational consultant (either by the district or by the architectural firm) to develop the document.* This individual should have knowledge and skills in both educational programming (curriculum and instruction) and facility planning.

• *Having personnel with the architectural firm that has already been retained complete the specifications.* Typically, they do this by interviewing district and school employees to obtain information about the scope and delivery of program.

• *Having district administrators complete the specifications with guidance from architects.* Typically, the administrators are given an outline of the information that they are to produce.

While the task can be effectively completed with any of these approaches, many school officials opt to use an educational consultant because they want the final product to be as objective as possible.

Accurate educational specifications play a pivotal role in determining if form will follow function in a school building. Thus, this document is one of the most important elements of planning. To ensure that adequacy is achieved, the specifications should accurately reflect what educational inputs would be used, the treatment of those inputs, and the intended outcomes. These tasks require a facilitator who has a deep understanding of curriculum, pedagogy, and school administration.

Control Specifications

Control specifications are concerned with regulating problems related to setting standards, fixing limits, and determining feasibilities. Legal and fiscal controls are two of the most common. Also included are organizational factors such as size of the school (e.g., setting enrollment parameters), site selection (e.g., eliminating certain types of sites), and resources available to support operations (e.g., maintenance budgets, maintenance staff). Another important control specification is the project budget, that is, placing a limit on the cost of a building.

The architects determine many control specifications, but some are developed collaboratively with school officials. Two examples of collaborative decisions are project budgets and site selection. Errors or omissions in control specifications can result in legal problems and detract from a school building's productiveness. For example, selecting a site that is too small may result in restricted outdoor facilities.

Construction Specifications

Construction specifications deal with interpretive engineering through design and material decisions. These documents are dependent on both educational and control specifications and result in design and engineering drawings and related construction decisions. Architects develop them, and in some situations, construction managers are involved.

Because construction specifications involve interpretations, school officials should ascertain how requirements established in the educational and control specifications have been treated. But in addition to checking for misinterpretations, school officials need to look for basic design errors. In designing a natatorium for a new high school, for example, an architect followed the program specification that called for seating 500 spectators. He designed concrete seating in a balcony overlooking the pool. Only after the bleachers were poured was a serious design error discovered. Spectators sitting in the top two rows of the bleachers could not see half of the lanes in the pool because of the site path.

Systems Components

Buildings are often analyzed in relation to nine components: spatial, sonic, visual, thermal, service, hygiene, safety and security, equipment, and structural. Each should be addressed in one or more of the specification documents.

Spatial Component. Spatial relationships include association, accessibility, arrangement, and fluidity of space. The shape and size of spaces, adaptability of given spaces, accommodations for traffic patterns, and the location of spaces are paramount issues. Some examples of spatial decisions include:

- Arranging grade levels in an elementary school (e.g., keeping the first grade classrooms together in the same wing as the kindergarten classrooms)
- Arranging departments in a middle school (e.g., locating language arts and social studies next to each other to accommodate teaming and block scheduling)
- Arranging space in a high school (e.g., locating departments that commonly use the media center near that area)

Decisions about space should be based on planned functions—that is, space allocations reflect what is needed and desired in a given area.

Sonic Component. Three dimensions of sound are important; they are quality, reduction, and control. Adequate acoustical treatments are a primary facet of this component. Sound control should address both airborne and structure-borne transmissions. Design decisions such as suppression and isolation of noise help to determine the sonic qualities of a school. Acoustical treatments should result in a good listening environment accomplished by "properly balanced reverberation time, the use of appropriately absorptive and reflective materials, adequate sound isolation and control of unwanted heating, ventilation and air conditioning noise and vibration" (Paoletti, 1989, p. 22).

Visual Component. The visual qualities of a school are more detailed than one might imagine. Proper lighting in a school has been linked to reducing physical tension, conserving energy, and increasing work efficiency. Less obvious is the importance of color in a school. Color schemes complement light by improving sight conditions; they also provide aesthetic qualities to space. Acting together, color and light can stimulate, relax, and provide an expression of warmth. Visual outputs in a school building include both natural and artificial lighting. Additionally, the visual component addresses light control (e.g., dimmers in classrooms to permit the use of audiovisual equipment).

Thermal Component. Heating, ventilation, cooling, and humidity control are aspects of the thermal component. The importance of proper controls can easily be observed by visiting an older school on a hot September day. Without air-conditioning or a highly effective ventilation system, the interior of the building becomes a detriment to instruction and a potential health hazard. Longer school years and expanded summer sessions have made cooling the primary thermal problem in many parts of the country.

Given the physical size of most schools, thermal control is one of the most difficult outputs to achieve and retain. Over the past few decades, energy costs have added to the importance of thermal controls. For example, older buildings—even in cold climates—were often designed with single-pane windows because heating fuels were relatively inexpensive at the time they were built. Today, these buildings are inefficient, causing serious problems for operating budgets.

Architects are expected to provide acceptable standards for thermal factors. Factors such as relative humidity and temperature must be considered together. For example, a relative humidity range of 40–60 percent is considered comfortable in a school with the upper limit being acceptable at a room temperature of 70 degrees Fahrenheit. But as the temperature increases, the relative humidity has to decrease to remain in the comfort zone (Knirk, 1979). Given the frequency of thermal problems in schools, administrators and others involved in planning should be prepared to ask questions about specifications for this aspect of the project.

Services Component. Service outputs pertain to facility provisions that improve the operation and utilization of the building. Included are accommodations for cleaning supplies and equipment, adequate security systems, two-way communication systems, and safe shipping and receiving areas. Utilities, such as adequate water, fuel, and sewage treatment, also are in this category. Deficiencies in service components are almost always attributable to omissions and errors in developing specifications. Two examples include not designing adequate spaces for custodial services or selecting a site that results in sewage treatment problems. Today, providing a barrier-free environment has become one of the most essential elements of the service component. Because of federal and state laws, such as the Americans with Disabilities Act, specifications for a barrier-free environment should be based on both legal and program requirements.

Hygiene Component. The hygiene component addresses features such as restrooms, lockers, waste disposal, and drinking fountains. Plumbing specifications, access to water, and waste disposal are central to these issues. Both original design features and the maintenance of those features are important.

Safety and Security Component. Not all administrators recognize that there is a fundamental difference between safety and security. The former addresses issues such as accident prevention, air quality, and fire or storm damage; the latter is concerned with preventing and responding to criminal acts and severe behavior (Trump, 1998). Safety components range from proper structural specifications to ensuring ample storage spaces. It is especially necessary to specify appropriate storage and disposal areas and equipment for chemicals or other potentially harmful materials. Security concerns range from forming spaces that are relatively easy to supervise and properly lighted to specifying hallways that have clear sight lines. Site location and placement of the building on a site also are important facets of this component.

Equipment Component. Frequently, sufficient attention is not given to the equipment component of a building project. Often school officials delay equipment decisions until the construction is completed or they make them incrementally as the project evolves. This can be a critical mistake. Equipment plays an important role in a facility's adequacy. Specifications for equipment should extend beyond quantitative data to address issues of durability, repair, and appropriateness with regard to decor. In addition, administrators should insist on seeing a nexus between intended program and equipment specifications. In designing a new elementary school, for instance, a decision about where students will store their personal belongings (e.g., coats) has direct implications for specifying classroom furniture and equipment.

Structural Component. The structural component includes decisions about the enclosure of space, the use of materials, keeping maintenance to a minimum, and the interfacing of space. Expansion of the structure, fireproofing, ability to withstand high winds, and load-bearing features exemplify aspects of this component. Structural decisions have become more challenging, because uncertainty about the future use of schools requires that spaces be both flexible and adaptable. Specifications for a structure are heavily influenced by geographic location and site.

OUTPUTS FOR FACILITY SYSTEMS ANALYSIS

As noted at the beginning of this chapter, a school is not adequate unless it is functional; that is, a functional building accommodates the purposes for which it was constructed. Thus, a determination of adequacy cannot be made accurately unless those purposes are known, and this is why looking at a school from a systems perspective is so essential. A system is an ordered grouping that identifies and relates parts. The process raises consciousness to the less obvious factors that enhance or deter adequacy. More important, a systems perspective allows administrators to identify deficiencies so that they can be addressed once a building is operational. To do this, one must use outputs as the means for reshaping inputs—in other words, systems analysis is an ongoing process. This relationship is illustrated in Figure 3–4.

Adequacy can be reduced by both errors of omission and errors commission. Unfortunately, many schools have been constructed with one or more of the following elements missing:

- Philosophical statements
- Needs assessment
- Ideas (formed by fusing philosophy and needs)
- Universal criteria
- Educational specifications
- Control specifications
- Construction specifications

In addition, some administrators have contributed to inaccurate definitions by either eliminating public participation or by failing to coordinate such participation. In the case of the former, planners assume that they know what the community believes, wants, and needs—and often they are wrong. In the case of the latter, they include community participants but fail to provide information, facilitation, and leadership. Under these conditions, decisions guided by personal values, beliefs, and biases result in a less-than-functional product.

CHAPTER SUMMARY

Most often, the adequacy of school buildings has been determined by state minimum criteria. This is understandable because state officials must establish

Figure 3–4
Total Systems Model for Determining Adequacy

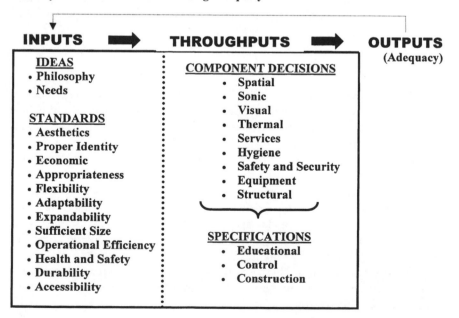

standards that are applicable to all schools. The disadvantage of such definitions, however, is quite obvious. Community philosophy and real needs are usually pushed aside when planners rely solely on minimum criteria to define an adequate educational environment. In addition, minimums are generally unreliable with respect to determining future adequacy. This is because programs and instructional approaches are constantly changing. More recently, litigation challenging state funding programs for school construction has led to another approach for determining adequacy: the interface of adequacy and equality. Within this perspective, a building is not adequate if it denies students educational opportunities that are reasonably equal to those given to other students in the same state.

When adequacy is defined from a systems perspective, both subjective and objective inputs are included. In addition, both specific needs and generic standards are considered. Consequently, school officials and the public gain a deeper understanding of how ideas get shaped into specifications that detail the building.

ISSUES FOR DISCUSSION

1. Why has adequacy been an ambiguous value in school facility planning?
2. What factors should determine the adequacy of a school building?
3. Why should adequacy consider the present and future?
4. Describe systems theory.
5. Are school buildings systems? Why or why not?
6. Some of the inputs discussed in this chapter are subjective. Which ones are they?
7. What is the difference between educational specifications and control specifications?
8. What is the difference between flexibility and adaptability?
9. Why are aesthetics important with respect to educational facilities?
10. How do rapid changes in society and the world affect definitions of building adequacy?
11. What are construction specifications?
12. Why is the relationship among spaces important in a school building?
13. What is the difference between trying to determine adequacy on the basis of inputs and trying to determine adequacy on the basis of outputs?

REFERENCES

Affleck, K., & Fuller, B. (1988). The integration of programming and educational specifications. *CEFP Journal, 26*(6), 9–12.

Arizona School Boards Association. (1998). *Students FIRST: A summary of the new school capital finance system* (Rev. ed.). Phoenix: Author.

Berne, R., & Stiefel, L. (1999). Concepts of finance equity: 1970 to present. In H. Ladd,

R. Chalk, and J. Hansen (Eds.), *Equity and adequacy in education finance: Issues and perspectives* (pp. 7–33). Washington, DC: National Academy Press.

Chan, T.C. (1988). The aesthetic environment and student learning. *School Business Affairs, 54*(1), 26–27.

Ehrenkrantz, E.D., & Eckstut, S. (1995). Today's new school can be state-of-the-art in 2055. *Electronic School, 1*(2), 30–32.

Guthrie, J.W., & Reed, R.J. (1991). *Educational administration and policy: Effective leadership for American education* (2nd ed.). Boston: Allyn and Bacon.

Knirk, F. (1979). *Designing productive learning environments*. Englewood Cliffs, NJ: Educational Technology Publications.

Kowalski, T.J., & Schmielau, R. (2000, April). *Liberty and equality provisions in state laws and policies for funding school construction*. Paper presented at the annual conference of the American Educational Research Association, New Orleans, LA.

Lewis, A. (1989). *Wolves at the schoolhouse door: An investigation of the condition of public school buildings*. Washington, DC: American Education Writers Association.

Owens, R.C. (2001). *Organizational behavior in education* (7th ed.). Boston: Allyn and Bacon.

Paoletti, D. (1989). Acoustical and audiovisual design considerations. *CEFP Journal, 27*(1), 22.

Swanson, A.D., & King, R.A. (1996). *School finance: Its economics and politics* (2nd ed.). New York: Longman.

Trump, K.S. (1998). *Practical school security: Basic guidelines for safe and secure schools*. Thousand Oaks, CA: Corwin Press.

Uline, C.L. (1997). School architecture as a subject of inquiry. *Journal of School Leadership, 7*(2), 194–209.

Worell, J., & Stilwell, W. (1981). *Psychology for teachers and students*. New York: McGraw-Hill.

PART II

Determining Needs and
Initiating Planning

CHAPTER 4

Factors Affecting Facility Needs

For much of the 20th century, school patrons assumed that school buildings needed to be replaced only because they were too old or improved only because they were too small to accommodate increased enrollment. While still relevant, these are not the sole reasons why nearly 50 percent of the nation's schools need to be replaced or refurbished. School reform, increased knowledge about the effects of environment on learning, and broadened educational expectations also have expanded the boundaries of adequacy. In addition, both the pace of societal change and the demands for educational improvement are accelerating— conditions that make it more necessary to reconfigure buildings during their normal life span.

As noted in the previous chapter, adequacy should be considered in relation to the present and the future; that is, a facility should be functional and remain functional during its life span. The purpose of this chapter is to identify and discuss four factors integral to evolving facility needs. They include demographic changes, school restructuring, technology, and the condition of existing buildings. These variables influence both the quantity and quality of spaces needed for contemporary elementary and secondary schools.

DEMOGRAPHIC CHANGES

Demography is the statistical study of human populations with special reference to size, density, distribution, and other related figures. National, state, county (or regional), and district population data provide critical information for educational planners. Because of state mandatory attendance laws, changes in school population are driven by changes in the number of school-age children in the general population. Consequently, demographic analysis provides an essential quantitative input for determining facility needs.

From a national perspective, three facets of demographic conditions are especially cogent for elementary and secondary education. First, the overall enrollment in public elementary and secondary schools is again increasing. In the aftermath of the baby boom that affected schools for several decades following World War II, total enrollment in elementary and secondary education declined in the 1970s and early 1980s (U.S. Department of Education, 2000). Some demographers (e.g., Caffarella, 1987) believe that a lesser baby boom started in 1973 and ended in approximately 1988. From 1973 to 1998, this "baby-boom echo" resulted in an overall enrollment increase in public schools of about 17 percent. In elementary schools the increase was about 18 percent, and in secondary schools it was about 14 percent (*Digest of Education Statistics*, 1999). Second, the profile of the school population is continuing to change. The following data showing percentages of public elementary and secondary school enrollment by race and ethnicity in 1986 and 1997, reported in the *Digest of Education Statistics* (1999), verify this fact:

	1986	*1997*
White	70.4%	63.5%
Black	16.1%	17.0%
Hispanic	9.9%	14.4%

Third, the number of public schools operating in the United States is changing. Following World War II, school consolidation swept across many states. In 1930, there were 262,000 public schools. This figure steadily decreased through the 1970s, and, today, there are approximately 90,000 schools. While the current number of public schools is substantially lower than what it once was, there actually was an increase of about 5,000 schools between 1990 and 1997 (*Digest of Education Statistics*, 1999).

At the state level, patterns of student enrollment in public schools vary considerably. From 1970 to 1997, for example, public school enrollment in Florida increased by about 61 percent. In Texas, the increase was 34 percent, and in California it was 27 percent. During that same period, however, some states actually declined in pupil population. Nebraska, for instance, declined about 15 percent, and North Dakota declined about 30 percent (*Digest of Education Statistics*, 1999). Figures for these selected states illustrate how population patterns—and thus the need for school construction—vary markedly across the country. While some school districts in Florida (where all districts are large all-county systems) have had to build one or more new schools every year for the past 15 years to accommodate enrollment growth, some districts in other states have been forced to close schools as a result of enrollment declines.

According to the U.S. Department of Education (2000), growth in elementary and secondary school enrollment is not expected to be uniform across regions of the country. Public schools in the Midwest and Northeast are likely to experience decreases in their share of the national enrollment in the next decade, while schools in the South and West are likely to experience increases. Much of the increase in student enrollment in the South and West has been due to Hispanic children. The percentage of Hispanic students in western states, for example, rose from 15 percent to 30 percent between 1972 and 1998. Even more revealing is the fact that in 1998, 48 percent of students in public elementary and secondary schools in western states were minority students (U.S. Department of Education, 2000).

At one time, many states had rather homogeneous population patterns. Today, conditions within all states vary to some degree because of factors such as land values, migration patterns, economic development, and employment opportunities. As a consequence, variables such as poverty, race, and educational attainment are not distributed evenly—even within states (Hodgkinson, 1999). Thus, school officials also must pay close attention to regional and county demographic trends to determine general and student population shifts.

Demographics at the local district present another challenge. Unless districts have extremely stable population patterns, administrators need to monitor changes among schools. Unstable student populations have been most prevelant in larger districts. Many urban districts, for instance, lost thousands of students because of general population declines and because of court-ordered busing during the 1960s and 1970s. But these downward trends have not always been permanent. The Indianapolis Public Schools lost approximately 10,000 students after a judge ordered a one-way busing program. School district officials had to close schools and decide whether to retain or sell the property. Approximately 25 years later, the busing plan is being phased out and the district now faces the prospect of substantial enrollment increases.

In summary, the overall enrollment in elementary and secondary public schools is once again increasing. Clearly, this will require new or larger school buildings. But the growth pattern is not uniform: not all districts are growing. In addition, the nature of the population is changing; at the same time the overall student population is increasing, the percentage of white students enrolled in public education is declining.

SCHOOL RESTRUCTURING

Another variable affecting definitions of school building adequacy is restructuring. During the 1980s, school reformers attempted to improve educational outputs by tinkering with existing organizational structure. The intent was to "fix" the institution by essentially making students and teachers do more of what they were already doing (referred to as intensification mandates). Prime examples included increasing the length of the school day, graduation requirements, and the length of the school year (Cuban, 1988; Raywid, 1990). Because they did not change the basic organizational structure of schools, these initiatives required little or no adaptations to school buildings.

More recently, however, reformers have embraced a different school reform perspective. They now conclude that schools will not be more effective unless roles, relationships, programs, and delivery of programs are reconfigured. More important, these transformations need to be site-specific—that is, the nature of the change will be shaped by the specific needs of local districts and schools and not by generic national standards. Thus, school restructuring is viewed as a school-specific process for school improvement. Whereas the reform initiatives of the 1980s had little effect on facilities, the concept of restructuring raises a number of consequential issues about school design (Goldberg, 1991).

From a process perspective, restructuring requires ample space to accommodate activities such as shared decision making, teacher collaboration, and team planning. Unfortunately, many existing schools are less than adequate in this regard. For example, they do not have sufficient spaces for small group activities, especially for small groups of adults. From a program perspective, restructuring often requires ample and appropriate spaces to accommodate emerging instructional strategies and curriculum modifications. Examples include using instructional teams in middle schools, some departmentalized instruction in elementary schools, and interdisciplinary courses in high schools. In general, restructuring requires schools to have sufficient and flexible spaces. However, a study sponsored by the General Accounting Office (1996) found that over half the nation's schools lacked these qualities.

One of the more popular restructuring ideas has been site-based management—a decentralization concept that makes the individual school more responsible for planning and program development. Principals involved in implementing this concept will readily acknowledge that new demands were placed on their facilities. For example, decentralization of authority almost always increases the number of meetings held in the school and increases parental involvement with the school. These changes usually require an interactive environment in which individuals can communicate freely and collaborate. The following are selected examples of reform ideas that have direct implications for school environments.

- *State Deregulation and District Decentralization.* Predicated on the idea that educational decisions are most effective when they are made closest to students, public education has shifted toward ideas such as site-based management. These concepts require more planning and policy decisions at the district and school levels. Consequently, facilities must accommodate both an increase in these activities and the technologies to support them.

- *Teacher Professionalism.* Greater autonomy for teachers requires more office and planning areas in schools. It also necessitates that teachers have access to technology that integrates voice, video, and data.

- *Shared Decision Making.* In traditional schools, the administrative areas are often limited in size because relatively few individuals had decision-making and management responsibilities. As the processes become more democratic, areas such as conference rooms become more essential.

- *Increased Community Involvement.* Most schools, especially elementary schools, were not designed to accommodate ongoing community involvement. Such involvement could include volunteer work, participation on committees, increased conferencing, and learning activities. Some new schools now include community pride rooms—areas that are used by adults to access the internet, to hold meetings, and similar activities.

- *Scheduling Modifications.* During the 1990s, several new approaches to scheduling education resurfaced. The most popular have included block scheduling (designed to intensify instruction), single-track year-round calendars (designed to reduce the negative effects of summer learning losses), and expanded summer programming (e.g., remedial courses for students who failed state tests). Such modifications affect both quantitative (e.g., amount of spaces needed) and qualitative (e.g., air-conditioning) dimensions of an adequate school.

- *Full-Service Schools.* Some communities have adopted the idea of providing full-service schools (sometimes called community schools). The initiative is premised on the idea that some children will not be able to reach their academic potential unless medical, social, emotional, physical, and psychological problems are addressed. Hence, the school facility must accommodate a range of specialists who provide these services on a full-or part-time basis.

School reform has also included specific curricular and instructional modifications that have implications for facilities. Among them, are the following:

- *Interdisciplinary Teams.* This concept is central to the middle-school philosophy and many expect it will become common in high schools. Teaming creates a need for planning spaces and diversified instructional spaces.

- *Technology Education.* The traditional curriculum in industrial education is rapidly being transformed into technology education. Hands-on courses such as woods and metals are being replaced with new courses such as electronics. Both the size of the instructional spaces and the nature of the equipment used are affected.

- *Increased Emphasis on Science.* More students are planning to attend college and enrollment in science courses is increasing. More and better-equipped labs are necessary. Many new elementary schools now have one or more science laboratories, which allows younger students to engage in active learning. Outdoor science areas (nature labs) also are becoming common.

- *Individualized Instruction.* A greater focus on individual learning styles and ability differences create the need for a greater variety of learning spaces. In secondary schools this may include areas for individual learning, and in elementary schools this may include areas for small-group instruction.

TECHNOLOGY

Adhering to the guiding principle that form follows function, architects who design educational environments recognize that operations affect appearance (Sabo, 1996). Unfortunately, there usually is a considerable lag time between the introduction of new programs, ideas, and equipment and the redesign of spaces. As an example, some schools designed in the early 1980s did not have computer labs, and some designed in the early 1990s did not have sufficient wiring and cable to provide widespread access to the Internet. The problem is made even worse by the fact that advancements in technology are occurring at an increasingly rapid rate. Thus, anticipating future advancements in technology has become one of the greatest challenges facing architects and school administrators.

Personal computers and their interconnectivity have had a substantial impact on many, but not all, schools in the past 25 years. A national study in the mid-1990s found that most schools did not fully use modern technologies and lacked access to the information superhighway (General Accounting Office, 1996). This was particularly true in the oldest schools. Of schools built in 1985 or later, 59 percent were connected to the Internet in 1995, whereas only 42 percent of the schools built before 1969 had such connections (U.S. Department of Education, 1999).

The extent to which technology has contributed to new definitions of adequate schools is exemplified by its deployment in teaching and administration. The digital revolution and real-time communication encourage educators to use integrated voice, video, and data in their daily activities. In the modern school, one would find

- Keyboarding (computer) labs,
- Computers in every classroom, office, conference area, and support area,
- Networking,
- Distance learning classrooms,
- Head-end and file server rooms,
- Visual information systems that allow visual tapes, Power Point presentations, telephone conferencing, and similar functions to occur in every classroom,
- Modern media centers equipped with a range of technologies (e.g., fax machines, electronic catalogs).

Technology also has affected all support services commonly found in schools. Examples include food services, energy management, facility maintenance, and inventory control. Today, most new school buildings are designed to incorporate structured wiring systems that integrate building automation, energy management, and fire alarm and security functions.

The infusion of technology into school buildings almost always increases space requirements. This is especially true with respect to the average classroom. For example, a second-grade classroom may have 900 square feet and accommodate 25 pupils. Once you put four or five computers in that space, the area becomes crowded—especially if the computers are dispersed around the room. Obviously, labs and operation rooms add to the overall size of schools. Almost always, technology increases the cost of constructing or renovating school buildings (Glass, 1999), a factor not always apparent to taxpayers. And the public does not always support increased costs due to technology. Some critics (e.g., Oppenheimer, 1997) have argued that there is little evidence to support the contention that computers have had a positive effect on learning. Such judgments, however, are myopic and ignore the reality that the computer has contributed to new ways of accessing and using information—and in this regard, they created new ways of learning.

CONDITION OF EXISTING BUILDINGS

Despite several national reports detailing a school facility crisis in America, many taxpayers still do not recognize the magnitude of the problem. In 1998, the average public school building in this country was 42 years old; the average age of a building in Northeast and Central states was 47, and in Southeast states it was 37 (U.S. Department of Education, 1999). In a 1995 study, the General Accounting Office (1996) discovered that almost 60 percent of the nation's schools reported at least one major building feature in disrepair, requiring extensive repair or replacement. Buildings in disrepair negatively affect the morale, health, and productivity of both teachers and students (Frazier, 1993). In the mid-1990s, it was estimated that public elementary and secondary education needed about $112 billion to address current deficiencies (General Accounting Office, 1996).

The projected life span of a school building is not uniform. While some are designed to last up to 70 years, others become obsolete in less than 40 years. Funding school construction, especially in those states requiring local taxpayers to assume all or most of the burden, is both an economic and a political issue (Kowalski & Schmielau, 2000). Often inexpensive facilities are constructed on the premise that the next generation of taxpayers will pay to improve or replace them. But when the next generation abdicates this responsibility, an even greater burden gets passed to a third generation of taxpayers. This philosophy and an overall neglect for proper maintenance have certainly contributed to the current facility crisis (Krysiak, 1999).

The utility of existing facilities also has been reduced by a greater awareness of health and safety standards. From a health perspective, environmental hazards such as radon gas and asbestos, lead paint, and poor indoor air quality are responsible for many older buildings being labeled as "sick schools" (Grubb & Daimantes, 1998). From a safety perspective, older schools were rarely designed to provide access control and pupil control. And because health and safety concerns present an immediate danger, many districts have had to use operating funds to resolve these problems (Ornstein, 1994)—an action that further reduces the effectiveness of schools.

In general, schools require some renovation and equipment replacement after just 20 years. Even when funds to do this have been available, some school district officials postponed action because limited resources earmarked for facilities were used to cover other educational needs (Marcus, 1995). Both deferred maintenance and an unwillingness to replace buildings at reasonable intervals have contributed to the existing crisis. In some communities, voters have repeatedly rejected recommendations for school construction, even when the need for such action was blatantly obvious. Most often, they did so because they rejected the premise that property taxes should be the primary funding source for school construction.

While funding school construction is both an economic and political issue, the political dimensions have typically been more dominant (Dahlkemper, 1997). In states that require local districts to cover all or most of the costs of school construction with property tax revenues, district officials have encountered fierce opposition from property owners who did not have children enrolled in the public schools. Differences in property wealth in these states have resulted in tremendous disparities in tax rates and in the quality of educational facilities. Consequently, districts most needing to replace or renovate schools often experience the greatest difficulty getting taxpayer approval for such initiatives.

The effects of neglecting school buildings have been compounded by the proclivity of governors and state legislators to mandate school improvement initiatives without providing necessary funding. For example, some states are restricting enrollment in primary grades—a supportable idea that nevertheless produces the need for more elementary school classrooms. Yet, these same policy makers have rarely provided districts with money to construct the additional classrooms. Reductions in class size, extended school years, all-day kindergarten or preschool programs, and expanded graduation requirements are common examples of state policies resulting in a need for more space.

CHAPTER SUMMARY

The adequacy of the nation's infrastructure for public education is being affected by four primary variables presented in this chapter. Enrollment is again rising, creating the need for more classrooms; for example, the 51.7 million students enrolled in elementary and secondary schools in 1997 is higher than the previous record of 51.3 million set in 1971 (Jones, 1997). In addition, the student population is becoming increasingly diverse—a condition that also presents challenges for programming and for facilities to house the programs.

School restructuring and technology also present new needs for school buildings. The process of restructuring requires areas for visioning and planning, community involvement, and collaborative decision making. In addition, the outcomes of the process are likely to require additional and different instructional spaces in many schools. The infusion of computers and other new technologies into schools over the past 25 years also add to space needs. More important, technology has already altered the ways in which many teachers and administrators work.

Finally, the infrastructure of America's schools is weakened by the fact that many existing buildings are old, unhealthy, and unsafe. A combination of antiquated state policies requiring total or near-total local funding, neglected maintenance, and increased environmental hazards are responsible.

ISSUES FOR DISCUSSION

1. In what ways do changes in migration and birth patterns affect the need for school facilities?

2. What factors might affect enrollment trends in a school district?

3. In what ways might increased diversity affect the design of school buildings?

4. What does school restructuring mean? Is restructuring a process or a product?

5. Both state deregulation and district decentralization have become popular reform ideas. What implications do these concepts have for school design?

6. What mandates in your state have contributed to an increased need for school facilities?

7. In what ways have computers contributed to the need for school construction?

8. What new technologies other than computers are commonly found in the modern school? How do these technologies affect definitions of adequacy?

9. What are some barriers in older schools that may physically prevent technology from being deployed?

10. How might technology affect the cost of school construction?

11. As many as 50 percent of the schools in this country need to be replaced or renovated. What has caused this crisis?

12. How does initial cost affect the life expectancy of a building?

13. Often, funding school construction is both an economic and political issue. Why?

14. In states where a majority of the cost of school construction comes from local tax revenues, how does district wealth (as measured by taxable property) deter or enhance a district's ability to improve school facilities?

REFERENCES

Caffarella, E.P. (1987). Effects of the baby boomette on school enrollment. *School Business Affairs, 53*(7), 26–28, 41–43.

Cuban, L. (1988). The fundamental puzzle of school reform. *Phi Delta Kappan, 69*(5), 341–344.

Dahlkemper, L. (1997). Rundown schools: Whose responsibility? *State Legislatures, 23*(8), 15–19.

Digest of education statistics. (1999). Washington, DC: National Center for Education Statistics, U.S. Department of Education.

Frazier, L.M. (1993). *Deteriorating school facilities and student learning*. (ERIC Document Reproduction Service No. ED 356 564)

General Accounting Office. (1996). *School facilities: America's schools report differing conditions*. Washington, DC: U.S. Government Printing Office.

Glass, T.E. (1999). Hidden costs of school construction. *School Business Affairs, 65*(7), 6–8, 10–12.

Goldberg, B. (1991). Redesigning schools: Architecture and school restructuring. *Radius, 3*(1).

Grubb, D., & Diamantes, T. (1998). Is your school sick? Five threats to healthy schools. *Clearing House, 71*(4), 202–207.

Hodgkinson, H. (1999). State differences: The key to demographics. *School Business Affairs, 65*(5), 32–36.

Jones, R. (1997). The kids are coming. *American School Board Journal, 184*(4), 20–24.

Kowalski, T.J., & Schmielau, R. (2000, April). *Potential for achieving liberty and equality in funding school construction: Analysis of state laws and policies at the end of the 20th century*. Paper presented at the annual conference of the American Educational Research Association, New Orleans, LA.

Krysiak, B.H. (1999). Keeping up with what you have. *School Business Affairs, 65*(7), 49–53.

Marcus, J. (1995). A sorry state of disrepair. *American School Board Journal, 182*(4), 37–39.

Oppenheimer, T. (1997). The computer delusion. *The Atlantic Monthly, 280*(1), 45–62.

Ornstein, A.C. (1994). School finance and the conditions of schools. *Theory into Practice, 33*(2), 118–125.

Raywid, M.A. (1990). The evolving effort to improve schools: Pseudo-reforms, incremental reform, and restructuring. *Phi Delta Kappan, 72*(2), 139–143.

Sabo, S.R. (1996). Shaping school design. *The American School Board Journal, 183*(10), 42–44.

U.S. Department of Education, National Center for Education Statistics. (1999). *How old are America's schools?* (NCES 1999–048). Washington, DC: U.S. Government Printing Office.

U.S. Department of Education, National Center for Education Statistics. (2000). *The condition of education 2000* (NCES 2000–602), Washington, DC: U.S. Government Printing Office.

CHAPTER 5

Planning Models

Unfortunately many superintendents and boards of education stumble into the facility-planning process, that is, considered selection and use of a structured planning model do not guide their decisions relative to replacing or renovating public buildings at a cost of millions of dollars. Frequently, this behavior is predicated on the notion that detailed planning is not necessary because the board and administration already know what the public needs and wants. Actions based entirely on such unfounded assumptions, however, often constrain and hamper future education programs, result in costly mistakes, create conflict, and damage a district's credibility for years.

No facility-planning project should begin unless three conditions have been achieved.

- The project has a clear purpose.
- An appropriate planning model has been selected.
- The planning participants and their roles have been determined.

While school construction projects serve the practical purpose of providing an adequate and safe environment for educators and students, they also offer an opportunity to improve services to the total community. Changing or augmenting the curriculum and instructional practices—outcomes made more likely by systems planning—accomplishes this. In fact, inclusive and comprehensive planning is the best way to ensure the bricks and mortar provide the necessary space and design for intended educational programs (Moore, 1991).

Figure 5–1
Attributes of Planning Models

Attribute	*Continua*

Linearity	Non-linear planning ————————————— Linear planning
Goal Orientation	Predetermined goals ————————————— Evolving goals
Time Parameters	Short-range planning ————————————— Long-range planning
Participation	Restrictive (administrators only) ————————————— Inclusive
Flexibility	Immutable goals ————————————— Flexible goals
Comprehensiveness	Issue focused ————————————— System focused

This chapter examines planning attributes and discusses their implications. In addition, five commonly used approaches to facility planning are explained and critiqued. Finally, the chapter provides criteria for selecting a planning paradigm.

PLANNING ATTRIBUTES

School officials routinely engage in planning that spans educational programs, staffing, financial management, and facility management.In assuming this responsibility, administrators have an opportunity to make important choices regarding the processes they will use. There are many approaches to planning, and selecting an effective process is as important as making the correct planning decisions once a process is in motion. Accordingly, administrators should adopt a planning model that they understand, have the ability to implement, and have the resources to implement (Howe & Schrader, 1997). Often administrators ignore this advice and select a planning paradigm simply on the basis of convenience.

Before discussing specific paradigms, it is helpful to understand the attributes that distinguish one model from another. Attributes relate to qualities that define the operational philosophy of a planning process. In the case of planning paradigms, there are six primary attributes as shown in Figure 5–1.

Linearity

Planning models are defined broadly as being *linear* or *nonlinear*. Linear models have been described as "prescriptive, providing the planner a sequential path to follow" (Kowalski, 1999, p. 219). Once the first step is completed, each successive step is dependent on the preceding step. Applying a linear model is akin to following a recipe when baking a cake. Linear models reflect the influence of rational decision making; that is, the overall task is broken into parts and each part is completed before the next commences. Theoretically, this permits planners to concentrate on individual components until each is completed properly. Linear planning has been dominant in educational administration because it is relatively straightforward and simple. This approach, however, has two potential pitfalls. First, planners can get stalled at a particular step causing time delays or sufficient frustration that scuttles the process. Second, different individuals may be assigned to work on different steps (largely on the basis of expertise) resulting in planning participants gaining only a small portion of information.

Nonlinear paradigms do not prescribe a specific set of steps for planning, and they allow various components of planning to occur simultaneously. The primary attribute of this approach is providing choices with respect to time and resources. Murk and Galbraith (1986), proponents of this concept, argued that because of the idiosyncratic nature of schools and communities, nonlinear planning allows administrators to determine the appropriate starting point based on the contextual variables that frame their work. They also noted that nonlinear models were more effective in dealing with system breaks (unanticipated occurrences that often derail linear planning). While they are more flexible, nonlinear models are more prone to generate conflict and they can be difficult to coordinate. Administrators who are inexperienced in planning usually find nonlinear models more threatening.

Goal Orientation

Planning may begin with one or more goals predetermined or the process may be structured to allow goals to evolve over time. Almost always, school districts engage in facility planning with one or more objectives in mind. For example, the superintendent appoints a planning committee to determine the best way to address a lack of facility space at a high school. The committee members accept the validity of this problem, and, thus, they concentrate on identifying and recommending the best solution. Rational planning exemplifies a paradigm in which one or more goals are predetermined. Most planning models have a goal orientation.

The purpose of allowing goals to evolve during the planning process is to encourage open communication and creativity. Instead of directing the planning committee to seek a remedy for crowding at the high school, the superintendent charges the committee with the responsibility of examining programming and facilities. In so doing, the superintendent is careful not to inject any conclusions or biases. Thus, as the planning committee moves forward with its work, the members may or may not decide whether there is a lack of space at the high school.

Time Parameters

The time dimension of planning is also an important variable. Short-range planning generally refers to time parameters of two years or less. This type of planning is further divided into two categories.

- *Problem-Based.* School officials must identify actions to address an existing problem (Lewis, 1983); for example, a plan is devised to determine how the school district will deal with asbestos removal from three buildings over a six-month period.
- *Operations-Based.* School officials must conduct plans in annual or biannual cycles (Lewis, 1983); examples include developing budget and staffing plans.

Because short-range planning is almost always focused on issues that fall within the domain of normal administrative operations, participation is usually limited to administrative personnel and a linear process is employed. However, short-range planning can be conducted in other ways.

Long-range planning generally addresses a period of more than two years. While some writers have treated long-range planning and strategic planning as being interchangeable, other authors (e.g., McCune, 1986) have defined them as different approaches, and they are not treated as being synonymous here. The reason is that not all long-range planning is strategic in nature.

Participation

Participation in planning falls along a continuum that ranges from closed to open. Closed planning refers to a process conducted in relative isolation with only a few select school officials participating. The notion of closed planning is nested in classical theory. Only high-ranking administrators are considered to have sufficient information and expertise to contribute to the necessary decisions (Hanson, 1996). Actually, involving other district employees (e.g., principals and teachers) and the public is viewed as counterproductive because their involvement is thought to reduce objectivity. Put another way, these individuals would only contribute their values and emotions thus reducing the objectivity of the planning process and increasing the likelihood of conflict. The presumed advantage of closed planning is expediency—that is, the process can be completed quickly because only a few individuals make the decisions.

Despite these presumed benefits, closed planning is almost always a poor alternative for public decision making. Inputs are limited, often resulting in judgment errors regarding needs and wants. In addition, excluding district employees and community representatives from planning almost always produces a negative political outcome: The public is less likely to support the planning outcomes (Kowalski, 1999). This is an especially crucial consideration in most states, because voter approval is necessary for the tax increases associated with construction.

Open planning is predicated on the assumption that planners make better decisions when they appropriately weigh the values, beliefs, and attitudes of the entire community. While this approach often sparks more conflict and takes more time to complete than closed planning, it is compatible with democratic philosophy. Kowalski (1999) cited the following advantages of open planning:

- Real needs are more likely to be identified because a broader range of individuals is involved.
- Planning provides a medium for individuals and groups with competing philosophies and ideas to exchange ideas and to possibly compromise.
- Planning participants are exposed to a substantial amount of information about education and the district; this information allows them to make informed choices about addressing needs.
- Planning participants often play a key role in building broader community support for the planning initiatives.

Since the 1970s, there has been a tendency for local districts to involve citizen committees in studying facility planning. However, the motives for shifting to open planning have been primarily political (the need to gain public support) and not philosophical.

Flexibility

Flexibility refers to the degree planners can change directions once planning has been initiated. Planning flexibility is described along a continuum from low to high. Low-flexibility models are designed to freeze both short-term and long-term goals for a specified period, preventing organizational officials from changing directions before the plan has had a chance to reach fruition. School boards in districts experiencing frequent changes in the superintendency, for example, may be inclined to use rigid planning in an attempt to reduce the negative effects of leadership instability (e.g., they adopt a plan with the proviso that goals cannot be altered for least five years).

The weakness of low-flexibility planning is exhibited by the fallacy of its assumptions. The planners assume that they know precisely where the organization needs to be at some future point (long-term goals) and that they know the precise incremental steps (or short-term goals) needed to reach that point. Rarely, if ever, are these assumptions valid—especially when planning spans more than one or two years. Consequently, low-flexibility planning encourages school officials to ignore changing organizational and community conditions— conditions that may clearly negate the validity of both short-range and long-range goals (Kowalski, 1999).

High-flexibility planning is based on different assumptions. The planners believe that organizational and societal changes they cannot initially predict will occur during the duration of the plan. Moreover, these changes may be sufficiently powerful to diminish or eradicate the utility of some of the plan's goals. Consequently, goals, both short-range and long-range, are considered mutable; that is, the planners change them as soon as new evidence suggests that it is advantageous to do so.

Comprehensiveness

The attribute of comprehensiveness is related to goal orientation, but yet it is different. A paradigm ranking low in this attribute focuses exclusively on a single function of an organization (e.g., facility planning in the case of school districts). Typically, focused planning can be completed more rapidly and planners are not prone to be distracted by other elements of operations in the organization. And because the planners are not studying the entire district, the process usually requires fewer resources. The primary weakness of focused planning is that it ignores the reality that specific aspects of districts and schools do not exist in isolation, rather they are part of larger systems.

Comprehensive planning is shaped by systems theory. Accordingly, the process is based on the assumption that all operations should be appropriately evaluated when making decisions about any specific part of the system (Carey, 1999). For example, plans for a new high school could be affected by community economic development decisions. Unless the planners examined all aspects of the district and community, they would not account for this contingency. Therefore, comprehensive planning is considered more effective than isolated or narrowly focused planning.

POPULAR PLANNING PARADIGMS

Differences among planning models are illuminated by the attributes discussed in the preceding section. If administrators are to make informed choices, they must know the planning options that are available and they must be able to evaluate the attributes in relation to contextual variables in their districts and communities. The five models discussed here represent a spectrum of the options available to facility planners and are the ones most frequently used by school administrators.

Rational Planning

Planning became an integral part of school administration in the 1950s when the profession embraced Herbert Simon's theoretical work on this topic. He held that organizations such as school districts were rational institutions working toward logical and preferred solutions to administrative problems (Simon, 1955). Therefore, the path or set of actions that led to solutions was both rational and linear. In essence, rational decision making relies on logic and science to make impartial choices related to one or more predetermined goals based on a pre-scribed format to ensure objective analysis (Giesecke, 1993).

Rational planning is intended to achieve ideal solutions. Drucker (1974) out-lined the following steps for the process:

- Defining the problem
- Analyzing the problem
- Developing alternative solutions
- Deciding on the best solution
- Converting the best solution into effective action (pp. 19–20)

Management by objectives and zero-base budgeting, popular concepts during the 1960s and 1970s, are examples of this model. Rational planning is predicated on three key assumptions.

- Planners have the ability to be completely objective.
- Planners have the ability to access all the information they require.
- All data can be assessed quantitatively. (Kowalski, 1999)

Despite the fact that these assumptions are rarely valid with respect to public education, rational planning has been the dominant paradigm used by adminis-trators for facility planning (Castaldi, 1994). One reason is linearity; that is, many administrators feel more comfortable using a step-by-step approach. An-other reason is that rational models are congruous with the hierarchical structure still found in most school districts (Earthman, 1992). In these bureaucratic-type organizations, a few top-level administrators assume that they have the infor-mation and expertise necessary to make ideal decisions on behalf of the public, and therefore they control the process.

Rational planning models have several shortcomings. Time is one of them. In the real world of school administration, superintendents and principals rarely have the time necessary to identify and evaluate all potential problems and solutions. Another weakness is resource limitations. Administrators usually do not have access to complete information; thus, they are unable to identify and evaluate all possible problems and solutions. Additionally, administrators often embrace aspects of Herbert Simon's work on rational planning while ignoring his caveats. For example, Simon (1970) noted that in order to make objectively rational decisions, an administrator must be able to

- View all decision alternatives in panoramic fashion prior to making a choice,
- Correctly identify all potential consequences that would follow each choice,
- Assign value to each alternative and select one on the basis of quantitative superiority.

In actual facility planning, administrators never have complete information, conditions are often ambiguous, and uncertainty is pervasive.

Bounded Rationality

Recognizing rational planning's limitations, theorists developed a variation known as "bounded rationality." This iteration was premised on the conclusion that rational planning's basic assumptions were flawed: the belief that organizations could be totally rational and the belief that planners possessed or could obtain complete information. However, bounded rationality does retain however, the attributes of goal orientation and linearity. Simon (1997) described bounded rationality in four actions.

- *Intelligence activity* (identifying problems)
- *Design activity* (identifying possible solutions)
- *Choice activity* (selecting a course of action)
- *Review activity* (evaluating outcomes)

By rejecting the assumptions of total rationality and complete information, bounded rationality does not purport to produce perfect decisions. Instead the concept often leads to "satisficing"—a process in which planners select a satisfactory but less than ideal choice (Hellreigel & Slocum, 1996). As an example, planners in a school district often recommend solutions for facility problems knowing that not all members of the community will be supportive. Bounded rationality models are considered an improvement over rational models because they recognize uncertainty, values, competing interests, and biases as pervasive organizational characteristics.

Strategic Planning

General Electric popularized strategic planning in the 1960s when executives in that company recognized that changes outside their organization would have a greater impact on future success than would internal controls. Many private corporations now use some form of strategic planning in an effort to achieve organizational transformations by infusing changes and trends from outside the organization into organizational decision making (Bradford & Duncan, 2000; McCune, 1986). In other words, strategic planning in the private sector has focused on determining strategic actions to plan products, achieve market shares, and enhance profit levels (Bradford & Duncan, 2000).

One of the distinguishing features of strategic planning is the integration of external information inputs. As an example, companies infuse market research studies as a way of determining what the public really wants and needs. The process is intended to get administrators to think "outside the box" of their own work, and in this vein, strategic planning is considered to have the power to transform an organization (Quong, Walker, & Stott, 1999). This can be accomplished in the following ways:

- Planners are encouraged to revise or replace the organization's mission.
- Planners are sensitive to external forces that have the power to determine the organization's success.
- Planners provide strategic directions allowing an organization to focus on its goals and to achieve its mission.
- Planners are required to assess the organization's capacity for improvement. (Rea & Kerzner, 1999)

The generic term "long-range planning" is often used to connote rational planning that spans more than a couple of years. This is one reason why strategic planning and long-range planning should not be treated as synonymous. In truth, any planning paradigm could involve long-term planning. Long-range rational planning is usually an internal planning process used to develop and achieve goals in a comparatively stable environment. Strategic planning is externally driven, examining the environment for information and analyzing what is happening in the community and world. Strategic planning typically is inclusive—that is, the process involves a broad spectrum of stakeholders (McCune, 1986). Put another way, rational planning usually views the organization as a closed system (i.e., closed to interventions from its external environment), whereas strategic planning usually views the organization as an open system that must change constantly to meet the challenges of an ever-changing world (Bryson, 1995).

The literature reflects a general agreement that a strategic planning model should include at least six processes to function effectively. They include:

- Database development
- Strategic analysis
- Development of the strategic plan
- Capacity analysis
- Action planning
- Establishing a planning cycle (Beach & Trent, 2000; Cook, 1985; Howe & Schrader, 1997)

In addition, the process should involve parents, other taxpayers, and staff so that they assume ownership in the plan (Bradford & Duncan, 2000). According to Cook (1988), implementation entails the following planning team activities.

- *Developing a Database*. This involves collecting quantitative and qualitative data.
- *Conducting Strategic Analysis*. Analysis of internal and external data is undertaken to identify trends that may affect future goal setting and implementation strategies; activity produces planning assumptions.
- *Developing the Strategic Plan*. A mission statement, strategic vision, and goal setting are completed.
- *Conducting Capacity Analysis*. Determinations are made regarding the sufficiency of current or projected resources in relation to the plan.
- *Establishing an Action Plan*. Strategies for goal attainment are developed.
- *Establishing a Planning Cycle*. The planning process is made continuous within specified cycles that culminate with evaluations.

Integrative Planning

In the 1960s, alternative models that were goal-free and developmental in nature emerged. These paradigms, collectively referred to as "integrative models," differed from rational models in that goals and targets evolved during the planning process rather than being predetermined. This paradigm is developmental in that stakeholders are involved from the outset, allowing them to participate in establishing the agenda, setting priorities, and determining both organizational and planning goals (Beach & Trent, 2000). The main advantage of integrative planning is that the participants are able to draw their own conclusions about needs and goals. Often the freedom to do this results in a deeper sense of ownership in the planning outcomes by a broad range of the community.

Integrative planning, however, can be conflict-ridden and chaotic, especially when the participants are uncertain about the overall process or about their respective roles in it (Beach & Trent, 2000). The model is considered best-suited for school districts experiencing considerable and rapid change. Because goals are not predetermined and organizations are not treated as rational entities, interactive planning requires strong leadership and facilitation from administrators who must coordinate the process, adjudicate philosophical and political disputes, and keep the planning participants on task. Rational models rely on predetermined goals and a prescribed process; interactive models allow planning participants to make critical decisions at times they deem appropriate.

Contingency Planning

With most planning models, including strategic planning, planners make two assumptions: They know precisely where their organization can and should be at some point in the future, and they can determine the precise steps that must be taken to move from the current status to the desired status. Accordingly, long-term goals are pursued incrementally by using operational (one-year) goals.

Selecting and pursuing a single goal can be problematic because contextual variables, many beyond the control of school administrators, can change rapidly. For example, information technologies are changing so rapidly that even well conceived plans frequently become obsolete well before they are implemented (Yorsi, 1993).

Both contingency planning and strategic planning rely on the assumption that the relevancy of goals and the organization's ability to attain them are dependent on a combination of organizational and environmental conditions. But contingency planning also is predicated on three other assumptions not integral to other planning paradigms.

- Rather than setting a specific long-range goal for an area of operation, organizations experiencing changing conditions should establish multiple potential futures that are possible based on current environmental and organizational conditions.
- Annual assessments (operational plans) are required to monitor trends and reevaluate the validity of contingency goals.
- Rather than protecting long-range goals until their intended implementation date, those that are found to be no longer valid should be eliminated or altered; new trends may require the addition of long-range contingency goals (Kowalski, 1999).

Contingency planning may be criticized if the organization is constantly shifting or changing its long-range goals. Doing this can create instability that deters true change. Thus, contingency long-range goals should only be deleted, altered, or added when there is clear and compelling evidence to do so.

COMPARING PLANNING PARADIGMS

In many instances, school officials have moved forward with facility projects without using any specific planning paradigm. This clearly is the least desirable alternative. Among those who have used a planning paradigm, rational and strategic models have been the norm. In an effort to provide a deeper understanding of the options available, the planning paradigms described in the previous section are compared to each other.

Primary Attributes

Planning paradigms differ with respect to what they are intended to provide: either as process or outcomes. Table 5–1 summarizes the perceived attributes of the planning models discussed here. Both rational planning and bounded rationality have an internal orientation; that is, they focus on internal operations of the organization while generally ignoring environmental factors. Including community representatives in facility planning is encouraged for at least two reasons: such participation provides more accurate information about real needs and wants, and such participation is critical to establishing political support.

Table 5–1
Paradigm Attributes

Attribute	Rational Planning	Bounded Rationality	Strategic Planning	Integrative Planning	Contingency Planning
Implementation	Easy	Easy	Difficult	Difficult	Difficult
Flexibility	Low	Low	Moderate	High	High
Scope of analysis	Limited	Limited	Broad	Broad	Broad
Community participation	Never	Rarely	Rarely	Always	Occasionally
Use of environmental data	Never	Rarely	Always	Usually	Always

Although strategic planning requires a significant amount of external information, it does not require that persons other than district employees be directly involved. While some authors (e.g., Carey, 1999; Quong, Walker, & Stott, 1999) encourage community involvement on the planning team, doing so has not been the norm. In many districts, only administrators are part of the strategic planning team. Strategic planning does encourage administrators to seek public reactions; for example, data are usually shared with citizens in an effort to ascertain their reactions and opinions (McCune, 1986).

Scope of analysis refers to the extent to which planning is conducted from a systems perspective. Both rational models and bounded rationality are likely to focus on a single concern (e.g., the need for a new high school). Complete data covering the entire community and district are not likely to be infused, since doing so is treated as an unnecessary distraction. The other three models rely on a systems perspective.

Flexibility has become increasingly important because the future has become less certain. In this vein, integrative and contingency planning, although difficult to implement, have become more popular models. Contingency planning is more structured and administrator-oriented than integrative planning.

Data Sources

The five paradigms examined here also differ markedly in the types of data required. Both rational models and bounded rationality depend on internal, quantitative data. Such data are considered to be less vulnerable to bias and subjectivity. The other planning paradigms use a broader range of data generated both internally and externally. Integrative planning, in particular, is oriented toward qualitative data.

Potential Problems

The types of problems likely to evolve from the planning models also differ substantially. Table 5–2 provides a listing of the most common difficulties. Administrators often are able to eliminate or avoid certain common concerns by modifying a paradigm. As an example, strategic planning is typically more effective politically if administrators opt to use an inclusive planning team (i.e.,

Table 5–2
Problems Associated with Planning Paradigms

Paradigm	Common Problems
Rational Planning	Goals are based on inaccurate judgments of real needs and wants because environmental input has been excluded; the effects of bias and subjectivity are ignored; often there is little political support among employees or taxpayers for outcomes.
Bounded Rationality	Goals are based on inaccurate judgments of real needs and wants because environmental input has been excluded; tendency to rely on "satisficing," which may produce marginal decisions.
Strategic Planning	Process can be quite inflexible if there is resistance to adjusting long-range goals annually; political support for outcomes may be low if citizens are not involved in the planning process; implementation can be quite time-consuming.
Integrative Planning	Can become chaotic if not properly coordinated; can be time-consuming and inefficient; likely to produce serious conflict; can produce highly subjective goals that may not reflect real needs.
Contingency Planning	If long-range goals are altered continuously, the planning process is attenuated because ideas never have an opportunity to reach fruition; the process is difficult and time-consuming.

a team that includes both citizens and employees). Or integrative planning can be less conflict-ridden and chaotic if administrators are adequately prepared to facilitate the process.

CRITERIA FOR PLANNING AND OUTCOMES

Planning would be much easier if there were a single paradigm ideal for all conditions. But this clearly is not the case. Communities, districts, and facility projects are not identical. Consequently, administrators need to ask two critical questions: What planning model is best suited for conditions in this district? What qualities should be expected in the planning outcomes? Answers to both queries can be guided by criteria that reflect good practice across all districts.

Criteria for Selecting a Paradigm

Arguably, all planning models have been effective at certain times and in certain locations. But selecting the most appropriate approach for a given situation requires an interface of contextual variables (i.e., conditions existing in a specific district) and general facility planning guidelines. These guidelines are stated here as criteria, and they include the following:

- *A systems perspective should guide planning.* Planning errors are far more likely when administrators separate a specific problem from the context of community and school district. School districts are complex entities, and decisions in any part of the organization are likely to affect the entire organization.
- *The planning process should be inclusive.* Planning is more effective when a broad

spectrum of the community and district is involved. Today, citizens who resist tax increases can scuttle even the best goals (Ray, Hack, & Candoli, 2001). Involving key individuals in planning is an effective way to reduce political resistance.

- *The planning process should rely on both quantitative and qualitative data.* Many important factors affecting facility decisions are not quantifiable. For example, school officials may not be able to determine the future needs of the science curriculum by studying past enrollment trends.

- *The process should be congruous with the district's resources.* No planning model can be effective if a school district does not have the material and human resources necessary to implement it properly.

- *The process should be sufficiently flexible.* The amount of flexibility required depends on the nature of the community and school district. Areas experiencing rapid change need highly flexible paradigms.

- *The focus of planning should be long-term.* New school buildings are expected to last 50 or more years. Even renovations are expected to prolong a building's life span by 25 or more years. Hence, decisions about facility planning should have a long-term orientation.

- *The process should recognize the importance of philosophical, political, and economic variables.* Regardless of the paradigm used, bias, subjectivity, emotions, and self-interests always affect decisions to some degree. Pretending that this does not happen only reduces the effectiveness of planning.

- *Planning should be continuous.* Most districts make the mistake of only planning when problems are obvious. The most effective facility planning occurs as part of an ongoing process of district planning. This does not mean that special planning is not necessary, rather it implies that facility planning should be an extension of district planning.

Outcome Criteria

Before choosing one planning model over another, administrators should weigh outcome criteria. These are expectations of what planning will produce. Castaldi (1994) suggests the following standards.

- The outcomes should provide a clear rationale demonstrating that the plan is logical.
- The outcomes should be flexible.
- The outcomes should be educationally defensible.
- The outcomes should be financially defensible.
- The outcomes should be within the parameters of public opinion.
- The outcomes should accommodate the future needs of the district adequately.

Ray, Hack, and Candoli (2001) add the following criteria.

- The outcomes should produce an action plan.
- The outcomes should provide sufficient information to facilitate decisions.

Most often, facility planning fails because administrators are unable to defend recommendations. Their inability to do so is usually associated with a disjunction among data, findings, conclusions, and recommendations—that is, the findings are not based on accurate data, the conclusions are not based on accurate findings, and the recommendations are not based on valid conclusions. In most communities, it is no longer sufficient for a superintendent to tell the board and public, "We need a new high school. Trust me."

CHAPTER SUMMARY

This chapter examined attributes of facility planning, planning paradigms, and criteria for selecting paradigms. Unfortunately, no one planning approach is best-suited for all situations. What will work best in a district depends on a multitude of contextual variables that relate to the community, the district, educational programs, resources, and the condition of existing facilities. Thus, administrators need to understand the range of planning models that are available to them, and they need to be able to evaluate these options using general criteria that permit them to interface their conditions with the strengths and weaknesses of these options.

Today, it is impractical to move forward with building initiatives without conducting planning. Many states require local districts to engage in planning, especially with respect to providing evidence that a need for construction exists. Liberty provisions in many states permit taxpayers to block tax increases associated with construction, and in the absence of compelling evidence of need, many of them have exercised this power (Kowalski & Schmielau, 2000). Most important, however, planning is necessary to ensure that construction is justified and shaped by real educational needs.

ISSUES FOR DISCUSSION

1. What is the difference between long-range and short-range planning? Why is long-range planning appropriate for facilities?
2. What is the difference between linear and nonlinear planning? Which is easier to implement and why?
3. What is the concept of "satisficing?" What are the advantages and disadvantages of "satisficing?"
4. What assumptions are made in rational planning? Are these assumptions valid?
5. In what ways is bounded rationality different from rational planning?
6. What is strategic planning? How does strategic planning treat information and data from outside of the school district?
7. What are the strengths and weaknesses of strategic planning?
8. What is integrative planning?
9. Under what types of conditions is integrative planning likely to be most effective?

10. What is contingency planning?

11. In what ways are contingency planning and strategic planning alike and different?

12. Why is it important to interface standard planning criteria with a district's contextual variables in selecting a specific planning model?

13. Some administrators will only examine issues directly related to a facility need in planning a new building and others will examine conditions across the entire school district. What are the advantages and disadvantages of both approaches?

REFERENCES

Beach, R.H., & Trent, J. (2000). Planning in public relations. In T.J. Kowalski (Ed.), *Public relations in schools* (2nd ed., pp. 247–271). Upper Saddle River, NJ: Merrill, Prentice-Hall.

Bradford, R., & Duncan, J. (2000) *Simplified strategic planning: A no-nonsense guide for busy people who want results fast.* Worcester, MA: Chandler House.

Bryson, J.M. (1995). *Strategic planning for public and nonprofit organizations: A guide to strengthening and sustaining organizational achievement.* San Francisco: Jossey-Bass.

Carey, K. (1999). Best-laid plans: Before you build, start with a comprehensive planning process. *The American School Board Journal, 186*(10), 36–38.

Castaldi, B. (1994). *Educational facilities: Planning, modernization, and management* (4th ed). Boston: Allyn and Bacon.

Cook, W.J. (1988). *Strategic planning for America's schools.* Arlington, VA: American Association of School Administrators.

Drucker, P.F. (1974). *Management: Tasks, responsibilities, and practices.* New York: Harper and Row.

Earthman, G. (1992). *Planning educational facilities for the next century.* Reston, VA: Association of School Business Officials International.

Giesecke, G.A. (1993). Recognizing multiple-decision making models: A guide for managers. *College and Research Libraries, 54*(2), 103–114.

Hanson, E.M. (1996). *Educational administration and organizational behavior* (4th ed.). Boston: Allyn and Bacon.

Hellreigel, D. & Slocum, J.W. (1996). *Management* (7th ed.). Cincinnati, OH: Battelle Press.

Howe, F., & Schrader, A. (Eds.). (1997). *The board member's guide to strategic planning: A practical approach to strengthening nonprofit organizations.* San Francisco: Jossey-Bass.

Kowalski, T.J. (1999). *The school superintendent: Theory, practice, and cases.* Upper Saddle River, NJ: Merrill, Prentice-Hall.

Kowalski, T.J., & Schmielau, R. (2000, April). *Liberty and equality provisions in state funding policies for school construction.* Paper presented at the annual conference of the American Educational Research Association, New Orleans, LA.

Lewis, J. (1983). *Long range and short range planning for educational administrators.* Boston: Allyn and Bacon.

McCune, S.D. (1986). *Guide to strategic planning for educators.* Alexandria, VA: Association for Supervision and Curriculum Development.

Moore, D. (Ed.). (1991). *Guide for planning educational facilities.* Scottsdale, AZ: Council of Educational Facility Planners, International.

Murk, P.J., & Galbraith, M.W. (1986). Planning successful continuing education programs: A systems approach model. *Lifelong Learning, 9*(5), 21–23.

Quong, T., Walker, A., & Stott, K. (1999). *Values based strategic planning: A dynamic approach for schools*. Englewood Cliffs, NJ: Prentice-Hall.

Ray, R., Hack, W., & Candoli, C. (2001). *School business administration: A planning approach* (7th ed). Boston: Allyn and Bacon.

Rea, P., & Kerzner, H. (2000). *Strategic planning: A practical guide*. New York: Wiley.

Simon, H.A. (1955). A behavior model of rational choice. *Quarterly Journal of Economics, 6*(9), 99–118.

Simon, H.A. (1970). *The new science of management decisions*. New York: Harper and Row.

Simon, H.A. (1997). *Administrative behavior: A study of decision-making processes in administrative organizations* (4th ed.). New York: The Free Press.

Yorsi, A. (1993). Say goodbye to strategic planning. *Computerworld, 27*(35), 33.

CHAPTER 6

Needs Assessment and Planning Studies

School districts may develop two types of facility plans. The district master plan is an overarching document that helps administrators make systemic decisions spanning multiple buildings. Typically, these plans are strategic in nature, and they may even be connected to overall planning for total district operations. Focused planning studies, by comparison, concentrate on verifying needs and recommending improvements for specific buildings. These documents are often called action plans. Ideally, focused plans are outgrowths or extensions of master facility plans.

Unfortunately, many school officials do not routinely engage in either master planning or focused planning. Rather, they retain architects and ask them to make critical decisions about facility improvements on a case-by-case basis—including decisions that have profound programmatic effects. When administrators totally relegate facility management decisions to persons outside of the school system they are acting neither responsibly nor professionally. If superintendents and other administrators are to provide the appropriate level of leadership and management, they must be able to assess existing needs, anticipate future needs, and build coherent plans that articulate how these needs will be addressed. This chapter examines these tasks.

NEEDS AND NEEDS ASSESSMENT

Reading the literature on needs and needs assessment can be confusing. Ambiguity exists because authors use different terms to refer to the same concept, give different definitions to identical terms, and confuse needs with wants

(Brackhaus, 1984). Thus, it is essential to define both needs and needs assessment to ensure that these terms are used properly in facility planning.

Needs

The word "needs" is relatively simple to define: it is the gap between what is and what is needed. However, it is often modified by an adjective. Listed below are definitions for modified terms that are cogent to facility planning.

• *Felt Needs.* These needs are self-identified and represent a conscious awareness by the individual of needs they seek to gratify (Monette, 1977). For example, a teacher in third grade may express a need to have a sink in her classroom. Although felt needs often cannot be satisfied for economic reasons, they are important because they convey feelings and attitudes that should be addressed during the planning process.

• *Ascribed Needs.* These are observer-generated needs and represent an attempt to be objective. Because they are based on opinion, they contain some bias and subjectivity (Kowalski, 1988). For example, a consultant may be asked to determine the adequacy of a media center; she looks at the space and renders a judgment that the area is too small. She has just stated an ascribed need: The media center needs to be larger. But by what standards? If all she offers is her professional opinion, there is no way of determining whether her standard is congruous with other standards (e.g., state standards or standards of the American Library Association).

• *Normative Needs.* These needs represent the difference between what is and a recognized normative standard. For example, assume that virtually all elementary schools in a region of the state have one or more science laboratories because science education experts recommend such spaces. A district in this region that does not have them has a normative need to add them.

• *Real Needs.* These needs may be felt, ascribed, or normative needs that are verified by required standards; that is, they are true gaps between what is and what is required (Kowalski, 1988). Assume that a school district owns a seven-acre site and intends to build a new elementary school on it. The state, however, requires a minimum of nine acres for such a building. The need to acquire two additional acres is a real need.

Each term is important to facility planning, and administrators should be able to differentiate among the various types of needs. Especially important is an administrator's ability to determine when felt, ascribed, or normative needs should be transformed into real needs.

Frequently needs are confused with wants. Wants involve motivation—the predisposition to achieve something. Alone, wants do not fully reflect needs. For example, a school district may need to close a school because of declining enrollment; however, the board and administration are not motivated to do this. Thus, the need exists but decision makers do not want to act to satisfy the need. Planners should include both needs and wants in their studies, so long as they accurately reflect conditions and community sentiments. Wants, although less important, can create political problems if they are ignored or simply dismissed.

In addressing needs and wants, however, administrators should distinguish between them and explain the differences to the planning participants and to the general public.

Needs Assessment

A needs assessment is a formal process of determining existing and anticipated needs (Brackhaus, 1984). But since there are varying forms of needs, the process may be structured in different ways. In addition, it is important to understand that measurement, assessment, and evaluation are different activities. Measurement involves empirical observations of some attribute or characteristic and the translation of that observation into a quantifiable amount. Assessment involves collecting data in some systematic way in order to make decisions. For example, testing and appraisals are forms of assessment. Evaluation is a judgmental activity involving the determination of a thing's worth, value, or quality (Worthen, Borg, & White, 1993). Assessment does not involve evaluation—an activity that takes place when assessments are completed and infused into the planning process so that conclusions and recommendations can be developed. Thus, needs assessment is defined here as *the systematic identification and categorization of existing and anticipated needs.*

All types of needs have some relevance for facility planning; however, the failure to categorize needs properly often leads to procedural errors and political problems. For example, a superintendent may say publicly that a new middle school needs a swimming pool when in truth a swimming pool is something the superintendent and others want. If it were a real need, the superintendent should be able to demonstrate that the school's program could not be fully implemented without it.

The most difficult aspect of a needs assessment is anticipating future needs. This is typically accomplished by conducting assessments that infuse trend analyses. With respect to facility planning, these assessments are commonly conducted in the following areas.

- *Demographic-Based Assessment.* Demographic analysis involves studying past and present population figures, trends that may have affected those figures, and emerging conditions that may affect future population figures. Both quantitative and qualitative data may be used; however, most analyses are quantitative in nature and they produce enrollment projections used to determine future space needs. This topic is addressed in detail in Chapter 11.

- *Community-Based Assessment.* Community-based assessments focus on shifting educational needs that are community-specific. These needs may be predicated on social, economic, or political conditions. For example, new businesses in the community may increase the need for high school graduates to be computer literate. Or, an influx of non–English-speaking residents may require bilingual education programs.

- *Education-Based Assessment.* Education-based assessments typically focus on either process or outcome needs. The former involve curriculum needs and the latter involve performance needs. For example, a school district may need to add more mathematics and science courses to make high school graduates more competitive applicants for admission to better universities. Or a district may need to raise student test scores to regain state accreditation.

- *Finance-Based Assessment.* Finance-based assessments focus on a district's ability to incur debt related to construction. For example, the need to raise additional taxes is examined in relation to fiscal ability (typically assessed valuation), fiscal effort (typically existing tax rates), debt analysis (typically level and duration of indebtedness and the quantity of existing debt), and fiscal impact (typically estimates of needed tax increases).

- *Facility-Based Assessment.* Facility-based assessments focus on needs directly related to a school building. The basis of the need may be the educational program (an additional science lab is needed to support course offerings) or the condition of the building (the roof needs to be replaced). Such assessments should include anticipated program changes. For example, the likelihood of funding all-day kindergarten programs prompts planners to anticipate the impact of this program change on facility needs.

All of the above assessments contribute to the overall planning process, and collectively they help to describe the types of facilities needed (Earthman, 1994; Ortiz, 1994).

DISTRICT MASTER PLANS

Facility master plans should serve as a resource guide for administrators and board members. If properly developed, the document combines policy, philosophy, and goals relative to the development, maintenance, and use of district-owned buildings. For this reason, master plans should be made readily available to all district employees and to everyone else who might have an interest in looking at them.

Despite their importance, far too many superintendents have not opted to create master plans. Among the reasons for not performing this important task are the following:

- The board and superintendent assume they know what is needed without a plan.
- The board and superintendent rely on crisis management; that is, they pay little attention to facility needs until problems become serious and unavoidable.
- Administrators neglect this responsibility because they are consumed with other tasks.
- No district personnel are qualified to prepare a master plan.
- District officials ignore planning assuming that architects will provide direction once a need becomes obvious.

In order to appreciate the value of having a district master plan, administrators need to understand the purposes served by this document.

Purposes

First and foremost, district plans provide long-term goals for facility management. Typically, the goals focus on reviewing, improving, or replacing specific buildings within designated time frames. Having these objectives helps to ensure that construction projects can be spread across several decades, thus avoiding sharp fluctuations in tax rates that might be necessary if several projects were done simultaneously. Second, the master plan includes general information that provides a framework for making decisions about specific projects. For example, the master plan may contain a policy stipulating the minimum and maximum enrollment of an elementary school. Third, the presence of the master plan serves to inform the public of the importance of facilities to the educational process. It is particularly helpful to keep the public informed about the necessity of continuously updating facilities.

Attributes

Master plans can be developed in many ways as described in the previous chapter. In general, the following attributes improve a plan's effectiveness.

- *The plan is predicated on a systems perspective.* Master plans should treat the school district as a social system. A decision in any part of the system can affect all other parts. Thus, the plan addresses all facilities—including those that have been recently constructed.
- *The plan should include an environmental analysis.* The plan should identify general environmental changes and assess their impact on the district (Morrison & Mecca, 1989). For example, socioeconomic changes in the community could affect the scope of instructional programs.
- *The planning cycle is continuous.* A master plan should not be written and then left alone for five to 10 years. The plan should be a "living" document evaluated annually and adjusted as needed.
- *The plan is highly flexible.* No portion of the plan should be immutable; often plans are placed in three-ring binders so they can be easily updated as conditions warrant.
- *The plan is coherent.* Given the purposes of the plan, the document should be written in language readily understood by employees and taxpayers, and all parts of the plan should be interrelated.
- *The plan provides sufficient direction without being unduly directive or restrictive.* The purpose of the master plan is to guide action, not to provide specific decisions. Thus, the document should include information and general directions without dictating decisions for present and evolving conditions.
- *The plan has a long-range focus.* Plans should extend at least 10 to 15 years into the future. Some elements of the plan (e.g., schedule of renovation or replacement) may extend well beyond 20 years.

Components

While there is no universally accepted table of contents for a master plan, certain elements are considered essential. Basically, the plan should include anticipated large expenditures and contingencies (Meglis, 1999). Specific components include the following:

- *Facility Philosophy Statement.* The document should include value and belief statements regarding the purposes of facilities, the importance of facilities to the educational process, and the community's obligation to support facility development. The statements should reflect a consensus of the district's leadership and the community.
- *Information about the Populations to Be Served.* This section of the plan should be both quantitative and qualitative; that is, it should include enrollment projections and related demographic data as well as general descriptions of the population served (e.g., socioeconomic status).
- *Organizational Structure of the District.* This section of the plan should identify the grade parameters for elementary schools, middle-grade schools, and high schools.
- *Summary of Policies Relating to Facilities.* This portion of the plan should identify policies related to facility operations, maintenance, and use.
- *Overview of Existing Facilities.* Each building should be described in terms of size, condition, and known problems. This section of the plan requires an appraisal of all buildings.
- *Technology Plan.* Districts should have separate technology plans (Ray, Hack, & Candoli, 2001). Either a summary of that plan or portions of it that affect facilities should be included in the district's master plan.
- *Known or Anticipated Program Changes.* Changes in curricular or extracurricular programming that affect facility usage should be summarized in this section. For example, if a new science course is to be added within the next three years, facility needs created by this change are detailed.
- *Calendar of Anticipated Facility Projects.* This portion of the master plan is perhaps the most important and widely used, because it should detail anticipated capital projects during the time period covered by the plan. Table 6–1 provides a sample calendar for a school district.

Each component of the plan should be updated at least every two years to ensure accuracy.

FOCUSED PLANNING STUDIES

The average American school district has four to six buildings that accommodate an enrollment of about 2,500 students (Glass, Bjork, & Brunner, 2000). Most district master plans, especially in large districts, are not sufficiently detailed to provide recommendations for specific construction projects. Therefore, administrators extend the master plan by engaging in action planning when it is

Table 6–1
Sample Calendar of Anticipated Facility Projects

Long-Range Schedule of Building Improvements

Year	School	Scheduled improvement
2005	Lincoln Middle School	Renovation and addition of 15,000 square feet
2009	East Elementary School	Renovation
2013	Taft Middle School	Renovation or replacement
2016	McKinley Elementary School	Renovation
2019	Central High School	Renovation and addition of 25,000 square feet
2023	Washington Elementary School	Replacement
2026	North Elementary School	Renovation

probable that specific needs must be addressed. Compared to the master plan, the focused plan is narrower (i.e., it addresses only one or several buildings) but deeper (i.e., it contains greater specificity and specific recommendations).

Purposes

Focused planning studies essentially serve three purposes. First, they validate general information contained in the district's master plan. For example, evolving conditions verified in the focused report may invalidate a scheduled renovation for a building. Second, focused studies contain much more specificity than is found in most master plans. For example, facility deficiencies may be described at this level of planning, whereas the master plan may merely list potential deficiencies. And third, focused plans are designed to produce specific recommendations for construction projects.

Attributes

Although district master plans and focused plans cover many of the same topics, the nature of the coverage is different. Focused plans should be

- *Specific.* Focused plans provide much more specificity than do master plans. For example, identified deficiencies are described in detail—especially as they relate to the intended school program.
- *Objective.* Since the ultimate purpose of the focused report is to produce recommendations for sizable expenditures of public funds, there is an expectation that the plan is objective. Districts often use consultants to prepare these plans because doing so increases the likelihood of objectivity.

Table 6–2
Basic Components of a Focused Planning Study for a Single School

Task	*Focus*
Demographic analysis	**General, district, and school populations and projection of future populations**
Program analysis	**Descriptions of district and individual school curriculum and extracurricular programs; identification of problems caused by facility deficiencies**
Facility appraisal	**Assessment of existing building in relation to adequacy standards**
Financial appraisal	**District wealth, tax effort, existing debt obligations, capacity to incur additional debt, projected tax impact**
Conclusions and recommendations	**Evaluation of conditions and needs based on total evidence and recommended solutions**

- *Factual.* The plan should be based on facts and not biases or emotions. The facts may reveal both needs and wants.
- *Comprehensive.* Recommendations produced by the plan should not be based solely on one criterion (e.g., funding). Rather, recommendations should be predicated on conclusions that collectively reflect demographic, program, building, and financial needs.
- *Clear.* Data, findings, conclusions, and recommendations should be stated with clarity, allowing all potential readers to comprehend the material.

Components

Focused planning studies also may vary in size and scope. For instance, some districts may study the feasibility of completing two or more projects simultaneously. Obviously, doing so would increase the volume of the plan. In addition, conditions in a district dictate what special components may be needed. At a minimum, focused studies have five components: demographic analysis, program analysis, facility appraisal, financial appraisal, conclusions and recommendation (See Table 6–2).

Demographic Analysis. Both master plans and focused studies include demographic data. The former usually includes district data; the latter usually includes both district and specific school data. Typically, demographic analysis includes census data, migration data, birth data, building-permit data, utility studies, and area planning-commission data (e.g., regarding approvals for subdivisions). Focused reports also provide analysis with respect to existing district attendance boundaries. Renovating and enlarging an elementary school, for instance, may necessitate redrawing attendance boundaries. The process of completing demographic analysis, including doing enrollment projections, is discussed in detail in Chapter 11.

Program Analysis. Perhaps the most overlooked aspect of planning—and yet the most important aspect—is program analysis. Again, this topic is addressed in both district and focused plans; however, content in focused plans is much more specific. Data in this section should be provided in the following areas.

- An interface of existing curricula with state mandated curricula
- An interface of existing curricula in a specific school(s) with curricula in schools at the same level in the district
- An interface of existing curricula with desired curricula
- Restrictions to implementing curricula (especially facility-related restrictions)
- Details of extracurricular programs and restrictions to those programs (especially facility-related restrictions)
- Staff felt and ascribed needs regarding programming
- A summary of performance data (e.g., test scores, college attendance, and dropout rates)
- A summary of program-based needs

In general, program analysis provides three vital pieces of information: what the school does, what the school needs to be doing, and gaps between what is being done and what needs to be done. The program analysis should clearly state the scope of activities that do and will occur in a building as well as the methodologies used to deliver those activities.

Facility Appraisal. The common procedure for determining facility-based needs is a formal appraisal of buildings. Spaces within a school are divided into three categories: instruction (e.g., standard classrooms), instructional support (e.g., media center), and general support (e.g., administrative and counseling offices). Estimates of building capacity are based solely on instructional spaces; the adequacy of instructional support and general support areas is assessed on the basis of the building's instructional capacity. For example, a middle school that has sufficient instructional spaces to accommodate up to 750 students should have a media center and cafeteria that can accommodate this many pupils under conditions of normal usage. School capacities are often confusing, because they are stated in two ways.

- *Design or Technical Capacity.* This figure is determined on the assumption of a 100 percent utilization level.
- *Practical Capacity.* This figure is determined on the assumption of a utilization level less than 100 percent; practical capacities assume that some spaces are needed for unanticipated functions or activities that do not occur daily.

Detailed information about calculating necessary instructional spaces and for determining practical capacities are discussed in Chapter 10 in relation to programming at the elementary, middle grades, and high school levels.

Appraisals typically include both normative and criterion-based measurements. Normative appraisal involves measuring existing conditions in relation to an established norm or requirement; the process constitutes a relative comparison. For example, by measuring the actual size of a classroom (700 sq. ft.) against an accepted norm for a classroom (900 sq. ft.) the appraiser provides information about how this building compares to other buildings. Criterion-referenced appraisal involves measuring existing conditions in relation to a well-defined domain of expectations (Worthen et al., 1993). For example, by determining whether a classroom has sufficient space to accommodate up to four personal computers, the appraiser provides information relative to the classroom's ability to accommodate expected functions.

Most often, school officials have educational consultants or architects conduct facility appraisals to enhance objectivity. If persons from outside the school district do the appraisals, administrators should always approve the type of instrumentation they will use. Instrumentation determines the form and scope of the appraisal outputs. A myriad of appraisal instruments are available, either commercially or from state departments of education. Most produce quantitative or a combination of quantitative and qualitative analysis in four areas.

1. *Condition of the Building.* Assessments of adequacy are made in relation to federal, state, and local codes.
2. *Educational Adequacy of the Building.* Assessments of adequacy are made in relation to accepted and evolving educational practices and norms.
3. *Capacity and Use of the Building.* Assessments of adequacy are made in relation to quantitative standards such as square feet per pupil, operating costs per pupil, and utilization levels for components of the building.
4. *Future Status of the Building.* Assessments of adequacy are made in relation to the building's life span and in relation to accommodating future programs.

Experienced educational facility planners are prone to rely on mixed methodologies to assess facilities (Earthman, 1994). As an example, they use (a) rating instruments that address facility capacities, adequacy, and performance levels (producing primarily quantitative data); (b) stakeholder interviews (producing primarily qualitative data); and (c) open-ended questionnaires (producing both types of data). The educational adequacy component may be ignored if the persons doing the appraisal lack the knowledge required to make these judgments.

Financial Appraisal. Laws and policies for funding school facilities vary significantly across the 50 states. However, most states require partial or substantial local funding for capital outlay (Kowalski & Schmielau, 2001). In those states, financial appraisals address the following topics.

- *Fiscal Capacity*. Fiscal capacity is defined as a school district's wealth (Alexander & Salmon, 1995). Wealth is measured by assessed valuation—that is, the aggregate value of property subjected to school district taxes. An appraisal of fiscal capacity includes past assessed valuation trends, factors affecting current assessed valuations, and projections of future assessed valuations. The last component is especially important, because projected assessed valuations provide a basis for estimated tax increases.

- *Fiscal Effort*. Fiscal effort is the extent to which taxpayers are supporting local public schools. This is commonly determined by either a ratio of revenue to the tax base (Alexander & Salmon, 1995) or by comparing the district's tax rates to the state's average tax rate for all school districts. In addition, trends for each individual fund are developed showing whether the tax rates for funds have been increasing or decreasing.

- *Debt Analysis*. Existing debt obligations are analyzed to determine debt leeway. Typically, this is accomplished by determining the ratio of existing debt (principal only) to assessed valuation. Once this is done, calculations can be made to determine how much additional debt the district can incur while remaining within specified debt levels. For example, assume that a district has an assessed valuation of $200 million and an outstanding debt principal totaling $20 million. The district's debt level is 10 percent. The district could incur an additional $20 million in debt if the goal is to not exceed a 20 percent debt level.

- *Tax Impact Estimate*. In some states, school districts are required to inform taxpayers of the estimated increase in the debt-service tax rate prior to officially approving a facility project. Even when this information is not required, many administrators prefer to make such data public. This calculation requires the projected assessed valuation for the year(s) being analyzed and the estimated size of the bond issue.

Conclusions and Recommendations. The final standard component of a focused study includes conclusions and specific recommendations. Conclusions should be based on findings of fact; recommendations should be defended on the basis of conclusions. Often, focused plans include an evaluation of several contingency solutions. The advantages and disadvantages of each are identified, and one of the contingencies is recommended as the preferred solution.

Optional Components. Optional components may be included in focused studies depending on conditions in a school district. The more common options include:

- *Analysis of Personnel and Staffing*. Staffing decisions may be relevant to facility decisions, especially if the district has restricted resources available to fund additional positions that may be made necessary by new or enlarged facilities.

- *Analysis of Joint Programs*. Districts in many states participate in joint educational services that may affect facility decisions. This is because some students receive instruction in facilities located in other districts. Joint services in special education and vocational education are examples.

- *Analysis of Transportation Services*. Often facility projects affect bus routes; thus, district officials may want to study the potential impact of a proposed building program on transportation efficiency and cost.

• *Site Acquisition Options.* Administrators contemplating building a new school may want to include a section in the focused study that identifies and evaluates potential sites.

As noted earlier, districts ideally should engage in both master and focused planning. Many school systems, however, only develop focused plans when they have to—either because state law requires evidence that a need for construction exists or because the public demands such evidence. Action plans usually take about six months to complete (Moore, 1991); however, the time parameters vary depending on the needs in question, the planning process, and the size of the planning committee.

CHAPTER SUMMARY

The value of comprehensive planning is exhibited by the problems created when this responsibility is ignored or done poorly. Consider the following three dilemmas.

• District administrators are placed at a severe disadvantage when they make recommendations without coherent long-range and systems-based plans. In other words, they have no frame of reference for evaluating how decisions for a given project will systemically affect the district.

• Thompson, Wood, and Honeyman (1994) observed that a lack of proper planning contributes to wasted scarce resources and the underutilization of facilities.

• Without adequate planning, it is improbable that sufficient attention will be given to current and future programming. Some districts, for example, have had to remodel schools just a few years after they were originally constructed to accommodate new programs, changing teaching patterns, and changing student needs (Earthman, 1994).

Effective facility planning is dependent on the ability of administrators to identify both needs and wants in the community and school district. In addition, administrators are expected to differentiate needs from wants and real needs from ascribed or felt needs. This information provides a nucleus for developing district master plans and focused plans. Both documents are especially powerful decision-making tools when they incorporate the attributes described in the previous chapter—especially broad-based participation allowing community representatives to help identify needs and make decisions.

ISSUES FOR DISCUSSION

1. What is the difference between a need and a want?
2. Should both needs and wants be addressed in planning documents? Why or why not?

3. What is the difference between real needs and ascribed needs? Between real needs and felt needs?

4. What are the primary purposes of a district facility master plan?

5. What are the essential components of a district facility master plan?

6. Focused plans are developed for specific projects. How do they differ from master plans?

7. Ideally, what connection should focused plans have to district master plans?

8. What is a facility assessment? What is the purpose of the assessment?

9. Why is objectivity important in relation to planning studies?

10. What purposes are served by analyzing a school's programs in relation to their physical environment?

11. What are some possible reasons why administrators ignore facility planning?

12. Why is it important to incorporate an analysis of financial conditions into a facility planning study?

REFERENCES

Alexander, K., & Salmon, R.G. (1995). *Public school finance.* Boston: Allyn and Bacon.

Brackhaus, B. (1984). Needs assessment in adult education: Its problems and prospects. *Adult Education Quarterly, 34*(4), 233–239.

Earthman, G.I. (1994). *School renovation handbook: Investing in education.* Lancaster, PA: Technomic Press.

Glass, T.E., Bjork, L., & Brunner, C. (2000). *The study of the American school superintendency, 2000.* Arlington, VA: American Association of School Administrators.

Kowalski, T.J. (1988). *The organization and planning of adult education.* Albany: State University of New York Press.

Kowalski, T.J., & Schmielau, R.E. (2001). Liberty provisions in state policies for financing school construction. *School Business Affairs, 67*(4), 32–37.

Meglis, E. (1999). Long-term planning and the building process. *School Business Affairs, 65*(7), 14–16.

Monette, M.L. (1977). The concept of educational needs: An analysis of selected literature. *Adult Education, 27,* 116–127.

Moore, D. (1991). *Guide for planning educational facilities.* Scottsdale, AZ: Council of Educational Facility Planners, International.

Morrison, J.L., & Mecca, T.V. (1989). Managing uncertainty: Environmental analysis/forecasting in academic planning. In J.C. Smart (Ed.), *Higher education: Handbook of theory and research* (vol. 5, pp. 334–382). New York: Agathon Press.

Ortiz, F.I. (1994). *Schoolhousing: Planning and designing educational facilities.* Albany: State University of New York Press.

Ray, J.R., Hack, W.G., & Candoli, I.C. (2001). *School business administration: A planning approach* (7th ed.). Boston: Allyn and Bacon.

Thompson, D.C., Wood, R.C., & Honeyman, D.S. (1994). *Fiscal leadership for schools: Concepts and practices.* New York: Longman.
Worthen, B.R., Borg, W.R., & White, K.R. (1993). *Measurement and evaluation in the schools.* New York: Longman.

CHAPTER 7

Public Opinion in Facility Planning

Public opinion is a critical variable in school facility planning because most states have liberty provisions granting district residents the opportunity to block intended facility projects. This power, expressed in state constitutions, laws, or regulations, is almost always exercised either through required tax referenda or through remonstrance procedures (Kowalski & Schmielau, 2001). Attitudes and perceptions about schools play a critical role in shaping voter decisions about specific issues (Spring, 1998); therefore, facility planners who have an insight into public sentiment have an advantage. This is especially important, given the fact that voters across the country defeated approximately 50 percent of the proposed tax increases related to school construction during the 1990s (Boschee & Holt, 1999). This failure rate for tax referenda includes both states that require partial local funding and states that require total local funding.

This chapter examines the process of conducting opinion polls. Such polls may be used to obtain public attitudes about facility needs early in a planning process, to determine attitudes toward possible solutions and to predict the outcome of a tax referendum. Regardless of purpose, the general rules for conducting polling remain the same. Special attention is given here to the options available for polling and to critical decisions that administrators must make once they have decided to conduct an opinion poll.

POLLING OPTIONS

Public opinion polling has become a common practice, especially in political elections. School districts have engaged in polling to guide decisions for routine matters and for infrequent but potentially controversial matters. Examples in the former category include setting of tax levies or publicly advertising proposed budgets. Examples in the latter category include school closings and tax increases to fund construction. In recent years more districts have been using public opinion surveys in conjunction with the initial stages of strategic planning (Phi Delta Kappa, 1999).

Polls are surveys based on samples drawn from populations. The purpose of conducting a poll is to make accurate inferences about population data collected from the sample. Because the value of polling depends on the accuracy of the inferences, scientific methods must be used to ensure confidence in the outcomes.

Opinion surveys may be conducted internally (by district personnel) or externally (by consultants). While large districts may have staff with the expertise necessary to conduct a scientific poll, most districts do not. Despite the fact that taxpayers often can and do derail facility projects, numerous school boards and superintendents fail to consider the consequences of not assessing public opinion and of not working to build positive opinions. This indifference frequently is caused by a most dubious assumption: They suppose the public will accept the validity of any need for construction they express collectively.

Using Written Instruments

Written instruments may be used in two ways to determine public opinion: questionnaires delivered and returned via mail (including electronic mail) and questionnaires that can be picked up and returned to a designated location. Although the results obtained from questionnaires provide valuable information administrators use to make decisions, they also can become a liability. Whether questionnaire data produce positive or negative outcomes depends largely on four questions.

- Were the questionnaires properly developed?
- Was the population properly sampled?
- Were the results interpreted correctly?
- Did the process do more than just uncover data?

If the answers to these queries are negative, the process is likely to do more harm than good. The last question is especially cogent, because the most effective opinion polling involves analysis, synthesis, and integration of the outcomes with the larger planning process.

Mail surveys are one of the most widely used techniques for identifying public opinions, especially among school districts. Compared to other alternatives for ascertaining public opinions, the mail survey

- Is usually less expensive,

- Is usually less labor-intensive,

- Has a greater likelihood of reaching persons who are difficult to contact,

- Has the potential of being used with large samples—a factor that can increase validity,

- Usually elicits more valid responses (because respondents do not have to identify themselves) (Mouly, 1970),

- Provides respondents time to reflect before responding (Place, McNamara, & McNamara, 2000).

Mail surveys also have potential pitfalls. Consider the following:

- There is a risk of only obtaining extreme positions; yet opinions of persons in the middle often are critical to determining whether the community will support a building program (Graham & Wise, 2000).

- Mail surveys tend to have a high non-return rate. This is noteworthy because non-respondents tend to differ from respondents in fundamental ways. However, no generalizations can be made about persons who did not respond (Place et al., 2000).

- Validity depends on the willingness and ability of the respondent to provide the information requested. Persons with less education and in lower income brackets are less likely to complete and return a mail survey.

- When questions are misinterpreted, there is no mechanism for providing direction. And there is often no way to detect whether misinterpretations occurred (Mouly, 1970).

- Questionnaires often contain clarifying information that may be interpreted by respondents as being prejudicial or manipulative (Place et al., 2000).

- There is no opportunity to evaluate non-verbal behavior.

McNamara (1994) identified three basic types of questions that could be used in surveys. The first is open-ended questions. This approach allows respondents to answer in any manner they choose. The second is open-ended questions with precoded answers. Here respondents answer as they wish, but the person(s) conducting the survey place the answers in predetermined categories. The third is closed questions. This is the most commonly used type of question, and the respondent is asked to select from precoded response choices that are closest to or best represent their opinion.

Dillman (1978) noted that questionnaires produce one or more of the following types of information.

- What people say they want (attitudes or opinions).
- What people believe to be true (beliefs).
- What people do or intend to do (behaviors).
- Who people are (attributes).

Mail surveys related to facility planning may involve all of these pieces of information. For example, district officials may want to collect demographic data about the respondents in order to determine if factors such as education, income, or having children attending school affect opinions.

From a standpoint of advantages and disadvantages, the "pick-up-and-deliver" approach is similar to the mail survey. However, with this technique, the district does not control sample selection—a factor that could skew results significantly. For example, only persons opposed to tax increases may be motivated to take the time to obtain, complete, and return a questionnaire. For this reason, school districts rarely use the pick-up-and-deliver approach.

Interviewing

Interviewing is another methodology for obtaining public opinion. Basically, interviewing can be structured or unstructured and be conducted face to face or in some other manner. Structured interviews are conducted using a predetermined set of questions and the interviewer reads the questions and records the responses (Graham & Wise, 2000). Unstructured interviews flow freely and the respondent may be able to control the content of the interview. The most common form of interviewing used by schools has been a structured telephone interview.

The primary advantages of the face-to-face interview are the opportunity for the respondent to request question clarifications and the opportunity for the interviewer to request response clarifications (Frey & Oishi, 1995). Another advantage is the opportunity to evaluate nonverbal behavior. A possible problem with this technique is that the environment of the interview may influence the outcome (Place et al., 2000). For instance, either the interviewer or interviewee may feel uncomfortable because of the setting in which the questions are asked. Also, face-to-face interviews are labor-intensive, and thus they tend to be relatively expensive.

The most common face-to-face technique used by school officials is a house-to-house survey. Districts often use volunteers to collect opinions; and if the volunteers are known in their assigned neighborhoods, this can positively affect interviewee cooperation. Concerns about this approach include the following:

- House-to-house canvassing can produce unreliable data, especially if district residents are segregated racially or economically by neighborhoods and either the contact or response rates are not reasonably uniform across neighborhoods.
- Training volunteers to conduct the interviews can be relatively expensive.
- The procedure is usually more time-consuming than either mailed surveys or telephone interviews.

Telephone interviews are a popular way to get public opinion. The following are perceived advantages of this technique.

- They can be relatively inexpensive, especially if long-distance calls are not necessary (Place et al., 2000). Thus, they are a good option when large samples are desired and mail surveys are not acceptable. There are differences of opinion, however, about the cost of telephone interviewing. For example, Lavrakas (1987), noted that administrators often overlook costs associated with developing an interview guide and transcribing information.
- The interviews can be closely supervised (Frey & Oishi, 1995).
- The interviewer and interviewee can interact; this is important with respect to clarifications.

Potential problems with telephone interviews include:

- Some persons cannot be contacted because they have unlisted telephone numbers.
- The increasing use of phone answering machines has diminished participation rates; some individuals never return a call or respond to follow-up calls.
- Widespread negative attitudes toward telemarketing prompts some individuals to hang up when confronted with any type of survey.
- Responses are subject to interpretations made by the persons who transcribe the messages.

District telephone surveys may be conducted on a school-by-school basis. This technique allows comparisons among respondents based on their location in the district. When multiple interviewers conduct the interviews, the use of a carefully designed instrument based on the information needed for facility planning is essential (Phi Delta Kappa, 1999).

With the development of the Internet and electronic mail, some districts are turning to e-mail interviews. This procedure basically has the same advantages and disadvantages of the telephone interview, except that more time is necessary to conduct the interview. In addition, the technique is not feasible in districts where a large proportion of the population does not use this technology.

Other Options

Another tool that has been used in conjunction with opinion polling is the focus group. This technique is a form of interviewing, but it is conducted in a group setting. The group members may be homogeneous (e.g., all realtors or all clergy) or heterogeneous (e.g., taxpayers selected at random). When homogeneous groups are used, administrators typically obtain data from multiple groups so that outcomes can be integrated and compared. The primary purpose of a focus group is to obtain information that individuals are unlikely to share on a survey or through a structured interview. The technique also may be used as a follow-up procedure to other survey methodologies; when used in this manner, the intent is to obtain deeper and richer information (Stewart & Shamdasani, 1990). The qualitative data produced by this technique reflect feelings and emotions that often surface in group discussions. In part, they surface in this format because the participants are allowed to talk freely and to describe their opinions in words that are meaningful to them.

While the focus group can produce information not normally accessible through more traditional survey methods, the procedure does have several potential pitfalls. First, the process is difficult to execute and the person conducting the sessions must be skilled in this methodology (Stewart & Shamdasani, 1990). Second, it is difficult to make generalizations to the entire population, especially if members were not selected scientifically or if the group was too small to represent the population in question. Typically, focus groups consist of only 12 to 15 persons.

Another technique frequently used by school districts—but not always endorsed by survey experts—is the public forum. These sessions tend to be dominated by a few speakers who are often critical of the district, and their comments appear in the media as being representative of the entire community. Even when speakers provide both positive and negative comments, the media often cast the differing opinions in a negative light (e.g., they cite the differences as evidence of pervasive conflict). If given ample media coverage, the negative views expressed by just a few speakers at a public forum could shape the opinions of thousands of taxpayers. Despite these concerns, the public forum is deeply embedded in this country's public school culture because the process is an expression of local control. Some states even require local districts to hold public hearings in relation to facility projects. In those instances, administrators should be prepared to present and defend their recommended actions. They do this by presenting a coherent plan, a rationale for action, cost estimates, and a list of perceived benefits for students and the community. In addition, effort should be made to get citizens supportive of the action to state their views at the meetings (Graham & Wise, 1999).

OPINION POLLING DECISIONS

Once school officials have decided to conduct a public opinion poll, they must answer several other critical questions. Who will conduct the polling? How will data be collected and analyzed? When will the polling begin and end? Who will be polled? In large measure, all of these questions are affected by instrumentation. The primary decisions facing administrators are shown in Figure 7–1.

Selecting a Polling Methodology

Every proposed polling technique has an underlying set of purposes, advantages, and disadvantages. Generally, the process is intended to produce a profile of opinions or to clarify existing information. In addition to determining if there is congruence between the district's needed information and the general attributes of a methodology, administrators need to consider the following questions.

Figure 7–1
Opinion Polling Decisions Facing Administrators

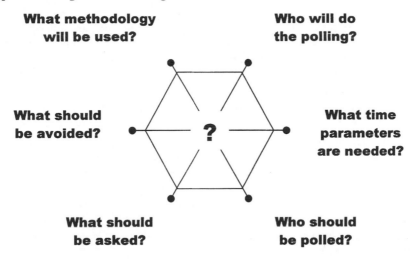

- Does the methodology require expertise available to the district (either in-house or through the use of consultants)?
- Can the polling be completed using the methodology within the established time parameters for planning?
- Does the school district have the financial resources necessary to use this methodology?
- Will the methodology produce the quantity and quality of data desired?

In some instances, administrators decide who will conduct the polling before they select a methodology. This is especially likely if administrators do not have much knowledge of the process and elect to retain consultants.

Selecting Persons to Conduct the Polling

Superintendents often decide to outsource public opinion polling to private firms. This option has advantages and disadvantages. Objectivity is one of the presumed benefits if the consultants have no vested interest in the polling outcome. Public opinion polling occurs frequently in the private sector; therefore, school officials should be able to find qualified consultants without much difficulty (Phi Delta Kappa, 1999). Another advantage of outsourcing is that administrators do not have to devote much time to the process—at least not until it is finished. One of the disadvantages may be cost. Another is the inability of the consultant to interpret unsolicited comments. This point is especially meaningful in light of the fact that about one-third of the persons surveyed in an educational poll are likely to provide such comments (Glass, 1997). Finally, some consultants may have little or no experience working with educational institutions; this could be detrimental with respect to structuring survey questions.

Conducting polling with district personnel or community volunteers often saves valuable resources. In addition, the persons involved usually know and understand the community and district. But using district personnel and volunteers requires careful coordination and proper training. But if none of the leaders possesses the requisite knowledge to conduct a scientific poll, no level of coordination and training will suffice. Two other potential problems associated with conducting polls with in-house personnel are the disclosure of information and bias. Some employees and volunteers may share partial outcomes inaccurately or prematurely. This can produce conflict and spawn erroneous media reports. In addition, employees and volunteers enter the process with their own opinions and bias; and when they have a vested interest in polling outcomes, they may not be objective in collecting or analyzing data.

In some districts, a community polling committee is established to either collect opinions or to oversee the process. If this approach is used, care should be taken to ensure that views on the committee are balanced and representative of the broad spectrum of the district and its communities. The committee's responsibility should be clearly articulated by the superintendent, and an administrator should be appointed to facilitate the committee's work (Council of Educational Facility Planners, International, 1995).

Time Parameters

Administrators often underestimate the amount of time necessary to conduct public opinion polls. This is because they fail to calculate the amount of time needed to prepare the instrument and to analyze the results. Obviously, time requirements vary according to population or sample size, the qualifications of the data collectors, and methodology. If done properly, the development of questions and their validation can take several weeks—especially if the task is not assigned to consultants.

Making a mistake with time parameters can present serious problems for the entire planning process. For example, the work of the planning committee or subcommittees may be stalled until the analyzed data are available. Therefore, the estimated time for completing polling should be coordinated with the overall planning calendar.

Determining Who Should Be Polled

Ideally, all residents should have an opportunity to voice their opinions. In all but the smallest districts, this is not feasible. Both time and cost limitations usually require administrators to rely on opinions drawn from a sample of the district's population. Administrators should use scientific random sampling techniques, because this process is the only way to ensure that every individual or household in a population has an equal chance of being chosen (Krathwohl, 1998). Random sampling can be completed in several ways including using computers or a table of random numbers that matches an individual's assigned number (Place et al., 2000).

When samples of a population are used to obtain opinions, the person conducting the poll must determine a reasonable margin of error and a reasonable confidence level.

The margin of error is a measure of how closely the information obtained from a sample represents the entire population. The level of confidence deals with acknowledging that in a few cases it is possible that the survey results are not as close to the population as the margin of error adopted. (Place et al., 2000, p. 318)

Assume that a school district conducts a mail opinion poll with a random sample of the district's population. Both the margin of error and the level of confidence are set at 5 percent. When the results are analyzed, the data show that 80 percent of the respondents expressed positive opinions regarding the need to build a new school. The margin of error indicates the accuracy of this outcome in relation to the actual opinions of the district's population. With a margin of error of plus or minus five percentage points, the assumption is made that the sample result of 80 percent means that between 75 percent and 85 percent of the district's population have a positive opinion toward the need to build a new school. The level of confidence indicates error probability; that is, a a 95 percent confidence level indicates a 5 percent chance that the sampling data are in error. Most experts (Henry, 1990; Place et al., 2000) indicate that a 95 percent confidence level is sufficient to ensure that results from the sample are acceptable for making necessary decisions. If the actual level of positive opinions in the population was outside the margin of error (i.e., the level of positive opinions is actually higher than 85 percent or lower than 75 percent), the 80 percent positive level would be obtained from fewer than five samples in 100. In other words, with a 5 percent margin of error and a 95 percent confidence level, the administrators could be highly confident that the results obtained from the sample are rather indicative of the district's population.

Determining sample sizes and calculating a margin of error require some knowledge of statistics. Survey research and statistics books detail the appropriate procedures for these tasks. For every sample size table, there is a second table used to determine error margins based on analysis and the percentage of returned surveys. Two general rules should be noted. First, the larger the overall population of a school district, the smaller the percent of population needed in the sample. Second, the higher the percentage of returns, the lower the margin of error (McNamara, 1994).

Determining What to Ask

Limiting the content of an opinion instrument may be difficult. Administrators, board members, and others involved in planning may want to use the public opinion poll to collect all types of data. Not focusing the opinion poll on issues directly related to facility planning can be problematic, because people are less likely to respond to extensive surveys or interviews that require more than 15 or 20 minutes of their time. Also, collecting data not related to facility planning may serve to confuse individuals who interpret the outcomes.

Often questions are included to collect opinions about the present and the future. This is especially important for facility planning, because construction decisions have such long-term implications. As noted previously, both existing and anticipated needs should be weighed in arriving at facility recommendations. How questions are structured is critical, and this is one reason why superintendents often seek consultants to assist them. For example, asking the question "Do you support building a new high school?" can be damaging. This is because some individuals with little information may feel obligated to defend a negative answer even after compelling evidence for the need to build a new school is presented to them. Rather, the questions might seek opinions regarding circumstances under which the respondents would be supportive of construction projects.

Another important consideration involves the types of questions used. They can be open-ended or closed-choice questions; and respondents could be given an opportunity to add unsolicited comments. Open-ended questions and unsolicited comments provide deeper insights into opinions; however, analyzing them can be very time-consuming. In all instances, questions should be worded clearly and as neutrally as possible.

In addition to obtaining information that informs facility planning, the polling instrument should collect demographic data. Such data enhance analysis and permit district officials to make conclusions as to whether the respondents are truly representative of the district's population. Common demographic items include

• Identifying respondents who have children enrolled in the district,
• Identifying the portion of the district in which the respondents reside,
• Identifying respondents' family income level,
• Identifying respondents' family size,
• Identifying the respondents' levels of education.

Demographic questions should appear at the end of the survey, and questions related to key issues should appear at the beginning of the survey to capture the respondent's interest (Cox, 1996).

Determining What to Avoid

Conducting a bad poll can be disastrous for administrators. Generally, there are two types of bad polls: those that produce inaccurate data because they were not constructed properly, and those that produce inaccurate data because they were designed to do so. In the first case, the persons administering the poll do not have sufficient knowledge to ensure scientific controls. In the second case, the persons administering the poll intentionally designed the process to suit their self-interests. In either case, polls that produce inaccurate outcomes harm the school district and the reputations of the administrators who sponsored or conducted them.

Specific problems often encountered by school districts when conducting public opinion polls include the following:

- Violating the rules of random sampling
- Creating an instrument that contributes to low response rates (e.g., it is too lengthy or too ambiguous)
- Failing to calculate or apply a margin of error and a confidence level
- Drawing conclusions that are not based on data collected
- Failing to establish adequate security measures concerning the distribution and return of the surveys

The last point is especially meaningful with respect to mail surveys. Unless adequate security measures are taken, some respondents may make multiple copies of the survey, complete all of them, and return them in separate envelopes. This type of mischief may occur when patrons have strong feelings about the issues in question. Proper security can be maintained by coding the surveys and envelopes so that counterfeit documents can be detected.

CHAPTER SUMMARY

Public opinion polling has become a common technique, especially in relation to decisions that involve aspects of government. Polling is particularly valuable in relation to school facility planning because competing interests are almost always present. Thus, public sentiment provides planners with insights that may determine whether their intentions are supported by a majority of taxpayers.

Various options for conducting polls are identified in this chapter. Largely because scientific controls and objectivity are so important, school officials are generally advised to use consultants for this activity. It is especially important that conclusions drawn from sample data are defined within the parameters of a margin of error and confidence level. Unless this is done, misinterpretations of outcomes are almost certain.

ISSUES FOR DISCUSSION

1. Identify the ways that a public opinion poll might be used in facility planning.

2. What is the difference between a structured and an unstructured interview?

3. Compare a mail survey to a telephone interview. What are the advantages and disadvantages of each technique?

4. What is a margin of error?

5. What is a confidence level?

6. Why is it essential to draw samples randomly?

7. What are the advantages and disadvantages of conducting an opinion poll with district personnel and/or volunteers?

8. Assume that administrators wanted to conduct an opinion poll in a district with 5,000 households. How would they determine how many households would have to be selected in the sample to achieve a 95 percent confidence level?

9. What is meant by bias? How might bias affect the way an opinion poll is structured and analyzed?

10. Polls allow administrators to make inferences about the district's population. Why are such inferences important to facility planning?

11. Are there possible political benefits associated with conducting public opinion polls? If so, what are they?

REFERENCES

Boschee, F., & Holt, C.R. (1999). *School bond success*. Lancaster, PA: Technomic Press.

Council of Educational Facility Planners, International. (1995). *Facilities planning manual*. Scottsdale, AZ: Author.

Cox, J. (1996). *How to build the best questionnaires in the field of education*. Thousand Oaks, CA: Corwin.

Dillman, D.A. (1978). *Mail and telephone surveys: The total design method*. New York: Wiley.

Frey, F.H., & Oishi, S. (1995). *How to conduct interviews by telephone and in person*. Thousand Oaks, CA: Sage.

Glass, T.E. (1997). Using school district public opinion surveys to gauge and obtain public support. *The School Community Journal, 7*(1), 101–116.

Graham, G., & Wise, G. (2000). Public relations in a funding campaign. In T.J. Kowalski (Ed.), *Public relations in schools* (2nd ed., pp. 339–359). Upper Saddle River, NJ: Merrill, Prentice-Hall.

Henry, G.T. (1990). *Practical sampling*. Newbury Park, CA: Sage.

Kowalski, T.J., & Schmielau, R.E. (2001). Liberty provisions in state policies for financing school construction. *School Business Affairs, 67*(4), 32–37.

Krathwohl, D.R. (1998). *Methods of educational and social science research: An integrated approach* (2nd ed.). New York: Longman.

Lavrakas, P.J. (1987). *Telephone survey methods*. Newbury Park, CA: Sage.

McNamara, J.F. (1994). *Surveys and experiments in education research*. Lancaster, PA: Technomic Press.

Mouly, G.J. (1970). *The science of educational research* (2nd ed.). New York: Van Nostrand Reinhold.

Phi Delta Kappa. (1999). *Pace: Polling attitudes of community on education*. Bloomington, IN: Author.

Place, W.A., McNamara, M., & McNamara, J.F. (2000). Collecting and analyzing decision-oriented data. In T.J. Kowalski (Ed.), *Public relations in schools* (2nd ed., pp. 315–338). Upper Saddle River, NJ: Merrill, Prentice-Hall.

Spring, J. (1998). *Conflict of interest*. New York: McGraw-Hill.

Stewart, D.W., & Shamdasani, P.N. (1990). *Focus groups: Theory and practice*. Newbury Park, CA: Sage.

PART III

Completing a Facility Project

CHAPTER 8

Professional Assistance

One of the primary responsibilities of a superintendent (or administrative designee) is to select professionals to provide services for a facility project. This task is challenging for at least four reasons.

- Many administrators have not previously performed this task; thus, they are unable to rely on personal experiences to guide them.

- Most districts do not have policies regarding the selection and use of consultants.

- Decisions about the scope of services to be provided are critical and require knowledge of the potential providers and their responsibilities.

- Selection and compensation decisions often generate controversy; thus, economic, professional, and political variables need to be considered.

In addition, the variety of consultants retained and the scope of their responsibilities usually depend on factors such as state laws, the resources of the school district, and the nature of the construction project.

This chapter explores the range of professional assistance that could be used in a facility project. Qualifications, responsibilities, possible services, selection procedures, and compensation are discussed. The intent is to provide a general overview of the decisions that must be made in relation to selecting and retaining professional assistance.

ARCHITECTS

Architects are licensed professionals who design buildings. In the case of school projects, their primary responsibility is to translate educational specifications into design and working documents. These documents span site development, building construction, and the identification and installation of equipment. States commonly require that all public buildings, including schools, must be constructed from plans developed by a licensed architect. To be safe, always make sure you know the laws in your state concerning this matter.

Duties and Responsibilities

School districts typically retain architectural services to design a new facility, renovate an existing facility, or expand an existing facility. Among the specific duties associated with these tasks are the following:

- Advise school officials on the issue of project budget
- Advise school officials on the issue of time parameters for the project
- Develop schematic designs
- Develop preliminary drawings and cost estimates
- Prepare final working drawings and cost estimates
- Provide direction and consultation with respect to developing bids and awarding contracts
- Evaluate contractor compliance with design and construction documents
- Review shop drawings, products, and material samples to confirm compliance
- Serve as the owner's agent if there are problems during construction
- Certify that various segments of the project have been completed properly
- Check contractor payment requisitions against work progress
- Keep the school officials appraised regarding the budgetary aspects of the project
- Do any necessary cost revisions
- Prepare and recommend change orders
- Provide final inspections and certifications for the owner
- Develop and implement a punch list
- Assist with building occupancy and start-up

District officials may decide to have the architect assume even broader duties. For instance, they may expect them to assist with pre-design activities, such as site selection and involvement in the development of educational specifications.

The scope of responsibilities often depends on the amount and expertise available among district administrative staff and the decision to use construction management (a concept that will be discussed later in this chapter). Some large

Figure 8–1
Selecting an Architectural Firm

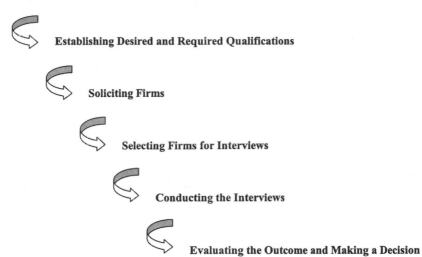

Determining the Selection Committee

Establishing Desired and Required Qualifications

Soliciting Firms

Selecting Firms for Interviews

Conducting the Interviews

Evaluating the Outcome and Making a Decision

districts, for example, employ full-time architects and they assume supervisory responsibilities once a project is started. A list of standard duties and potential duties are available in various documents available from the American Institute of Architects (AIA).

Selecting an Architectural Firm

As a general rule, on architectural firm should be selected as early in a project as possible. The search can usually commence once school officials know the nature of the work they want completed (Madden & Coughlin, 1985). The selection process recommended here is linear and can be used across all districts for all types of projects in states where local districts have the liberty to select their own architects. Each step in the process (see Figure 8–1) is discussed separately.

Determining the Selection Committee. Deciding who will be involved in architect selection is influenced by both district philosophy and size. Historically, school board members, the superintendent, and other administrators constituted the selection committee; but, today, there is a growing trend toward wider involvement. Some districts employ a planning committee for the entire project, and architect selection becomes one of many committee responsibilities. Typically, broad-based committees include principals, teachers, parents, influential community leaders, and even students. When more inclusive procedures are used, the superintendent has the responsibility for ensuring that someone on the administrative staff will provide leadership and facilitation. Regardless of what method is used, the school board ultimately approves the selection of an architect because a legal contract is necessary.

Establishing Desired and Required Qualifications. Objectively selecting an architectural firm is virtually impossible unless qualifications are predetermined. Criteria should be based on the needs of a particular school district (Smith, Stevenson, & Pellicer, 1984); however, the following general criteria can be used.

- *Reputation for Designing Schools.* A firm's general reputation may not be indicative of its reputation for school design.
- *Experience in Designing Schools.* Some firms have designed over 100 schools while others have never designed a school.
- *Stability.* Because school buildings are expected to last 50 or more years, the stability of a firm is relatively important. Well established firms are more likely to still be in business decades after the school is opened.
- *Size of the Firm.* The size of a firm may range from one person to over 100, with the average being about 10 to 15. Size of firm may be important in relation to project complexity.
- *In-House Services.* Firms differ with respect to in-house specializations. While some larger firms have their own landscape architects, mechanical engineers, electrical engineers, structural engineers, interior designers, and acoustical engineers, smaller firms typically subcontract for these services.
- *Location.* Some districts prefer to work with in-state or in-community firms; others prefer to recruit architects on a national basis.
- *Availability.* Districts often have general time lines for starting and completing construction. It is important to know whether firms can meet these schedules.
- *Philosophy.* Firms differ with respect to their values and beliefs about planning, decision making, and accountability.

Too often, school officials move forward without predetermining qualifications— an error that almost always results in political conflict. If the superintendent is not a member of the selection committee, selection criteria should be approved by the superintendent before the committee moves forward.

Soliciting Firms. A first step in selecting an architectural firm is creating a request for proposal (RFP). The RFP typically is divided into three sections. The first is an information section detailing the school district's intentions. This usually includes the following information.

- Description of the community
- Desired starting and ending date
- Project site (if known) (Madden & Coughlin, 1985)
- Project type (e.g., new construction, renovation)

- Project level (e.g., elementary school, high school)
- Project size and types of spaces needed
- Approximate budget
- Responsibilities to be assumed by the architects
- Level of involvement of architects in general planning (Smith, Stevenson, & Pellicer, 1984)

   The second section is essentially a questionnaire to be completed by an individual in the architectural firm. The following information is usually requested.

- General information about the firm (name, mailing address, telephone number)
- The name of the contact person in the firm
- A description of the size of the firm (number of employees by category)
- A list of past and present school district clients
- A list of references
- A statement of philosophy about working with clients in general and educational clients specifically
- An approximation of fees
- Availability to assume additional work within specified time parameters
- Information about any past and existing legal or financial difficulties (e.g., lawsuits, bankruptcy)
- Promotional materials (e.g., brochures, awards)
- Availability for an interview

   The AIA (1987) identifies the following potential services by project stages.

- Predesign Phase
  - predesign services (e.g., analysis of existing facilities)
  - site analysis services
- Design Phase
  - schematic design services
  - design development services
  - construction document services
- Construction Phase
  - building or negotiation services (e.g., project administration)
  - construction contract administration services (e.g., inspections, construction change directives)
- Post-Construction Phase
  - post-construction services (e.g., warranty reviews)

• Supplemental Services

  • range of special services (e.g., life-cycle cost analysis, computer applications, energy studies)

Although architecture is a profession, some variability in skills, expertise, and interests in doing school design work exists across firms (Levin, 1991).

The final section of the RFP should include details for submitting a proposal. Included here are the name and address of the contact person in the school district, the process for responding to the RFP, and the deadline for responding. A statement should be included indicating that no responses received after the deadline will be considered.

Once the RFP is designed, the selection committee needs to establish a list of potential firms. In most states, competition among firms seeking to work with school districts is intense; some superintendents report being contacted by as many as 35 firms when it becomes known that the district is considering a construction project. Thus, superintendents need to decide whether they want to be inundated with responses to an RFP. If they do not, then they need to take steps to limit the applicant pool. This is accomplished by compiling a list of no more than 10 to 20 firms. Common criteria for being placed on the list include a reputation for school design, experience with school design, size of the firm, and a location that facilitates a close working relationship with the district. Superintendents in districts having had recent projects, officials in state departments of education, and officials with the state school board associations may be helpful in identifying firms that meet the desired criteria. In some communities, local firms are automatically included on the list for political reasons even though they may not meet these criteria.

Selecting Firms for Interviews. Determining how many firms will be interviewed is an important step in the selection process. Unless school officials are willing and able to meet with all representatives from interested firms, the RFP should be designed to elicit specific information for a paper-screening process; that is, the responses need to be sufficiently detailed so that members of the selection committee can evaluate the firms and issue interview invitations. Typically, selection committees interview about 6–10 firms. Firms not selected should be sent a timely letter thanking them for their interest.

Conducting the Interviews. Interviews serve several purposes. Among the most important are the following:

• Allowing firms to elaborate on the written information they supplied

• Allowing firms to demonstrate the quality of their work (e.g., video presentations)

• Answering questions from committee members

• Providing the firms with more detailed information about the community, district, and project

- Assessing the compatibility of the district's and the firm's philosophies
- Pursuing more detailed information about responsibilities and compensation

The issue of philosophical compatibility is especially important because different beliefs about responsibility, performance, and communication usually produce conflict (Moore, 1989).

The goal of the selection committee should be to conduct fair and impartial interviews. Largely for this reason, the time parameters, location, procedures, and standard questions should be predetermined to prevent any one firm from having an unfair advantage. Any effort to bias the committee should be avoided (e.g., allowing members of a firm to contact committee members personally; allowing the firm to take the committee members to dinner before or after the interview).

Evaluating the Outcome and Making a Decision. If the selection is to be based on merit, the committee members must be able to compare the competing firms using uniform criteria. These criteria should be established at the very beginning of the selection process. They are assessed and evaluated at two stages: the written responses to the RFP and after the interviews.

Firms are typically required to state their fee schedule either in their response to the RFP or during the interview. Architectural fees may be structured in several ways. The most common are

- *Fixed Fee.* With this option, the services are provided for a specified amount (e.g., $1 million fee regardless of project cost). Often, firms will determine a fixed fee on the basis of project or construction costs but will present it as a fixed fee.

- *Percentage of the Construction Cost.* With this option, services are provided on the basis of a percentage of the construction costs; thus, if the construction costs were $20 million and the fee was 6 percent, the firm would receive $1.2 million. Typically, construction costs constitute about 75 percent of the project cost. The reason this option uses construction costs is because architectural services have no direct bearing on the remaining costs (typically called "soft costs," they include items such as land, interest payments during construction, and legal fees). The percentage fee is the most common compensation method and the one preferred by most firms.

- *Actual Costs for Services Without Parameters.* With this option, the firm bills the client for services using a mutually agreed upon daily or hourly rate; there is neither a minimum nor a maximum fee. This option is rarely used because both management (not knowing what the total costs will be until the project is finished) and political (the potential for paying an unusually high fee) problems are possible.

- *Actual Costs for Services With Parameters.* With this option, the firm bills the client for services using a mutually agreed upon daily or hourly rate; however, the total fee paid to the architect may not exceed a predetermined maximum fee. This option is not used very often because it requires additional work for the architect (e.g., preparing billing statements based on hourly or daily work) and the district administrators (e.g., verifying that the work was done).

Fees may or may not include expenses incurred by the architects in conjunction with the project. These costs are commonly called "reimbursables." They might include mileage, telecommunication charges, meals, and lodging (Madden & Coughlin, 1985). If the firm's fee does not cover reimbursables, these costs should be included in the project budget.

Comparing fees in architect proposals can be difficult, especially if the RFP did not stipulate a format for the fee statement. For example, some architects are likely to state a fixed fee while others will state a percentage of construction costs. Although all fees can be converted to a percentage, the actual construction costs are not known at the time a firm is employed. Thus, the comparisons must be based on an estimate of construction costs.

Before selecting a firm, the decision makers also should have a clear understanding of the personnel who will be directly assigned to the project. This includes the design architect, the principal in the firm who is assigned overall responsibility for your project, and the project architect (the person who will oversee construction). In fact, it is useful to tell firms that these three individuals should be present at the interviews so the decision makers know who they are.

Without predetermined criteria, persons selecting an architectural firm are much more vulnerable to two possible errors. They either select a local firm purely for political reasons or they select a firm simply because it submitted the lowest fee bid. These two factors may be important, but selecting a firm solely on either them is indefensible.

In districts using a selection committee, the superintendent should communicate expectations before the committee begins its work. This includes specifying that the committee should provide a rationale for its recommendation. Such direction enhances the likelihood that the committee will not make a purely subjective decision.

Employing an Architectural Firm

Once a firm has been selected, the next task is to execute a contract. Firms almost always prefer using the standard AIA contract. In fact, the general practice in many states has been that principals in the firm and not the school district officials prepared the contract. Consequently, most firms have used the form made available to them by their international association. Some critics (e.g., Levin, 1991; Sargent, 1996) suggest that the standard AIA contract is more protective of a firm's interests than it is of the school district's interests. In addition, some superintendents and school boards have approved a firm developed contract without having it reviewed by their own legal counsel. Responding to this concern, the school attorneys' association in North Carolina identified specific amendments to the AIA contract that would likely benefit and protect local districts (Punger, 1989).

In all instances, the school board's attorney should review the contract and suggest amendments before it is approved. If the standard AIA contract is not being used, the school attorney should either develop the contract or do so in collaboration with the firm's attorney (Uhler, 1988). The board's attorney cannot perform either of these functions if he or she does not have a clear understanding of the district's expectations of the firm's performance and compensation package. The board attorney's involvement helps ensure that the school district's administrative and legal interests are protected.

CONSTRUCTION MANAGEMENT

Prior to the 1970s, construction management (CM) was a relatively unknown concept (Tropf, 1972). But over the past three decades, it has been used with increasing frequency in conjunction with school construction (Kowalski & Coopman, 1997). In part, the growing demand for CM was fueled by demands that public officials be held accountable for tax revenue expenditures. The purposes of CM, the concept's assumed advantages and disadvantages, and issues related to contracting for services are discussed here.

Purposes

Largely because of its title, many erroneously assume that CM only provides supervision during the construction phase of a project. In truth, CM may span all segments of the project including design, bidding, construction, and post-construction. Goldblatt and Wood (1985) identified the following major functions.

* Material design and selection
* Cost estimates and budgets
* Schedules and coordination
* Supervision of actual construction
* Certification of payments to contractors.

Haltenhoff (1987) identified eight management functions integral to CM: cost management, value management, decision management, scheduling management, information management, risk management, contract management, and quality management.

During the pre-construction phase of a project, a CM firm may be involved in the following activities.

* Developing a project schedule
* Reviewing design studies and documents prepared by the architects
* Informing the architect about labor and material costs (Horowitz, 1974)
* Recommending bidding procedures and prepurchase requirements (Stukhart, 1987)

- Projecting cash flow (Haltenhoff, 1987)
- Developing a list of potential bidders
- Providing information about potential local subcontractors (e.g., experience, performance record)
- Assembling bid packages to take advantage of local conditions (Goldhaber & Jha, 1977)
- Evaluating bids in conjunction with the architect and district officials
- Issuing work orders to the successful bidders (Haltenhoff, 1987)

During the construction phase, the CM firm may provide the following services.

- Site security
- Warehousing materials
- Establishing and furnishing a field office
- Establishing safety and labor relations programs
- Providing on-site supervision (General Services Administration, 1976)
- Coordinating communication among district personnel, architects, and subcontractors
- Establishing procedures for processing documents such as shop drawings, material catalogs, test results, and change orders
- Preparing and approving progress payments
- Facilitating the as-built records, warranties, and guarantees
- Expediting the order and delivery of equipment and materials (Haltenhoff, 1987)

Perhaps the most important of these tasks are those that pertain to monitoring costs and work schedules (Warszawski, 1984).

During the post-construction phase, the CM firm may become involved in coordinating the following:

- Final inspections
- Warranties
- Punch lists
- District acceptance of the completed project
- Occupancy

In the first few months of occupancy, a CM firm may provide technical assistance with basic building systems and equipment.

Perceived Advantages and Disadvantages

School administrators are generally divided over the merits of CM. This is not especially unexpected because the concept has always had proponents and detractors. The list of perceived strengths include

- Cost savings via more competitive bidding,
- Cost savings attributable to completing projects on time,
- Protection of client's interests in relation to decisions made by [the architect] and subcontractors,
- Sufficient cost reductions to pay for the service itself,
- Quality control in relation to materials and equipment,
- Daily supervision of construction that reduces problems and the need for change orders (Dubray, 1993).

For many school officials, a position on using a CM firm is predicated on costs. Weinert (1987) articulated a standard argument made by providers and their advocates: "While the CM fees may appear to be an added expense because they usually [appear] as a separate line item on the project bid, the general contractor fees are hidden in the lump sum bid or buried in subcontractor's mark ups, or both" (p. 18). Potential cost savings associated with CM fall into two categories: those related to construction costs and those related to supervision costs. With regard to the former, Kluenker (1987) argued that the multiple-bid approach of CM reduced overall costs significantly when compared to the general-contractor format. With regard to the latter, proponents contend that CM provides indirect cost savings by ensuring daily and intense project supervision. Although architectural services commonly include some of this oversight, L'Hote (1983) asserted that the level of scrutiny provided by CM contributed to construction being completed on time and within budget.

Although cost savings are important, they are not the sole reasons why intense supervision is important. Some writers (e.g., Wright, 1996) have stated that the ultimate contributions of CM are superior management and improved project control. Weinert (1987) identified three types of projects in which daily and intense scrutiny of CM was likely to be most useful.

- Projects that must be designed to budget and subsequently require close fiscal control
- Projects that are unusually complex
- Projects that require completion in a timely manner

CM detractors view the service very differently. The points they accentuate include the following:

- In many states, CM is not a licensed practice and it may not be a professional practice. Whereas school officials can evaluate an architect's professional education, licensing status, and experience, they often must rely on experience alone when retaining CM services.
- There are no industry standards or state guidelines for compensating CM firms, and, as a result, some districts end up paying very high fees.
- CM firms cannot do anything more for a project than a reliable and trustworthy general contractor can do; yet, costs for CM are usually much more substantial.
- The results of using CM have been mixed.

In a recent Indiana study, Kowalski and Coopman (1997) found one of these criticisms to be valid and another to be invalid. Fees paid for CM by Indiana districts between 1992 and 1995 ranged from a low of 2.09 percent to a high of nearly 13 percent of construction costs (all fees were converted to construction costs for comparison purposes). This finding supports the contention that a lack of industry standards and state guidelines for compensating CM firms can be a serious disadvantage. On the other hand, the Indiana study found that the vast majority of school superintendents who used a CM firm were satisfied. This finding suggests that results of CM in Indiana—a state in which approximately 50 percent of school construction projects involve CM—have not been mixed.

Retaining Construction Management Services

Eight variables are especially important to retaining CM services.

- *Philosophy.* Both the administration and the school board should believe in the service and be committed to utilizing the concept to its full potential.
- *Qualifications.* States vary markedly with regard to statutes governing CM (Goldblatt & Wood, 1985). In some states, providers are not licensed as are practitioners of architecture and engineering. In these states, it is particularly important for superintendents to establish and evaluate the credentials of potential providers.
- *Experience.* Since CM is still a relatively new concept, a firm's experience should be determined and evaluated. This is especially true with respect to school projects.
- *Past Performance.* Knowing how a firm performed on previous school projects is essential. This is why school district officials should always compile a list of recent clients and seek permission to contact these individuals.
- *Independence.* Given the nature of the service provided by CM firms, they should have no legal attachment to the project architects. Large architectural firms may either provide CM services or own their own CM firms. In some states, it is illegal to retain a CM firm owned by the project's architectural firm. Even if such an arrangement is legal, it defeats the purpose of having the CM firm protect the client's interests.
- *Trust.* School officials must be able to trust the CM provider because they will be acting on behalf of the school district. In the absence of credibility, CM may create more conflict than it will resolve.

- *Ability to Communicate.* CM providers must be good communicators. This means that they are able to construct and deliver information in a timely and clear manner. It also means that they are good listeners who actively seek to obtain information from all participating groups and individuals.

- *Fees.* Although the literature on CM during the 1970s and 1980s indicated that the service was provided on a fixed-fee basis, this does not hold true across the country today. Many CM firms prefer to be compensated on a percentage of construction costs—the same standard embraced by most architectural firms. Given the CM firm's responsibility to serve as the district's representative, a fixed-fee contract is probably a safer political and economic option. This is because the CM firm would not benefit directly from decisions that escalated construction costs (e.g., change orders).

Additional Design/Construction Personnel

In this age of modern technology, new needs are surfacing with regard to facility projects. These needs often require the inclusion of highly specialized individuals to assist with the design and construction phases. These specialists may include acoustical consultants, computer consultants, and telecommunication consultants. The integration of voice and video, for example, is having a profound impact on educational programming. Often consultants in highly technical areas are not part of either architectural or CM firms. Their services must be obtained independently. The owner should establish at the time of entering into a contract with an architectural firm or a CM firm the scope of specialized services that will be required and who will be responsible for retaining and paying for such services.

OTHER PROFESSIONAL SERVICES

While the services provided by an architectural firm and a CM firm may be broad, school officials almost always retain the services of several other consultants. In some states this action is mandatory (e.g., retaining a bond attorney or retaining an educational consultant). In situations in which it is not, decisions about using consultants are usually based on the school district's human resources and the dispositions of key officials. In large school systems, for example, personnel may be available to perform highly specialized tasks such as developing performance specifications or preparing a bond prospectus. In addition, some administrators and board members have negative attitudes about the need for and value of consultant services.

In addition to facility design and construction, school districts commonly engage the services of consultants in four basic areas. They are educational programming, technology, legal services, and debt management. Soliciting and selecting consultants for these services are not clear-cut tasks because qualifications and potential roles vary substantially. In general, the following actions improve decisions about using consultants.

- Districts should have a policy for using and selecting consultants (Zinger, 1995).
- District officials should have a clear perspective of the services they are retaining.
- The intent should be to retain the best services that are available.
- Selection decisions should be objective and based on qualifications.

Education Consultants

Education consultants are commonly retained to assist with pre-construction planning. The most common tasks include:

- Conducting a needs assessment study that details program deficiencies associated with the physical environment of a school
- Conducting a feasibility study that details how existing needs can be met
- Developing educational specifications: a statement of how the school's program will be delivered by administrators, faculty, and staff
- Helping to monitor the design phase by evaluating the interpretation of educational specifications into actual design

Education consultants should be highly educated individuals (usually possessing a doctorate in educational administration) who have a vast amount of experience with school facility planning. The most common providers have been professors of educational administration who conduct research and teach courses in this specialization; however, some large architectural and CM firms and some state departments of education also have individuals who can perform these services.

The selection of an education consultant should be guided by two principles. The first is that the individuals who are being considered have expertise that will make a difference. Ethical practice mandates that the selection be based on merit and that the consultant is given free reign to work objectively. The second principle is that the consultant has a record of being objective. This means that he or she evaluates the situation candidly and reports outcomes accurately.

Equally important is the appearance of objectivity. Taxpayers who are predisposed to opposing construction are especially prone to criticizing recommendations made by consultants who appear to have ulterior motives. This is why most school districts avoid using consultants who are employees of architectural and CM firms and why they do not involve the education consultant in selecting an architectural or CM firm.

There is no certification or board registration for education consultants; thus, school officials must exercise great care in selecting one (Castaldi, 1994). School officials should always require potential consultants to provide a list of previous clients so that work quality can be evaluated. The contract for services should detail what is expected, the time parameters for the work, and the fee and reimbursables.

Technology Consultants

Technology has become one of the major forces determining how schools function (Sabo, 1996). Technological innovations, and especially computers, are essential in today's educational system. Accordingly, designs for new and renovated buildings must accommodate their use. Technology consultants are specialists who provide direction for at least three critical aspects of a facility project: the scope of technology that will be provided, the nature of technology, and the placement and use of technology. Because technology consultants are not licensed, persons with varying backgrounds attempt to provide such services.

Ideally, technology consultants involved in school construction planning should have considerable knowledge of both available technologies and the applications of those technologies in elementary and secondary education. School officials should carefully weigh their needs and determine the amount of expertise that is needed in each of these areas.

Compensation for technology consultants has varied considerably. In part, this may be due to the fact that the service is relatively new and superintendents are unaware of industry standards. In addition, there are relatively few consultants working in this area and the demand for their service often allows them to charge relatively high fees. State departments of education and state associations may be able to supply information about fee practices for technology consultants. Increasingly, technology design services are provided by the architectural firm designing the school—either through in-house personnel or through consultants retained as part of the architect's fee.

Legal Consultants

Many legal services associated with school facility projects are detailed in state statutes. Typically, the school board's regular attorney handles routine matters such as contracts, building codes, property acquisition, and labor disputes. Since facility projects are not common occurrences for most school systems, attorneys are typically compensated separately for this service (i.e., an amount that is in addition to their regular fee/retainer for serving as the school district's attorney).

In a number of states, bond sales also require school districts to retain the services of a bond counselor—an attorney who specializes in municipal bonds. This is especially true when it is necessary or advantageous to have an expert issue an opinion on the tax-exempt status of the bonds. Since bonds are almost always sold by competitive bid on the open market (in some states negotiated sales are permitted), the reputation of the bond attorney can be quite important. The attorney should have a national or regional reputation and be someone (or a firm) acceptable to the seller and the buyer (Stollar, 1967). Duties of a bond counselor can involve the following services.

- Drafting the original bond resolution or ordinance
- Developing a notice of bond election (if required by law)
- Developing a ballot for the election
- Reviewing the prospectus
- Reviewing the notice of sale
- Reviewing other financial advertisements
- Reviewing all materials presented to underwriters
- Reviewing the budget for the entire project
- Rendering a legal opinion regarding the tax status of the bonds
- Rendering a final opinion after the sale of the bonds

Fees for a bond counselor may be based on a percentage of construction costs, a flat rate, or an hourly rate; the percentage option has been most common. Since conditions for funding capital outlay are so diverse across the states, superintendents are advised to determine legal requirements for using attorneys in conjunction with school construction by contacting both the state department of education and the state school boards association.

Financial Consultants

Financial consultants are specialists who assist with a variety of tasks related to financing capital outlay. Like educational and technology consultants, the practice of these individuals may not be regulated. Providers may include attorneys, accountants, and professors specializing in school finance. One misconception about the services of financial consultants is that their sole purpose is to help sell bonds. In reality, they can perform a number of functions as illustrated in the following list developed by Kowalski (1988).

- Analyzing the existing financial status of the school district and determining the district's ability to incur further debt
- Estimating the impact of added debt
- Creating/coordinating the planning calendar for the entire project to ensure that deadlines pertaining to finance are met
- Helping to develop a project budget
- Assisting with securing special loans (e.g., some states have special loan programs available for school construction projects)
- Providing information to other specialists involved with the project (e.g., conferring with attorneys, the architect)
- Assisting with the bond sale
  - Determining the timing of the sale
  - Preparing the prospectus

- Preparing legal ads for the sale
- Distributing the prospectus
- Answering inquiries about the bond sale
- Interpreting bids
- Recommending selection of bids
- Appearing at hearings to help represent the school district (e.g., before state tax boards)
- Recommending conditions for debt management

The prospectus (the official statement for the sale of the bonds) is a very important document because it plays a pivotal role in attracting potential bond buyers. Superintendents should realize that nonprofessional brochures are immediately apparent to purchasers, and such products tend to alienate sophisticated buyers (Guthrie, Garms, & Pierce, 1988). In addition to having expertise about public finance and municipal bonds, a good financial consultant understands legal, political, and economic issues specific to school construction.

CHAPTER SUMMARY

Planning for school construction is a complex task that requires the assistance of several professionals who would normally not be employed by a school district. This chapter examined the services provided by these individuals and discussed issues related to their employment. Deciding what consultants are necessary and actually selecting them are often difficult tasks because economic, political, legal, and professional factors may be involved. Administrators are more likely to make appropriate decisions if they understand what consultants can do and if they understand the choices available with regard to compensating them.

The total amount of fees paid to an architectural firm, a CM firm, and consultants typically exceeds 10 percent of the construction cost. In many states, competition among providers is intense—a condition that raises the probability of political tension and conflict. Unfortunately, there have been instances in which administrators have violated ethical and even legal standards when making these critical decisions. To avoid these problems, administrators should (a) know the scope of the project they want to pursue, (b) set expectations for consultant services before seeking assistance, (c) make decisions that are in the best interest of the school district, and (d) follow ethical and legal standards.

ISSUES FOR DISCUSSION

1. What are the laws in your state regarding the use of architects on school construction projects?
2. What are the differences between an architect and an engineer?

3. What is CM? What are possible advantages and disadvantages of using CM for a school construction project?

4. Why should school districts avoid using CM firms that are affiliated with their architectural firm?

5. What is the legal status of CM in your state? Who can function as a CM provider?

6. What are the possible disadvantages of paying [architects] or CM providers on the basis of a percentage of construction costs?

7. Many school districts now retain the services of technology consultants for school construction. What services may these consultants provide? What are some possible criteria for selecting them?

8. Assume that you are the superintendent in a district that will build a new middle school. Identify criteria that you would use in selecting an architectural firm.

9. What is a bond attorney? What services does he or she provide?

10. What qualifications would you look for in an educational consultant? What are the advantages and disadvantages of using an educational consultant who is employed by an architectural firm?

11. In your state, what responsibilities are assumed by the board's attorney in conjunction with a construction project?

12. What criteria might you use to select a financial consultant?

13. What questions would you ask an architect in an interview to ascertain his or her philosophy about working with educational clients?

REFERENCES

American Institute of Architects. (1987). *You and your architect.* Washington, DC: Author.

Castaldi, B. (1994). *Educational facilities* (4th ed.). Boston: Allyn and Bacon.

Dubray, B.J. (1993). Master builder: Why use a construction manager? *The American School Board Journal, 180*(4), 37–38.

General Services Administration. (1976). *Using construction management for public and instructional facilities.* Washington, DC: Public Technology, pp. 18–29.

Goldblatt, S., & Wood, R.C. (1985). *Construction management for educational facilities: Professional services' procurement and competitive bid statutes.* (ERIC Document Reproduction Service No. ED 268 670)

Goldhaber, S., & Jha, C. (1977). Pros and cons of construction management. *Journal of the Construction Division CO, 4*(103), 668.

Guthrie, J., Garms, W., & Pierce, L. (1988). *School finance and education policy* (2nd ed.). Englewood Cliffs, N.J.: Prentice-Hall.

Haltenhoff, C.E. (1987). Construction management services. In B. Jones (Ed.), *Schoolhouse planning* (pp. 65–71). Reston, VA: Association of School Business Officials International.

Horowitz, S. (1974). *CM for the general contractor: A guide for construction management.* Washington, DC: Associated General Contractors of America.

Kluenker, C. (1987). Construction management and local contractors: A good team for the owners. *School Business Affairs, 53*(1), 22–23.

Kowalski, T.J. (1988). Variety consulting. *American School and University, 61*(1), 36h–361.

Kowalski, T.J., & Coopman, J.T. (1997). Using construction management for school facility projects in Indiana. *The Facility Planner, 35*(3), 8–11.

Levin, M.I. (1991). *Contracting with architects: A school district's perspective.* Alexandria, VA: National School Boards Association.

L'Hote, J.D. (1983). Educational facility construction—A role for the owner. *CEFP Journal, 21*(5), 4–6.

Madden, M., & Coughlin, T. (1985). *Selection and compensation of architectural services for school facility construction: Guidelines for school districts.* (ERIC Document Reproduction Service No. ED 267 485)

Moore, D. (1989). A new approach to selecting architects. *CEFP Journal, 27*(1), 35–37.

Punger, D.S. (1989). *The AIA standard form of agreement between owner and architect.* (ERIC Document Reproduction Service No. ED 306 653)

Sabo, S.R. (1996). Shaping school design. *The American School Board Journal, 183*(10), 42–44.

Sargent, N. (1996). Protecting yourself from liability: Architectural contracts by design. *School Business Affairs, 62*(2), 11–12.

Smith, E., Stevenson, K., & Pellicer, L. (1984). Follow these nine steps to select the architectural firm that can design a new school to your exact specification. *The American School Board Journal, 171*(5), 36–37.

Stollar, D. (1967). *Managing school indebtedness.* Danville, IL: Interstate Printers and Publishers.

Stukhart, G. (1987). Construction management responsibilities during design. *Journal of Construction Engineering and Management, 113*(2), 94–96.

Tropf, C.F. (1972). Construction management: The team concept. *CEFP Journal, 10*(5), 4–7.

Uhler, S. (1988). Scrutinizing architectural contracts. *School Business Affairs, 55*(12), 57–58.

Warszawski, A. (1984). Construction management program. *Journal of Construction Engineering and Management, 110*(3), 298–299.

Weinert, R.A. (1987). Construction management: A sensible alternative when building new schools. *School Business Affairs, 53*(1), 16–21.

Wright, D. (1996). The merits of construction management: A sensible alternative when building new schools. *School Business Affairs, 53*(1), 16–21.

Zinger, D. (1995, October). *Creating a successful consultant selection process for your school building project.* Paper presented at the annual meeting of the Association of School Business Officials, Nashville, TN.

CHAPTER 9

Designing and Constructing Buildings

Once a school board has made a commitment to pursue a facility project, and once decisions about professional assistance have been made, activities related to designing and constructing the building begin. The building planning process is generally divided into three parts: pre-construction activities, construction activities, and post-construction activities. Some administrators mistakenly conclude that they only need a minimum amount of knowledge about these tasks because architects and other consultants have the responsibility for completing them. However, without a substantial amount of knowledge regarding these tasks, school officials will be unable to ensure that the building is being planned properly.

The intent of this chapter is to broadly define the essential stages of design, construction, and building occupancy. State manuals on school construction usually provide specific provisions regarding the completion of these steps. The material is presented chronologically; however, certain tasks within the major categories may be completed simultaneously on certain projects.

PRE-CONSTRUCTION TASKS

Pre-construction tasks focus primarily on design activities. The initial steps of assessing needs and selecting professional assistance already have been discussed. The involvement of architects and a construction manager (if one is used) should begin as soon as possible and continue until the building is occupied.

Determining Legal Requirements

All states have laws, policies, codes, and rules governing the construction of public buildings, including schools. In addition, local codes affecting construction may be relevant. Collectively, these legal boundaries are a primary planning input. The project's architects should compile a list of these requirements before any specific design activity occurs. If a planning team is involved, the general nature of these requirements should be explained to them. Such requirements might include time lines for approvals, site selection criteria, options for funding, fire and safety codes, and so forth.

Determining a Delivery System

One of the first decisions school officials must make is the selection of a delivery system. State laws and regulations may place restrictions on the options that can be considered. The most common approach to school construction continues to be design–bid–build. With this approach, districts enter into separate contracts for design and construction. After the design is completed, competitive bidding is used to employ either a general contractor or multiple contractors if construction management is being used.

A second option is referred to as "construction management at risk." This option also separates design and construction; however, a district selects a contractor who performs both the construction and construction management responsibilities. The contractor is usually selected during the early design phase allowing him to have significant input in the design process (Konchar & Sanvido, 1998).

The third delivery option is design–build. With this option, a district enters into a single contract with a firm that provides both design and construction. The firm may either perform all of the work or elect to subcontract parts of the project (Konchar & Sanvido, 1998). The purported advantage is that the district has a single contract to manage. The term "design–build," has also been used to describe a process in which a school district elects to use a generic design owned by an architectural firm. The advantage of this is reduced design fees; this process also has been labeled a "cookie-cutter" approach to school construction.

One reason why school districts continue to rely heavily on the design–bid–build delivery system is competitive bidding. Another reason relates to ensuring checks and balances; that is, many administrators believe they benefit from having separate firms perform design, management, and construction responsibilities.

Educational Specifications

Educational programs should be the nucleus of facility planning. Ideally, districts and individual schools should have long-range plans that provide a frame-

Figure 9–1
Four Sources of Information for Educational Specifications

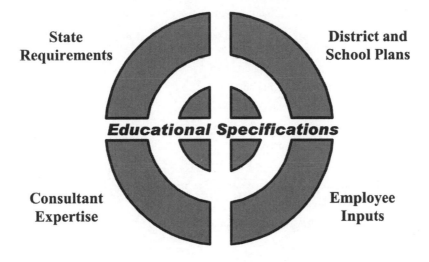

State
Requirements

District and
School Plans

Educational Specifications

Consultant
Expertise

Employee
Inputs

work for a specific project. Such district plans normally include an educational philosophy, a mission statement, a vision statement, and goals. Educational specifications are both an extension of these documents and written statements identifying needs, describing programs, describing program delivery systems, and translating program needs into space requirements (Earthman, 1994). Educational specifications are also referred to as *program specifications*, *performance specifications*, or *program requirements*.

Educational specifications are completed before any design activities are started. Four sources of information are used to shape this document as shown in Figure 9–1. They are state requirements, district/school plans, employee input, and consultant expertise. As noted earlier, educational specifications can be completed in several ways, but the preferred method is for a district to retain the services of an independent educational consultant. Some superintendents elect to have the architectural firm prepare the program statements—partly because the cost for the service may be hidden in the firm's fee and partly because superintendents do not fully understand the nature of this task. Persons developing educational specifications should have knowledge of pedagogy, curriculum, emerging educational trends, and facility development. They also should be objective and represent the best interests of the school district. If these qualities are missing, the superintendent may receive educational specifications that are nothing more than a wish list articulated by teachers and administrators. When this happens, the superintendent may be required to revise the document to ensure that it is economically and programmatically acceptable.

The primary purpose of educational specifications is to communicate to the design architects what functions will occur in the school. Typically, the document includes

- Guiding statements (e.g., philosophy, mission, vision),
- Details of the school's curriculum and extracurricular programs,
- A summary of the school's organizational structure (e.g., administration, departments),
- General specifications pertaining to the entire building (e.g., accessibility for the disabled),
- A list of learning spaces and support spaces,
- A statement of each space's function,
- The desired and essential relationships of spaces,
- Quantitative statements for furniture and fixtures,
- Intended capacity of each space,
- Site development standards,
- Technology plan or criteria,
- Acoustic criteria,
- Design criteria (e.g., flexibility, adaptability).

Ideally, the document should exhibit:

- *Connectivity*. The document is congruous with the district's master facility plan (if one exists).
- *Clarity*. The document includes statements that can readily be understood by various audiences.
- *Completeness*. The document addresses all segments of the school's programming.
- *Specificity*. The document includes both quantitative and qualitative data detailing intended functions.

Equally important are considerations of what should not be included in educational specifications. First, the document should not include design ideas. When administrators and teachers insist on designing their workspaces, they limit the creative potential of architects and attenuate the primary benefit of having architectural designs (Holcolm, 1995). School employees, however, should be given the opportunity subsequently to critique the architect's design ideas. Second, unless there are reasons to do so, the educational specifications should not include state regulations, codes, and other standards. Architects are expected to know federal and state standards, and they are expected to detect any conflicts between the specifications and standards once they start designing the building. Placing them in the educational specifications merely lengthens the document.

Once the first draft of the educational specifications is completed, it should be reviewed by all parties who contributed to the document to ensure accuracy of data and interpretations. After any necessary corrections are made, the document should be formally approved by the school board and officially given to the design architects.

Technology Plan

Technology has become a central issue in school facility design. While many administrators recognize that networking, hardware, and the integration of voice, video, and data are expensive, they often are less aware that the infusion of technology also affects space requirements in a modern school. As an example, placing three to five individual computers in a standard classroom has become common, and doing so increases minimum space requirements for these areas (McDonough, 2000). And although most educational institutions have taken steps to incorporate technology into learning environments, relatively few have done so in conjunction with a well developed technology-learning plan (Keown, 1999).

Several approaches may be used to develop a technology plan. Ideally, the plan is either developed in conjunction with educational specifications (and attached to the specifications as an addendum) or the plan is developed as part of educational specifications. Some administrators, however, have ignored technology plans or allowed the architectural firm to make technology decisions independently. Because technology has become integral to instruction, planning in this area should not be delayed until actual design activities begin. Rather, educational specifications and the technology plan should be the primary inputs for the design architects. Technology specifications increase the likelihood that appropriate raceways, ducts, and channels for wiring and cable will be integrated into the building design (Earthman, 1994).

The technology plan should focus on the implementation of technology across the building. This includes administration, instruction, and other support services. The integration of voice, video, and data; wide area networks; media services; and administrative services are primary foci. One of the key decisions relates to specifying an infrastructure for technology systems (e.g., using wired or wireless networks) (Fielding, 2000). The technology plan should provide the design architects with sufficient information for a delivery system, including:

- Specific requirements for each type of technology needed
- Salient features of each type of technology
- Access and control of the various technologies
- Descriptions of intended uses of the various technologies

If the district does not have a technology master plan, one should be developed prior to a facility project. The individual school plans should be an extension of the master plan.

Site Selection

State laws and policies almost always specify characteristics of school sites, such as size. These requirements constitute minimums; and therefore, administrators should be cognizant of all facets of acceptable sites.

- *Size*. Most states specify minimum acreage required for elementary and secondary schools. Planners should always anticipate the possibility that a school could be expanded after initial construction, so having land for possible expansion is advised.

- *Shape*. Since sites typically accommodate a building and outdoor facilities, the shape of a parcel of land is important. For example, locating athletic fields or playgrounds in desired areas may depend on the site's configuration.

- *Access to Utilities*. Whenever possible, it is preferable for schools to avoid using wells and septic systems because high installation and maintenance costs and environmental problems are likely. In today's information age, telephone and cable television services also are critically important.

- *Health and Safety Considerations*. Much greater attention is being given to locating schools in areas free of environmental hazards. Examples of problems to be avoided include high voltage electrical transmission lines, oil or petroleum products transmission lines and storage facilities, hazardous chemical or gas pipelines and storage areas, railroad tracks, busy highways, industrial parks, high-noise areas (e.g., airports), and hazardous-waste sites.

- *Location*. The site should be accessible, reasonably close to other schools and community services, and at or near the center of the population being served. Land in a flood plain or adjacent to lakes, ponds, and rivers should be avoided.

- *Availability*. Although schools have the legal option of acquiring land through eminent domain, such action almost always is politically unpopular and expensive. Consideration should be given to land that can be acquired without litigation.

- *Cost*. School officials often make the mistake of purchasing a site solely on the basis of cost. Often there are good reasons why the value of land varies. Selecting the lowest-cost option could mean buying a number of unforeseen problems. Over the life cycle of a school building, the initial cost of land is not a major expense—yet a poor decision about a site could seriously detract from a school's adequacy. Thus, cost should be weighed against quality as measured by the other criteria.

Some districts form site selection teams as part of the planning process. Often this is done when there are differences of opinion as to where the school should be located. When such teams are used, at least some members should have the expertise necessary to make judgments about the site quality (Haun, 1995).

Building Design

The design process has three stages. The first is commonly called "the schematic design phase." This is the point in planning at which the architects translate educational specifications and the technology plan into proposed schematic solutions. The products are outlines of different design conceptions. The process entails determining the quantity of space, the placement of the building on a site, and possible space arrangements; both floor plans and the exterior appearance of the school are developed. Decisions about the allocation of spaces on the site (e.g., athletic fields, parking lots) also are addressed.

Many administrators and planning participants find the schematic design stage to be the most exciting part of planning because ideas start to take form. Although the architects may develop literally dozens of different concepts, they typically present district officials with only a handful they consider to be best. Planning participants should be given an opportunity to study the schematic drawings, ask questions, and suggest possible improvements. In other words, the design architects, the planning team, administrators, and the school board engage in brainstorming. Changes in design concepts are easiest before detail for mechanical systems and materials have been developed. Thus, the schematic phase is the best time to evaluate general concepts for a building's design. The final decision to accept a specific concept rests with the school board.

The second stage of the design process is the design development phase. Basically, the ideas generated and accepted in the schematics are refined. Dimensions, structural systems, mechanical systems, electrical systems, and construction materials are now added. And because the building is starting to take shape, the architect usually starts communicating with various agency officials who must issue permits for the project. This is also a time when cost estimates for the project may be revised. If it appears that the project might exceed budget, the architects usually initiate discussions about materials and design options that might lower costs. For example, the advantages and disadvantages of using less expensive floor surfaces may be discussed. Again, the school board should formally approve the design development drawings before the architects move to the next design stage.

The third and final design stage is called the construction documents phase. At this point, the architects complete their work with the consultants and engineers, and detailed documents that will be used for contracts and construction are completed. For example, base drawings are sent to the engineers for drafting; building codes are rechecked; materials are selected; input from the special design consultants (e.g., kitchen, media center, technology) is integrated; site designs are finished; and architectural sheets for all aspects of the project are completed.

There are two basic parts to construction documents.

- *Working Drawings.* These are drawings of floor plans, elevations, and rooms that cover the entire building. They include dimensions and materials information. At the very least, working drawings have four divisions: structural, electrical, plumbing, and mechanical (heating, ventilation, and air-conditioning).
- *Construction Specifications.* These documents detail the materials and construction methods that contractors are expected to use. Specificity is essential. For example, equipment manufacturers and model numbers are provided.

Although the architects do not complete all the drawings and specifications (some are completed by engineers and special consultants), they have the responsibility for coordinating the collective efforts of the design team.

The construction documents should exhibit three qualities: they should be complete, they should be clear, and they should be accurate (Brooks, Conrad, & Griffith, 1980). Construction management personnel, if involved, usually provide an independent assessment to the school board regarding whether these standards have been met. Most important, the construction drawings should precisely delineate the scope and requirements of the work performed by contractors. Again, if necessary, cost estimates are revised and the school board approves the construction documents.

A relatively new concept that may be used to reduce the number of design errors is the Pre-construction Coordination and Constructibility Review (PCCR). Architects and engineers who have design expertise across disciplines conduct the PCCR. The purpose is to check the separate disciplines against one another to determine interferences and discrepancies at points of interface. According to Barrett (1997), the PCCR not only reduces change orders, it tightens bids, reduces the number of requests for information during construction, eliminates construction delays, and keeps the project within budget. The review should be conducted when the construction documents are 95 percent to 100 percent completed and before the bidding process.

Construction Calendar

After the construction documents have been approved, the architectural firm can now prepare the calendar detailing when the remaining phases of the project are to be completed. This document is especially important for schools because the timing for completing projects affects the delivery of educational services. For example, administrators prefer to occupy new facilities at the beginning of a school year. This means that a project needs to be completed prior to August. Often, however, there is a tension between scheduling a project to coincide with the start of a school year and scheduling a project so as to maximize bid competition (Delaney, 1983). Hence, it is a good idea for the superintendent to discuss timing priorities with representatives of the architectural firm very early in the planning process.

Construction calendars should be sufficiently detailed so that school officials can readily detect if projects are falling behind schedule. Some architects complete the construction calendar at the same time they complete the construction documents.

Construction Bid Documents and Contracts

Most states require school districts to use competitive bidding for awarding construction contracts. In order to attract prospective bidders, architects provide bid documents. Coordination of the bidding process usually rests with the architectural firm, unless this responsibility has been assigned to a construction management firm. The documents basically include the working drawings and the construction specifications. Typically, state laws dictate how the bidding process is to be conducted, including details for advertising and accepting bids.

Some states require school districts to accept the lowest bids, while others require acceptance of the lowest and best bid. The latter concept allows school officials to blend cost factors with product quality and performance. When such leeway is permitted, four criteria are often used to award construction contracts: experience, reputation, present and anticipated workload, and the bid amount. The person coordinating the bidding process (either architect or construction manager) is expected to make recommendations regarding the awarding of contracts. Depending on state laws, school officials may select a successful bidder, negotiate with one or more of the bidders in hopes of reaching a contract agreement, or reject all bids and start the process again. This last option is used when there is reason to believe that better bids can be obtained by restructuring the bid packages or by conducting the bidding at a time in the future when competition will be more intense.

State laws vary regarding requirements for submitting bids and issuing contracts. Generally, bidders are required to submit both a bid bond and non-collusion affidavit. The bond is a form of insurance protecting the school district in case the bidder defaults; the affidavit is a sworn statement stating that the bidder did not conspire with competitors to fix prices. In addition, many states require successful bidders to post a performance bond in the amount of the contract. The bond protects the school district from performance defaults.

Architects should recommend the establishment of a contingency fund in conjunction with awarding contracts. Such a fund is used if there are unforeseen circumstances resulting in added costs after the contracts are awarded. Typically, contingency funds are set at a percentage of the overall construction costs (e.g., 5 percent).

Risk Management

A school board's broad responsibilities include stated and implied powers for the protection of public funds and property (Burrup, Brimley, & Garfield, 1999). Before starting a construction project, school officials should be prepared for the following possibilities.

- *Property loss* (e.g., natural disasters, theft, vandalism)
- *Tort action* (e.g., lawsuits over contracts)
- *Accidents* (e.g., personal injury or death)
- *Construction delays* (e.g., strikes or material shortages that result in indirect cost increases)

The primary responsibility of school administrators is to eliminate risk exposure, and this involves insurance policies held by the board, architects, construction managers, and contractors. Property insurance contracts may have a myriad of provisions (Hack, Candoli, & Ray, 1998); therefore, both the school board's attorney and representatives of the architectural firm should be consulted regarding coverage during construction.

A relatively new concept for risk management is called "wrap-up." With this approach, the district purchases a comprehensive construction insurance policy that includes general liability, excessive liability, workers' compensation, and builders' risk insurance. Advocates claim the approach results in competitive pricing, safety incentives, lower claim costs, more competitive bidding, and improved policies (Ferraro, 1998).

Communication Procedures

One of the most overlooked tasks prior to starting construction is determining how communication among the various participants will occur. Large projects usually involve construction management, contractors, and subcontractors. Without predetermining communication, administrators may be insufficiently informed about possible delays, conflicts, and other important project matters. This is why it is critically important to establish and consistently use clearly defined communication channels (Metzner & Feifer, 1998).

Key questions that need to be addressed about communication include the following:

- *Who will be the district's official contact person during construction?* In smaller districts this is often the superintendent; in larger districts it may be an assistant superintendent, business manager, or director of facilities.

- *Who will have the primary responsibility for providing information to the school district?* Almost always architects are the key communication link between the owner and the contractors. If construction management is being used, the architects and the construction manager may share this role.

- *How can open and two-way communication be maintained without creating conflict?* School administrators should create channels that permit them to distribute and receive information in a timely manner. However, allowing every contractor and subcontractor unlimited access to the district's coordinator may result in serious conflict, especially when key participants such as the architects and construction managers feel that they are being bypassed. Typically, the district's primary representatives at the construction site are encouraged to share all pertinent information.

- *How often should progress reports be prepared?* The frequency of progress reports should be agreeable to the school board, the architects (or other primary representatives of the district during construction), and the superintendent.

- *How will communication occur?* Thought should be given to determining how information will be transferred. While some data might be forwarded via e-mail, other communiqués may need to be in writing.

TASKS DURING CONSTRUCTION

The responsibility of administrators does not end when construction starts. Regardless of how much professional assistance is being used, one administrator should be designated as an internal coordinator. The amount of time this individual will have to spend on this specific assignment obviously depends on the scope of the project, the effectiveness of the district's on-site supervisor (typically an employee of the architectural firm or the construction management firm), and the frequency of problems. Even when the construction is proceeding smoothly, there is a need to keep the school board, district employees, and the community informed.

Monitoring Progress

Once construction has started, the district's on-site representative has the responsibility to review the work and document progress. Typically, this on-site representative is an employee of the architectural firm or an employee of the construction management firm. In some situations in which the general-contractor approach is used, the district may employ a "clerk of the works"—an individual who provides daily on-site supervision. Information from the on-site supervisor should be transmitted to the in-district coordinator who then makes it available to the superintendent and school board. Such periodic reports should include

- A report of progress in relation to the construction calendar,
- A report of compliance with the construction documents,
- A summary of activities for the period being covered,
- Details for any problems and recommended solutions,
- Requests for directions or decisions that may come from the board or administration.

It is especially important that the district's on-site representative notify the superintendent and school board if changes to the construction calendar become necessary.

Keeping the School Board and the Public Informed

Once the superintendent has received the progress reports, he or she needs to make the information available to the school board and the public. In some instances, information about employees or potential litigation may not be made public. Typically, superintendents request that they receive the progress reports at least one week prior to a board meeting so that they can prepare a written and verbal summary for the meeting. Some superintendents prefer to have the on-site representative and the district's coordinator present the progress report directly to the school board.

Providing information to the media via timely news releases is one way to ensure that the public will be kept informed. School districts that publish newsletters typically may also use this medium for that purpose. Larger districts may employ a full-time public relations director; this administrator is typically a key person in the communication process. Some districts provide monthly updates of construction progress at school board meetings.

Dealing with Change Orders

Once construction contracts are in effect, it may be necessary to alter the architectural drawings or a technical specification. These modifications, referred to as "change orders," may be caused by circumstances such as

- An error in the construction documents,
- An omission in the construction documents,
- An opportunity to use an improved technique or material,
- Needs created by unforeseen conditions (e.g., site problems),
- The unavailability of specified materials,
- Needs created by changes in educational programming (e.g., the need to alter the configuration of a laboratory).

The first two problems listed here, errors and omissions, are the most common causes of change orders (Fewell, 1998).

Change orders may be initiated either by the district or by contractors. Because procedures or materials involved in change orders were not part of the competitive bidding process, costs are usually high (Earthman, 1994). School board members and administrators usually react negatively to change orders that are perceived to be necessary because of design errors. This is especially true when the change orders increase construction costs and when the architects are being compensated on a percentage of the construction costs. These conditions result in a situation in which compensation to contractors (or the architect) may actually be increased because of their error. Therefore, "the rate the contractor is to recover for changes should be agreed upon and defined in the prime contract document between the owner and contractor" (Epperson, 1983, p. 7). Continuous change orders during construction are reflective of inadequate design, a poor review of construction documents, or both (Brooks et al., 1980).

POST-CONSTRUCTION TASKS

Some of the most important responsibilities executed by administrators occur after construction has been essentially completed. In general, these duties involve certifying that construction has been completed as planned, that the building is ready for occupancy, and that the school program can be implemented.

Accepting the Completed Building

When a building is nearing completion, the contractors request a Certificate of Substantial Completion from the architectural firm. Representatives of the firm then inspect the project and identify items that still need to be completed; they also evaluate if all elements of the project meet specifications. These tasks are done using one or more "punch lists" of items to be completed or corrected. A school building may be occupied before the school board officially accepts it as a completed project, provided that appropriate permits and approvals are obtained from government officials (e.g., the fire marshal). Occupying a building before it is entirely completed may be necessary at the beginning of a school year or semester. When this is done, however, it is important for the administrators to have a written statement identifying what work needs to be completed after occupancy.

It is not unusual to withhold a percentage of the contractors' payment (e.g., 5 percent) until all work is completed. Before making final payment, administrators should check to ensure that all warranties and guarantees are in order. Final acceptance of the project should be done by formal board action subject to the correction of any remaining irregularities. Once the district accepts ownership, the contractors' responsibilities are limited to the remaining items on the punch lists (Brooks et al., 1980).

Preparing to Operate the Building

Today, districts are more likely to include all furniture and fixtures in the overall construction contracts. When this is not the case, school officials must determine what furniture is necessary, specify the products they want, conduct a bidding process, and award contracts. This involves a substantial amount of work, and this is why most superintendents prefer to include these items in the construction contracts.

In today's larger and more complex buildings, both general and specific orientation sessions are often held. The general sessions address features used by all building occupants; health, safety, and comfort concerns are examples. Technology features also may be discussed when all employees are present. Specific sessions focus on information pertaining to job functions (e.g., instructing custodians about the mechanical systems). Orientation sessions also are necessary for students. Of special importance here are tours of the building and information about safety and emergency situations.

Orientations to the building should cover several important issues. They include the layout of the building and the site, intended usage of the building and the site (including an overview of policies and rules), explanations of equipment (operations and access), and procedures for dealing with problems.

Dedication and Public Relations

School buildings represent a sizable investment of public funds; therefore, they are a source of community pride. As such, administrators should carefully plan and execute a public relations program regarding the completion and occupancy of a building. This includes a well planned dedication ceremony. Every effort should be made to make the taxpayers see the facility as their school. Typically architects have participated in building dedications, and they can provide suggestions for planning the program.

Brochures detailing the cost of the building and its most attractive features should be made available to the media and the public. The principal and superintendent should consider taking the media on a tour through the building, allowing them to take pictures and ask questions. Pictures of the school should be placed in areas of the central office (e.g., in the board room) where the public can see them. In general, administrators should accentuate the positive; they should point out why the new facility makes an essential contribution to the community and to the education of students. If taxpayers focus on negative aspects of a facility project, they may be extremely reluctant to support the next proposed building project.

Correcting Problems

Administrators should always anticipate that there will be some problems once a school is occupied. These problems need to be identified and corrected as soon as possible—partly because of warranty periods, but primarily because they negatively affect programming. Consequently, frequent (e.g., monthly) checks for problems should be conducted during the first year of operation. Postoccupancy evaluations usually become less frequent after the first year, but they generally continue for at least five years (Ortiz, 1993). The principal should be aware of procedures for addressing problems, and district administrators should have a clear understanding of the architect's responsibilities after occupancy.

CHAPTER SUMMARY

This chapter examined the responsibilities assumed by administrators prior to, during, and after construction. These duties are more expansive than most superintendents and principals realize. They can be extremely time-consuming, especially when the administrators have had little or no previous experience with school construction. Determining precisely what will be expected is impossible because of differences in state laws, district human resources, and the types of professional assistance used. For example, using construction management may reduce the amount of supervision that needs to be provided by district personnel.

The best way to avoid problems is careful planning. Thus, it is especially essential that administrators understand the range of responsibilities involved and the options they have for meeting them. Even with the best architects and contractors, problems are inevitable. Successful practice requires an ability to anticipate and deal with these problems.

ISSUES FOR DISCUSSION

1. What is the purpose of educational specifications?
2. What are the advantages and disadvantages of having the architects prepare the educational specifications?
3. What are schematics? Why are they important?
4. At what stage of design is it easiest to make changes?
5. What is the difference between working drawing and construction specifications?
6. What is risk management? Why is it important during a construction project?
7. What is the difference between a bid bond and a performance bond?
8. What is a non-collusion affidavit?
9. Construction managers may be able to break the primary elements of a construction project into smaller packages. Why might this be an advantage for the school district?
10. What is a change order? Who may initiate a change order?
11. Why do some board members and superintendents react negatively to change orders?
12. What are the best ways to avoid excessive change orders?
13. Why is it important to dedicate a new facility?
14. Why is it important to conduct orientation sessions before starting to use a new school building?

REFERENCES

Barrett, J.R. (1997). RFIs and change orders made simple. *School Business Management, 63*(12), 34–36.

Brooks, K.W., Conrad, M.C., & Griffith, W. (1980). *From program to educational facilities.* Lexington: College of Education, University of Kentucky.

Burrup, P.E., Brimley, V., & Garfield, R.R. (1999). *Financing education in a climate of change* (7th ed.). Boston: Allyn and Bacon.

Delaney, J.B. (1983). School construction scheduling. *CEFP Journal, 21*(5), 8–9.

Earthman, G.I. (1994). *School renovation handbook: Investing in education.* Lancaster, PA: Technomic Press.

Epperson, D.R. (1983). Construction contract changes. *CEFP Journal, 21*(5), 6–8.

Ferraro, M. (1998). "Wrapping up" your construction insurance. *School Business Management, 64*(1), 56–59.

Fewell, D.A. (1998). Interdisciplinary coordination reviews: A process to reduce construction costs. *Facilities Manager, 14*(2), 42–43, 45, 47–48.

Fielding, R. (2000). Wired vs. wireless. *School Construction News, 3*(2), 25–26.

Hack, W.G., Candoli, I.C., & Ray, J.R. (1998). *School business administration: A planning approach* (6th ed.). Boston: Allyn and Bacon.

Haun, G. (1995). Building an effective site investigation team. *Educational Facility Planner, 33*(4), 4–7.

Holcolm, J.H. (1995). *A guide to the planning of educational facilities* (3rd ed.). Lanham, MD: University Press of America.

Keown, C. (1999). A learning curve. *American School and University, 71*(12), 116–119.

Konchar, M., & Sanvido, V. (1998). Project delivery systems: What's the difference? *School Planning and Management, 37*(7), 22–26.

McDonough, J. (2000). Engaged learning. *American School and University, 72*(9), 60, 63–64.

Metzner, R.R., & Feifer, I.J. (1998). On the right track. *American School and University, 70*(11), 28, 30, 32.

Ortiz, F.I. (1993). *Schoolhousing: Planning and designing educational facilities*. Albany: State University of New York Press.

CHAPTER 10

Programs and School Buildings

The current status of public education has been shaped by a myriad of factors ranging from philosophical reforms to societal changes to political actions. Understanding these forces and their effects is critically important to planning educational programs and, thus, critically important to school facility planning. This chapter identifies the more cogent forces that affect school buildings. In addition, programming and school buildings at the three basic levels of education—elementary, middle grades, high school—are discussed.

FORCES AFFECTING PUBLIC EDUCATION AND SCHOOL BUILDINGS

In its formative years, America's public education system pursued the concept of the common school. This initiative was predicated on the belief that all children should receive a basic education consisting primarily of of reading, writing, and arithmetic. Children of all ages received instruction from one teacher in a one-room structure. The plain wooden building's only function was to protect the occupants from the elements.

The establishment of local school districts in cities and the need to broaden the curriculum prompted the development of separate grammar schools and high schools. Even though one-room schoolhouses were replaced with larger and more complex buildings, many education officials continued to view the physical environment of schooling as relatively unimportant. Consequently, most schools looked like factories.

In the late 1950s, the Soviet Union's launching of the first man-made satellite,

Sputnik, influenced the direction of public education. This accomplishment was viewed as a threat to the nation's security, and the finger of blame was pointed at public schools. The passage of the National Defense Education Act provided substantial funding to local districts to better prepare academically talented students to pursue college study in areas such as physics, chemistry, engineering, and mathematics. This federal intervention was followed by other initiatives that tossed public schools between the seemingly incompatible goals of excellence and equality. Consider the following key events.

- In the aftermath of the passage of the Civil Rights Act and racial unrest in the 1960s, public education entered a period of experimentation. Aided by the Elementary and Secondary Education Act, promulgated as part of President Lyndon Johnson's "Great Society," school officials began to concentrate on issues of equality and domestic tranquillity. New courses and instructional initiatives stressed social justice, citizenship, and racial equality (Kowalski, 1981).

- Title IX, a section of the 1972 Federal Education Amendments that prohibits discrimination on the basis of sex in any education program or activity receiving federal financial assistance, required schools to revamp their extracurricular programs. Secondary schools, in particular, suddenly experienced a shortage of athletic facilities.

- Partly because of mounting dissatisfaction with the experimentation that was occurring in public schools, the "Back-to-Basics" movement gained momentum in the mid-1970s. Supporters argued that educators had abandoned their responsibility to teach basic skills in favor of making students feel good about themselves.

- The shift toward excellence was made even more obvious when the stinging report *A Nation at Risk* was published in 1983. Claiming that the ineffectiveness of public education had jeopardized the nation's status as the world's economic leader, the reform document spawned countless intensification mandates that essentially made students and educators do more of what they were already doing. Examples of these mandates included longer school years, expanded summer-school programs, and increased graduation requirements.

- More recently, school restructuring—the quest to redesign the organizational structure of schools—and the infusion of technology have raised the possibility that programs across districts in a given state will become less uniform.

Each of these events has had either direct or circuitous effects on educational programs and definitions of facility adequacy.

One of the few certainties about educational change is that it is accelerating. But what will public school programs look like in 2015? Will public schools still enjoy the status of being a quasi-monopoly? Will children still attend school five days a week for approximately nine months each year? Factors such as the Internet, distance learning, charter schools, and vouchers and tax credits already provide the potential that traditional approaches to schooling will become outmoded. Even so, administrators have the responsibility to provide leadership to their districts and communities so that schools can operate in facilities that support rather than hinder instruction. This responsibility necessitates an understanding of the programming and the buildings at all three levels of public education.

ELEMENTARY SCHOOLS

The organizational patterns for elementary schools are more limited than they are for either middle schools or high schools. In large measure, this is because the primary focus of programming is the development of basic skills—especially in the first few years of schooling. Because of this limited focus, curriculum and instructional practices have been relatively uniform in elementary schools. Today, however, the possibility for change is greater than ever. State deregulation and district decentralization increase the possibility of experimentation with new organizational patterns and instructional paradigms.

Historical Perspective

Educational experts consistently assert that philosophy, curriculum, and instructional strategies should determine the organizational structure of elementary schools. In reality, organizational decisions often have been shaped by economic and political pressures outside the school. All schools can be studied in relation to their vertical and horizontal plans. Initially, the vertical plan for elementary schools was based on grade levels. In fact, the schools were often called "grade schools." Under this configuration a student progressed from grade level to grade level until the program of study was completed; and the program of study was initially determined by the number of years required to complete a state-mandated common education (Snyder & Peterson, 1970). Prior to World War II, this was usually up to grade 8.

Although the graded-school concept remains the primary vertical plan for elementary schools, the number of grade levels included has gradually declined. In part, this reduction reflected new organizational ideas, such as the junior high school; but more often than not, grade-level decisions were based on fluctuations in enrollments, fiscal constraints, and available classroom space. In many districts, for example, decisions about where to place a grade level were made on the basis of space availability and convenience. In some districts, the grades included in elementary schools varies from building to building—a clear indication that something other than philosophy and programming ideals is shaping grade-organization decisions.

Over the years, the graded-school concept has been criticized on the grounds that it does not adequately address differences in student ability, achievement, and learning styles. In essence, the graded school operates on the premise that students of the same chronological age can benefit from uniform instruction. In response to the obvious weaknesses of the "one-size-fits-all" approach, some districts have experimented with nongraded schools. The intent of this concept is to base instruction on progress and not age. In the late 1980s, Kentucky adopted the nongraded concept in the primary grades as part of its statewide reform act.

The primary horizontal plan for elementary schools has been the self-contained classroom. This approach has several advantages. Many educators believe that students adapt to school more readily when they are placed in one classroom with a single teacher and a relatively small group of students. But the concept also is favored because it is efficient, orderly, easy to administer, and understood by parents. There have been periodic experimentations with different horizontal plans. In the late 1960s and early 1970s, for example, quite a few open-space elementary schools were constructed. These facilities offered an opportunity for teachers to work together and to deliver instruction in unique ways. However, most teachers in these schools continued to teach as they always had—a condition that led to many of the schools being reconfigured into traditional designs. Another alternative to the self-contained classroom is departmentalized teaching. Some elementary schools utilize this concept in the intermediate grades.

Contemporary Conditions

Today, the most common grade configurations for elementary schools are K–5 and K–6, not K–8. A few districts have adopted a vertical organizational plan of K–2, 3–5, 6–8, and 9–12. In these districts, K–2 schools are called primary schools and the 3–5 schools are called intermediate schools. The kindergarten center is another relatively new concept: This is a school with a single grade that serves all of a district's kindergarten students.

Although the vast majority of elementary schools continue to use the graded school and self-contained classroom plans, programming is becoming more expansive. Consider the following factors that create facility needs.

- Providing special teachers for art, music, and physical education has become the norm.

- Programming for disabled students and other students with special needs continues to evolve. Most recently, the concept of inclusion has required administrators to reconsider facility needs for special education.

- The number of students with only one parent or with two working parents has increased dramatically since the 1950s. Consequently, demands for preschool programs and all-day kindergarten programs are growing. In some districts and states, these programs already have become major political and economic issues.

- There are a growing number of extracurricular activities offered in elementary schools. They include both athletic programs and extended learning opportunities (e.g., school choirs).

- The scope of student services offered by elementary schools is increasing; some schools already have counselors, psychologists, and social workers.

- The length of school days, the length of school years, and expanded summer school programs are resulting in higher utilization of facilities. In addition, some districts are experimenting with year-round education.

- The use of teacher aides, including parent volunteers, continues to increase.

- The use of technology has increased markedly. Most classrooms now contain one or more computers.

- Programming for gifted and talented students is now relatively common at the elementary-school level.

- The amount of small-group and individual instruction also is increasing. These activities create the need for appropriate spaces (e.g., areas for teacher aides to work outside classrooms).

- Reductions in class size, especially in the primary grades, increase the number of needed classrooms.

- Because of decentralization concepts (e.g., site-based management) and increased parental activities (e.g., conferences), more small-group and large-group meetings are taking place in elementary schools.

Size

There are different opinions about the ideal size of an elementary school. Clearly, there are effective small schools with only one class at each grade level and effective large schools with as many as six or seven classes at each grade level. Generally, three to four classes at each grade level is considered to be the optimum size. Such a configuration in a school housing grades K–5 results in enrollment of approximately 300–500 pupils. At this level, the school can function with only one art room, one music room, and one gymnasium. When elementary schools get larger, more special instruction areas are needed.

Arguments have been made for and against large elementary schools (i.e., schools greater than four sections per grade level). While larger schools have the potential for greater operational efficiency, a broader curriculum, and teacher specialization, they present concerns about faculty unity and student adjustments. Size is considered especially important for schools serving large proportions of disadvantaged students. A recent study of schools in Chicago, for example, found that schools enrolling less than 400 students simply were more effective (Lee & Loeb, 2000). Size appears to be especially important in creating a sense of community and building strong school cultures, that is, shared values and beliefs about schooling.

Utilization level is another size consideration. A utilization level represents the actual usage of the building in relation to its design or technical capacity. Schools operating at 100 percent or more of design or technical capacity almost always have problems. This is because there are no spaces available for non-routine needs. These needs might include meetings, extracurricular activities, and conferences. Ideally, an elementary school should operate at about 90 percent of design capacity; often the 90 percent level is referred to as the building's practical capacity.

Buildings

Historically, elementary school facilities did not receive the attention or fiscal support given to secondary schools. In many communities, outdated high schools were converted into elementary schools after new high schools were built. This misguided approach to facility planning was shaped primarily by two assumptions. The first was that the quality of instructional space in an elementary school is relatively unimportant because of the self-contained classroom mode. The second was that it was far more important to provide modern facilities for high schools because these buildings housed more complex programs and because they had the most visibility in the community. But converted high schools often were less than inviting facilities for young students, and these buildings frequently restricted programming. Ideally, elementary school buildings should be bright and inviting, and they should have a positive effect on student attitudes.

Spaces in an elementary school can be divided into three categories.

• Instructional spaces (e.g., classrooms, art rooms, and music rooms)
• Instructional support areas (e.g., media center)
• General support areas (e.g., administration, cafeteria)

Some spaces, such as the gymnasium, may fall into more than one of these categories.

Most of the rooms in an elementary school are standard classrooms. These rooms should be approximately 900–1,000 sq. ft. and provide adequate storage space, light control, and modern technologies—including two to four computers, a telephone, and a television monitor. Rooms used for the primary grades often have some special features to accommodate instruction; lined chalkboards and a student restroom are examples. In most elementary schools, classrooms used for the same grade level are located together, allowing teachers to collaborate. Some elementary schools have been designed using "pods," a concept that separates grade levels by placing them in different wings of the building.

Kindergarten classrooms should be larger and more flexible than standard classrooms. They should contain approximately 1,100–1,300 sq. ft., including student restrooms. Part of the room should be carpeted, and a storytelling area is essential. Most schools are designed so that kindergarten rooms have direct access to a playground. If a school provides pre-school programs, the kindergarten rooms should be located near the area where these programs are offered. In most elementary schools, kindergarten rooms are located next to the classrooms used for the primary grades. Historically, kindergarten has been a half-day program; thus, two classes are able to use the same classroom (one in the morning and one in the afternoon). Ongoing pressures for state legislatures to fund all-day kindergarten could result in the need to create many new spaces in elementary schools.

Special instruction and general support areas have become increasingly important in elementary schools, largely because programming has expanded. Twenty-five years ago, for example, it was relatively rare to find a counselor's office in an elementary school. Rooms for special education typically include both resource rooms and self-contained classrooms. The former are commonly used for learning disability programs; the latter are used for students who are not involved with inclusion. Table 10–1 contains a list of these spaces with selected comments about them.

Restrooms are another important consideration. Both student and adult restrooms must be provided. Smaller schools (one or two sections per grade level) often have two sets of restrooms: one set for the primary grades and one set for the intermediate grades. Larger schools should have three or more sets of restrooms. At least two sets of adult restrooms are recommended. Plumbing codes determine the number of restrooms and fixtures required. As a general guide, Hawkins and Lilley (1986) produced the following formula:

Lavatories:

    1 for every 30 students if total enrollment is below 300

    1 for every 40 students if total enrollment is above 300

Water Closets:

    1 for every 40 boys plus 1 urinal for every 30 boys

    1 for every 35 girls

These same standards are applicable to secondary schools.

Other areas that must be considered for an elementary school include a mechanical/service area and general storage and articulation (hallways) spaces. The architect and planning consultants should provide parameters for mechanical and storage areas. Articulation spaces should include display cases and wall surfaces that permit student work to be displayed. Lively graphics and colors are usually preferred for elementary schools. Fire codes determine the means of egress and minimum corridor widths.

Table 10–2 provides a summary of recommended space requirements for elementary schools with a designed capacity of 600 students.

Typically, the minimum site size for an elementary school is seven acres. Indiana guidelines suggest that one additional acre should be provided for every 100 students beyond 200 students. Thus, a school with an enrollment of 400 would have a minimum site size of nine acres. Site development needs for all levels of schools typically include

Table 10–1

Special Instruction and General Support Areas for Elementary Schools

Area	Selected Comments
Media Center	This space should be a focal point of the building. It should be centrally located and accommodate a minimum of 10 percent of the students at any given time. Typically, a modern media center includes several spaces in addition to the main reading room (e.g., office, work area, storage rooms). Access to technology and security provisions is essential in this area.
Art Rooms	These rooms should be approximately 1,200–1,500 square feet. They should include ample storage for materials and projects, large sinks, and a kiln area with proper ventilation. The floor surface should be easily cleaned. Some natural light is essential.
Music Rooms	General music rooms should be located away from low-noise areas. They should be approximately 1,000–1,200 sq. ft. Storage for equipment and materials and acoustical treatments are essential. Some elementary schools also have instrumental music rooms used for individual lessons and band.
Computer Labs	A computer lab should accommodate 25–30 students. The layout, lighting, electrical systems, and provision of dedicated phone lines are special considerations. Proper climate control and security are essential.
Administration	The administrative complex should be located at the main entrance of the school. Included are a reception area, a principal's office, a conference room, a workroom, a records storage area, and restrooms. Depending on the size of the school, an assistant principal's office also may be included.
Health Clinic	This area for the school nurse should include a restroom, storage space, and several areas for children who are ill. Often this facility is located in the administrative complex, especially if the school does not have a full-time nurse.
Speech/Hearing Clinic	This space is used for therapy and should be large enough to accommodate the therapist and up to six students.
Gymnasium	Most elementary schools have a standard-size gym floor, allowing the facility to be used by community groups and secondary school athletic teams when school is not in session. A small office and a storage area are common. The intended uses as identified in the educational specifications should determine whether spectator seating and locker rooms are included. Some elementary schools opt to use synthetic rather than wooden floors in gyms. Schools serving more than 500 students are likely to require two gyms. Gyms are used for physical education, athletic programs, and recreation (indoor recess). Both acoustics and ventilation are important design considerations.
Cafeteria	The cafeteria should be large enough to accommodate either 50 percent (if two lunch periods are used) or 35 percent (if three lunch periods are used) of the students at one time. Decisions must be made as to whether food will be prepared on site (requiring a kitchen) or elsewhere (requiring accommodations for warming and serving food). In addition, some schools opt to have "cafetoriums"—a combination of a cafeteria and auditorium. The selection of tables and seating is often an important decision reflecting how this space will be used before and after lunch.
Conference Areas	Elementary schools should include at least two conference rooms large enough to accommodate up to 12 individuals. One should be located in the administrative complex and one adjacent to the media center. In addition, modern schools have smaller conference areas where teachers and administrators can meet with parents during the school day.
Other Services	Additional spaces could include a counseling office, a testing room (for individual testing), rooms for instructional aides to work with individual students outside the classroom environment, a faculty workrooms, faculty lounge, a bookstore, a mechanical room, and a custodial office/storage area.

Table 10–2
Summaries of Recommended Room Sizes for Elementary Schools

Area	Suggested Size (sq. ft.)	Capacity	Comments
Classrooms			
Kindergarten	1,100-1,300	23	Easy access to outdoors
Standard	900-1,000	25	
Art	1,200-1,300	25	Includes storage
Music	1,000-1,200	25	Includes storage
Computer laboratory	900-1,100	25	
Special education (self-contained)	900-1,000	13	
Special education (resource room)	300-600	10	
Media center			
Main reading room	1,600-2,000	60	
Conference room	250-350	15	
Office/storage	400-800		
Physical education			
Gymnasium	6,500-8,000	250	Capacity for spectators
Locker rooms	300-400	25	One boys and one girls
Storage	200-300		
Teacher aide workroom	150	4	Ideally, 1 per grade level
Cafeteria			
Student dining	2,400-2,900	200	Based on 3 lunch periods
Kitchen	1,200-1,400		
Serving area	150-200		
Faculty dining/lounge	300-400	10	
Special education			
Self-contained	1,000	12	
Resource room	500	6	
Speech and hearing clinic	150-250	6	
Administration			
Principal's office	200-250		
Assistant principal's office	150-200		
Reception area	300-500	3	
Records storage/vault	200-300		
Counselor's office	150		Often located away from administration
Conference room	250-350	15	
Teacher workroom	300-500	5	
Health suite	500-700	4	3 cots and restrooms

Note: This table does not include some noninstructional spaces such as mechanical rooms and all restrooms.

- physical education and athletic facilities,

- parking (for students, faculty, and visitors),

- security provisions (e.g., lighting, fencing),

- sidewalks and entryways,

- health and safety provisions (e.g., restrooms, concession facility),

- spectator provisions (e.g., ticket booths, bleachers),

- vehicle traffic patterns (for automobiles, buses, and delivery trucks),

- landscaping,

- identification features (e.g., signs).

Two additional points deserve mention with regard to elementary school environments. One is the variance in the physical stature of children who occupy the school. A kindergarten student, for example, could weigh as little as 46 pounds and a sixth grader could weigh over 160 pounds—over three times as much. Likewise a small kindergarten student may be less than four feet tall, while a sixth grader could be over five feet eight inches tall. These are significant differences that deserve more than casual reflection in designing a school. Such consideration is especially needed for the common areas of the building used by all students.

Second, elementary schools are definitely becoming larger and more costly in most parts of the United States. They are becoming larger because of

- new programs (e.g., computer instruction, guidance services),
- smaller class sizes (especially in the primary grades),
- increased programming (e.g., full-day kindergarten, preschool programs),
- broader extracurricular activities (e.g., more organized athletic programs).

Many older buildings erected prior to the 1960s have less than 100 sq. ft. per pupil. Today, new elementary schools in some parts of the country have as much as 145–160 sq. ft. per pupil—a size that used to be considered appropriate for a high school. It is important to note that geographic location has affected school size. In general, schools in warm climates have had less space per pupil than schools in cold climates (because of differences in design features such as hallways and insulation), and schools in rural settings have had less space than schools in urban settings (because of program scope and overall enrollment) (Brubaker, 1988).

Outdoor facilities for elementary schools should include adequate and safe playgrounds. Often two playgrounds are provided: one for the primary grades and one for the intermediate grades. The design and selection of equipment for these areas are also important planning considerations. The development of athletic fields on an elementary school site varies considerably. Typically a baseball diamond and a soccer field are needed for physical education. Some elementary school sites are used for weekend and summer recreational programs (e.g., soccer, little league baseball). In addition, middle school and high school athletic teams may use athletic fields located at an elementary school if accommodations at their sites are inadequate.

SECONDARY SCHOOLS

There are several types of secondary schools.

- Junior high schools (typically grades 7–9)
- Middle schools (typically grades 6–8)

• Junior–Senior high schools (typically grades 7–12)
• High schools (typically grades 9–12 or 10–12)

In almost all instances, secondary schools are organized into instructional departments. The number of departments depends on the size of the school. For example, a small high school might combine mathematics and science into a single department. Secondary schools are discussed here in two categories: middle-level schools and high schools. Since junior–senior high schools are essentially high schools, they are addressed in the section on high schools.

Middle-Level Schools

Schools in the middle provide a transition experience for students between the self-contained environment of elementary schools and the departmental environment of high schools. Junior–senior high schools are really high schools that extend down to a lower grade level unless they operate a "school-within-a-school" concept. These schools almost always exist in small school systems (i.e., districts with enrollments below 1,500 pupils).

Historical Perspective. The junior high school emerged as the result of several major studies of the vertical organization of schooling. One of the most influential, published by the Commission on the Reorganization of Secondary Education in 1918, advocated movement away from the 8–4 grade organizational pattern to a 6–6 configuration (i.e., six years of elementary education and six years of secondary education). The secondary experience was to be divided into two, three-year segments (the junior high school and the senior high school). The most prevalent arguments for establishing junior high schools included

• Young adolescents would have a more suitable educational environment.
• Students in 7th and 8th grades would have access to a broader curriculum.
• Opportunities to participate in activities would be greater.
• Teachers would be better prepared to teach subjects in a departmentalized mode.
• Students would receive better guidance services.
• Students would experience a smoother transition from the self-contained classroom to departmentalized teaching (Anderson & Van Dyke, 1963).

Junior high schools became especially popular in districts that had reorganized. Merging two or more school districts into a single unit often created serious political problems. Administrators and school boards often tried to mollify disgruntled tax payers by placing elementary and junior high schools in local communities while erecting new high schools at a central location. The junior high schools were often the former high schools.

Several criticisms of the junior high school evolved in the 1950s and 1960s. The more cogent included the following:

- Critics charged that junior high schools had become miniature versions of high schools. Thus, they did not provide the transition experiences for which they were intended.

- Often the most experienced and competent teachers were assigned to senior high schools, leaving junior high schools with inferior faculties.

- Many teachers used the junior high school as a stepping-stone to the high school; they were not interested in dedicating themselves to the needs and problems of middle-grade students. Many junior high school teachers behaved as though they were working in a senior high school.

By the early 1970s, an alternative to the junior high school—the middle school—was gaining popularity. Philosophically, the middle-school approach was intended to be a real transition period, and the modal grade organization was 6–8 instead of 7–9. Middle schools are generally defined as schools with no grade lower than fifth and no grade higher than eighth. The shift toward middle schools and away from junior high schools, however, was not always based on sound educational principles. Some critics (e.g., Alexander & Kealy, 1969) charged that opportunistic superintendents adopted the middle-school concept not because of values and beliefs, but rather because they faced administrative problems such as inadequate facilities. Supporting this conclusion, Schubert (1986) wrote:

A new school plant was built ostensibly to overcome certain difficulties found in working with junior high school students. In fact, the slight alteration in grade level (taking the sixth grade out of the elementary school) was done for economic rather than educational reasons in many places. (p. 105)

Those created for the wrong reasons were middle schools in name only. Principles such as integration, exploration, guidance, differentiation, socialization, and articulation were generally ignored. Fortunately, principals and teachers in many middle schools have been able to incrementally adopt central concepts such as teacher teaming and block scheduling.

Contemporary Conditions. The curricula of junior high schools and middle schools essentially consist of two components: required courses and electives. In most states, a good portion of the curriculum is mandated by state requirements (laws and regulations). The elective courses may be referred to as exploratory courses. Typically, students are required to take social studies, language arts, mathematics, science, physical education, and health. Additional courses common at the middle-level schools include art, music, foreign language, home economics, typing, and industrial technology.

Extracurricular programs in junior high schools are usually well developed and reflect a range of athletic and club activities. Middle schools also may have this broad range of opportunities; however, some middle schools purposely deemphasize competitiveness to allow more students to participate in extracurricular activities.

Some junior high schools and middle schools employ the concept of core classes, a process that entails combining two or more subject areas. For example, social studies and language arts are combined, and the student is assigned the same teacher for both subjects in a single block of time. Mathematics and science are likewise often joined. The core class provides a transition between the self-contained classroom and departmentalized teaching.

Middle schools make a conscious attempt to develop learner independence. As a result, individual learning activities are emphasized and individual student use of special resources such as computers and the media center are encouraged. In elementary schools, ability grouping usually occurs within classrooms. In the schools in the middle, grouping is addressed by placing students in separate classes or courses (e.g., placing students in one of three levels of 8th grade mathematics).

Size. The size of junior high schools and middle schools varies considerably. Some are as small as 100 students while others are over 1,500. In the mid-1990s, 69 percent of all middle schools enrolled between 150 and 749 pupils (National Center for Education Statistics, 2000). As a general rule, experts believe that middle schools should be small enough to give students opportunities to be highly involved in school activities but large enough to support a broad curriculum and diversified faculty.

Schools below 250 often have difficulty providing elective courses, and students often have the same teachers for three or more classes while attending the school. Schools with more than 1,000 students often find it difficult to involve all students in activities. Thus, the preferred enrollment range for middle level schools is between 500 and 900, with 300 to 1,000 being acceptable. Many experts (e.g., Spencer, 1988) establish the optimum between 600 and 800. When planning a facility, decisions about school size can be made in one of three ways.

- Administrators can first decide which grades will be placed in the school then calculate the enrollment that must be served. This approach is prevalent in districts having only one middle school; selecting grade levels first is usually reflective of an emphasis on educational programming.

- Administrators can determine a maximum enrollment and subsequently determine which grades get placed in the school. This approach also is prevalent in districts having only one middle school; selecting size first is usually reflective of an emphasis on social adjustments.

- Administrators can set an enrollment maximum and select grade levels simultaneously. This approach is only applicable in districts operating more than one middle school.

Ideally, the practical capacity of middle school is about 85 percent of its design or technical capacity.

Buildings. Educational programming obviously gets broader after elementary school; thus, middle-level schools almost always have more space per pupil than do elementary schools. Today, an average of 165–200 sq. ft. per pupil in a contemporary middle school is common. While high schools and middle-level schools contain many of the same spaces, there are differences. Middle schools, for example, often have teacher team planning spaces rather than traditional departmental offices, and special instruction areas (e.g., science laboratories) are not as large and extensive as those in high schools.

Table 10–3 identifies some basic considerations for the various spaces in a middle school with a designed capacity for 750 students. Other cogent features usually found in middle schools include

- Student Lockers. Lockers are usually placed along hallways, although some schools have locker bays (areas off a hallway where all lockers are concentrated). Many principals do not like the locker-bay concept because they believe it presents a supervision problem.
- Commons Area. This is an open space, usually adjacent to the cafeteria, where students congregate when they are not in class.
- In-School Suspension Rooms. These rooms are usually located adjacent to the administration area so they can be properly supervised.
- Independent Study Rooms. These are spaces for independent student work; they are usually located adjacent to the main reading room in the media center.
- Outdoor Facilities. Middle schools require outdoor accommodations for physical education and athletic programs; some also have outdoor science laboratories.

Occasionally, middle-level schools have a swimming pool. Many of these schools are designed using the school-within-a-school concept that allows the grade levels to be located in separate areas of the building. This concept also facilitates teaming.

Ideally, middle schools should have ample space for outdoor facilities—usually more than 15 acres. While the site development features listed under elementary schools are applicable here, middle schools commonly have more diversified athletic facilities (e.g., football fields). In addition, the buildings should have their own identity in the community. In part, this is accomplished by exterior design that differentiates these schools from both elementary schools and high schools. There are differing opinions about locating middle schools adjacent to high schools; some administrators believe that the schools function more effectively when they are on separate sites.

High Schools

High schools receive more community attention than either elementary or middle schools. In part, athletic programs are responsible. From an academic perspective, high schools are viewed as barometers of student success. Statistics such as dropout rates, SAT scores, the percentage of students entering college, and the percentage of students passing state graduation tests are often used by

Table 10–3
Selected Space Requirements for Middle Schools

Area	Suggested Size (sq. ft.)	Capacity	Comments
Classrooms			
Standard	900	27	
Large-group instruction	2,000-2,200	75	
Small-group instruction	300-400	15	
Art			
Classroom	1,200-1,400	25	
Office/storage	200-350		Includes kiln area
Science			
Labs	1,000-1,200	22	
Classrooms	900	25	
Storage	150		
Special education			
Self-contained	1,000	12	Sink and restroom included
Resource room	500	6	
Home economics			
Unit lab	3,000-3,200	25	Combination foods-clothing lab
Foods	1,600-2,000	22	
Clothing	1,200-1,400	22	
Classroom	800-900	25	
Office/storage	200		
Computer laboratory	900-1,100	25	
Keyboarding room	1,100-1,200	25	Used for business education, typing
Music			
Instrumental	1,600-1,800	50	Tiered-floor surface
Vocal	1,100-1,200	40	Tiered-floor surface
Practice room	50-125	2	At least 2 provided
Office/storage	400-600		
Physical education			
Main gymnasium	8,000-9,000	1,000	Spectator seating
Auxiliary gymnasium	7,000-7,600	250	Spectator seating
Locker rooms	800-1,200	25	At least 2 provided
Faculty locker/office	250-500	5	
Restrooms	250-300		
Athletic office	100-150		
Athletic storage	500-1,000		
Instruction storage	200-300		
Technology education (industrial technology)			
Unit shop	2,400-2,600	25	
Planning-design area	1,000-1,100	25	Can be used as a classroom
Activity storage	200-300		
Equipment-material storage	300-500		
Media center			
Reading room	1,800-2,200	70	
Office	120-200		
Conference room	350	15	
Listening-viewing area	150	3	
Workroom	120-300		Running water, shelves, and cabinets

Storage	400-800		
Administration			
Principal's office	200-300		
Assistant principal's office	150-200		
Reception area	400-600	3	
Conference room	350	15	
Record storage room and vault	200-250		
Workroom	200-250		Running water, shelves, and cabinets
Student services area (counseling center)			
Offices	120-150		At least 3 provided
Reception/materials	100		
Conference room	200	10	
Storage	150		
Individual testing room	50	1	
Teacher support			
Team room or department office	250-400	10	At least 5 provided
Lounge	300-600	12	
Health clinic	600-700	5	At least 4 cots
Cafeteria			
Student dining area	3,750	250	
Kitchen	1,500		
Serving area	200		
Faculty dining	400-600	13	
Speech therapy	150-250	6	
Auditorium			
Stage	1,500-1,800		
Seating area	4,800	400	

Note: This table does not include some noninstructional spaces such as mechanical rooms and all restrooms.

taxpayers to pass judgment on a district's effectiveness. But high schools also are symbols of community commitment to public education. Thus, these buildings are commonly the largest, newest, and most expensive structures in a district.

Historical Perspective. With very few exceptions, high schools in this country fall into one of these categories:

• 9–12 schools

• 10–12 schools (often called senior high schools)

• 7–12 schools (often called junior-senior high schools)

The modal configuration is 9–12, and the 7–12 arrangement is found almost exclusively in small districts. This is because the rationale for having junior-senior high schools is small enrollment rather than educational philosophy. In very small districts, four-year high schools might have fewer than 150 pupils—a condition that makes it difficult to provide a diversified curriculum and a teaching staff with necessary specializations in all subjects.

Since their beginnings, high schools were guided by three ideals: mental discipline, social efficiency, and civic responsibility (Butts, 1978). In reality, the goal of preparing students for the workforce was dominant at least until the late 1950s. Describing high schools in the 10 years following World War II, George, McEwin, and Jenkins (2000) wrote, "Except for the dramatic growth in vocational and general education tracks, traditional programs and approaches remained at the center of high school life and practice" (p. 19).

Experimentation during the 1960s and 1970s occurred in high schools just as it did in elementary and middle-level schools. Concepts such as team teaching, mini courses, and open-concept schools emerged and then retreated as excellence resurfaced as a dominant value. Through all of this philosophical meandering, the basic organizational structure of high schools essentially remained unaltered.

Contemporary Conditions. Prompted primarily by changing social values and declining public confidence, state legislatures and governors virtually forced high schools to become more academically oriented in the early 1980s (Perrone, 1985). Many states increased the number of credits required for graduation and some even implemented mandatory graduation tests. These modifications have had a significant effect on programming and facility utilization. For example, enrollment in English, mathematics, social studies, and science have generally increased, while enrollment in some elective courses have been decimated. The number of class sections in subjects such as home economics, art, and music has actually declined more than 50 percent in some high schools since 1990.

High school programming also has been altered by the transitions from a manufacturing society to an Information Age and global economy (Roberts & Cawelti, 1984). Consider the following developments.

- Vocational schools and industrial education departments, once considered the dumping ground for lesser-ability students, have come under intense scrutiny. As a result, most high schools have moved from an industrial education curriculum (primarily a hands-on approach to developing manual skills) to an industrial–technology curriculum (primarily a problem-solving approach to technical problems) (Bensen, 1988). And in vocational schools, more rigorous mathematics and science courses have been integrated with on-the-job training (George et al., 2000).

- The number of graduates entering college is increasing across the country. Both students and parents are expecting high schools to provide better preparation for all students who harbor this goal. This has resulted in higher enrollment in basic courses, such as English, mathematics, and science.

- Foreign language courses have expanded because of increasing student demands and improved technologies. Until recently, most high schools offered just one or two languages—usually French and Spanish. Today, many of them offer German, Russian, Japanese, and Mandarin Chinese—either via direct instruction (in larger schools) or via distance learning (in smaller schools).

- There is a more open attitude toward experimentation. For example, independent study and interdisciplinary teaching are growing in popularity.

- More rigorous graduation requirements have prompted new forms of learning assessment. For example, students often complete projects as part of courses so that they have material evidence of their ability to apply knowledge (George et al., 2000).

Despite these continuing transitions and the effects of modern technologies, the subject-oriented curriculum persists at the high-school level. With a few exceptions, academic study is still divided by departments and departmental courses. Reluctance to change the traditional organizational structure is attributable to a national school culture that resists change (Sarason, 1996) and to traditional standards for graduation (e.g., credits and units) and teacher licensing (e.g., specialization to teach specific subjects) (Kowalski, 1999).

Size. The optimum size of high schools has been a point of controversy for some time. During the 1950s and 1960s, some large-city districts built schools to accommodate over 5,000 students. The decisions were based entirely on economic efficiency. The overall standard for the size of a high school is the same as for a middle-level school; that is, the school should not be so large that it prevents student participation in activities, and it should not be so small that it restricts the scope of curriculum and staffing. Brooks, Conrad, and Griffith (1980) suggest that high schools should be between 500 and 1,500 students, with 1,000–1,200 being the optimum size. Spencer (1988) also set the optimum at 1,000–1,200. Ideally, the practical capacity of a high school is 85 percent of its design or technical capacity.

Buildings. The high school curriculum is broader than either the elementary school or middle school curriculum, especially in the area of elective courses. Consequently, there is less uniformity in programming across all high schools— a condition that results in less uniformity in facilities. Consider the following examples illustrating how programming and facilities may differ from one high school to another.

- Some schools send students to area vocational schools while others offer vocational education courses on site.
- High schools differ in the degree of special spaces provided. For example, not all have swimming pools, auditoriums, or planetariums.
- The structure of the daily class schedule varies; some schools have traditional six or seven-period daily schedules while others use block scheduling (and there are variations of this concept).
- Smaller high schools are becoming increasingly reliant on distance learning to provide instruction in low-enrollment classes or in areas where licensed teachers are unavailable. Examples include physics, advanced mathematics courses, and foreign languages.

Accordingly, high schools vary considerably in the amount of space provided per student. Some of this variance, as noted earlier, is attributable to climate. High schools can vary from less than 150 sq. ft. per pupil to over 300 sq. ft. per pupil; the average size is around 210 sq. ft. per pupil. Selected guidelines for room sizes in a high school designed for 1,000 students are shown in Table 10–4.

A site of more than 22 acres is usually needed for a high school; a school with an enrollment of 1,200 should have a site of approximately 30 acres. While the site development features listed under elementary schools are applicable here, high schools commonly require many more athletic accommodations (e.g., football fields, softball diamonds, baseball diamonds, tennis courts, quality outdoor track).

School buildings are often judged by their exterior appearance. Thus, landscaping and other site development features can contribute to positive perceptions.

Other features that may be found in high schools include

- a commons area,
- a planetarium,
- a swimming pool,
- indoor racquet courts (tennis, handball),
- community pride rooms (areas that can be used by taxpayers for meetings or technology use).

High schools usually house programs that function outside the regular school day. Adult education and recreation programs are examples. Any usage of a school building during the evenings or on weekends raises security questions. Often, buildings are designed to have security zones. For example, part of a building could be used without jeopardizing security in the entire building.

ESTIMATING CLASSROOM REQUIREMENTS

In elementary schools, administrators typically determine how many sections of classes will be offered at each grade level. These data provide most of the information necessary to decide how many classrooms will be needed. However, in secondary schools, the process is more complicated. Offered here are two formulas that can be used to accomplish this task. Nelson (1972) developed the first. His calculation is as follows:

$$TSS = (AE \times TW) / (ND \times CS \times TO)$$

where:

TSS = teacher stations required for a subject

AE = anticipated enrollment (total number to be accommodated in this subject); it is determined from actual needs or estimates (e.g., 70 percent of 1,000 need to take mathematics; thus, 700 is the AE)

TW = time distribution per week (number of periods the class meets per week)

Table 10–4
Selected Space Requirements for High Schools

Area	Suggested Size (sq. ft.)	Capacity	Comments
Classrooms			
Standard	900	25	
Large-group instruction	2,000-2,200	75	1 or 2 rooms needed
Small-group instruction	300-400	10	4 to 6 rooms needed
Art			
Classroom	1,200-1,400	25	
Office/storage	200-350		Includes kiln area
Science			
Labs	1,200-1,600	22	
Classrooms	900-1,000	25	
Office/storage	550		
Home economics			
Unit lab	3,000-3,200	25	Combination foods-clothing lab
Foods	1,600-2,000	22	
Clothing	1,200-1,400	22	
Classroom	800-900	25	
Office/storage	400		
Computer laboratory	900-1,100	25	
Keyboarding	1,100-1,200	25	Used for business education, typing
Music			
Instrumental	1,600-1,800	50	Tiered-floor surface
Vocal	1,100-1,200	40	Tiered-floor surface
Practice room	50-125	2	At least 2 provided
Office/storage	400-600		
Special education			
Self-contained	1,000	12	
Resource room	500	6	
Physical education			
Main gymnasium	11,000-13,000	3,500	Spectator seating
Auxiliary gymnasium	7,500-8,500	500	Spectator seating
Locker rooms	800-1,200	25	Minimum of 4 provided
Faculty locker/office	350-600	6	One male and one female
Wrestling room	600-900	16	Proper ventilation required
Weight room	300-600	15	Avoid wood floors
Training room	250-400	10	Direct access to locker rooms
Restrooms	250-300		
Athletic office	150-200		
Athletic storage	700-1,200		
Instruction storage	400-600		
Technology education (industrial technology)			
Unit shop	2,400-2,600	25	
Planning-design area	1,000-1,100	25	Can be used as a classroom
Activity storage	200-300		
Equipment-material storage	300-500		
Media center			
Reading room	2,700-3,500	100	
Office	150-200		
Conference room	350	15	

Workroom	250-400		
Storage	500-900		
Student project rooms	100-150	4	For independent student work
Administration			
Principal's office	200-300		
Assistant principal's office	150-200		
Reception area	500-700	4	
Conference room	350	15	
Record storage room and vault	250-350		
Counseling center			
Offices	120-150		At least 3 provided
Reception/materials	150		
Conference room	250	12	
Storage	200		
Individual testing room	50	1	
Teacher support			
Department office	300-800		Depends on size of department
Lounge	400-800	15	
Health clinic	700-900	5	Cots for 5
Cafeteria			
Student dining area	3,750	250	Based on 4 lunch periods
Kitchen	1,600		
Serving area	200		
Faculty dining	500-700	16	
Speech therapy	250-300	6	
Auditorium			
Stage	1,600-2,000		
Seating	6,000	500	

Note: This table does not include some noninstructional spaces such as mechanical rooms and restrooms.

ND = number of divisions (number of activities to be carried out in a single space at the same time); (e.g., if a gym had a divider and housed two classes of physical education during the same period, the ND would be 2)

CS = class size (largest class size anticipated)

TO = time occupied (represents the extent to which the station is to be utilized for a given activity); (i.e., periods per week less periods per week that room is to be free)

Assume that a high school has an enrollment of 1,000. All students are expected to take English. English classes meet five times per week for 50 minutes. There are seven periods in the school day and only one class will meet in a room at a given time. The maximum class size is 25 and the classroom utilization is set at 85 percent (i.e., rooms are to be unassigned 15 percent of the time). Accordingly, the formula would be

$$TSS = (1,000 \times 5) / (1 \times 25 \times (35 \times .85)) \text{ or}$$

$$5,000 / (25 \times 31.5) \text{ or}$$

$$5,000 / 661.5 = 7.56 \text{ or } 8 \text{ classrooms}$$

Nelson's formula is especially useful for schools using nontraditional scheduling such as modules. It allows calculations for large-group instruction (via the ND factor) and varying time utilizations (via the TO factor), which are not possible in more basic formulas.

An alternative and more basic formula may be more useful for traditional programming formats. The one that follows is widely used by planners.

$$NR = (1.15 \times (ns/cs)) \times (npw/swp)$$

where:

NR = number of rooms required

ns = number of students taking a course

cs = desired class size

npw = number of periods per week that the class meets

swp = number of school-week periods

1.15 = some allowance for variance

As an example, assume that there are 306 students who need to take 8th-grade science. The science labs can accommodate a maximum of 22 students. The class meets five days per week. The school has seven periods each school day with 45 minutes in each period. Therefore, the formula for determining how many labs are needed is as follows:

$$(1.15 \times (306/22)) \times (5/35) \text{ or}$$

$$(1.15 \times 13.9) \times (.143) \text{ or}$$

$$15.99 \times .143 = 2.29$$

Thus, either the school must provide three science laboratories or increase the size of the sections to a point where only two labs would be necessary. Working backward, you can check this calculation. If the three science classes were used seven periods a day, they could accommodate 21 sections of 8th-grade science. With a total of 306 students, each class would have an average of 15 students—well within the limit of 22 per class.

In planning a new school the administrator must project future needs as well as existing needs. One relatively simple way to do this is to use the same formula but to adjust the total enrolled by a percent obtained from the enrollment projection. Imagine a district where enrollment at the middle-school level is expected to increase from 800 to 1,000 in the next 10 years. This is a 25 percent increase. Thus in estimating the number of needed classrooms, the current num-

Figure 10–1
Average Sizes of New Schools

(square feet of space per pupil)

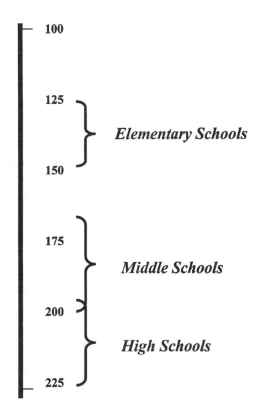

ber of 8th-grade students (306) enrolling in science would be increased by 25 percent. The resulting figure, 383, is then used in the formula. This method is relatively simple and effective.

CHAPTER SUMMARY

Although some critics conclude that schools and their programs have not changed much over the past 50 years, this is essentially untrue. Many new ideas have been introduced at all levels of schooling. Incrementally, curricula are becoming broader, instructional paradigms are becoming more diverse, and experimentation with organizational structure is more accepted. Collectively, these conditions are serving to make school buildings larger and more complex.

This chapter reviewed the basic programs for elementary, middle-level, and high schools. Recommended space requirements were provided for three schools.

- An elementary school programmed for four sections per grade level (capacity of 600 students)
- A middle school with a programmed capacity of 750 students
- A high school with a programmed capacity of 1,000 students

Generally, elementary schools require less space per student than do secondary schools. Ranges for school size are provided in Figure 10–1.

Perhaps the greatest challenge facing facility planners is to simultaneously accommodate current programming while ensuring preparedness for tomorrow's uncertainty. In large measure, this is why school facilities need to be flexible and adaptable.

ISSUES FOR DISCUSSION

1. Some elementary schools house grades K–2, some house K–5, and others house K–6. What are the possible reasons for this variance?

2. What curricular changes have occurred in elementary schools in the past 50 years? What are the potential implications of these changes for school facility planning?

3. There are varying opinions regarding the optimum size of an elementary school. What do you consider to be the optimum enrollment? Provide a rationale for your response.

4. The middle-school concept emerged as an alternative to the junior high school. What criticisms of the junior high school contributed to the growing popularity of the middle-school concept?

5. What are some of the characteristics of an ideal middle school? How does a middle school differ from the traditional junior high school?

6. Critics suggest that many districts opened middle schools because of facility needs and not because of educational philosophy. How may facility-related needs contribute to a decision to adopt the middle-school concept?

7. Middle schools often use teacher teams and block schedules to deliver instruction. How may these features influence school design?

8. What arguments could be made for and against designing middle schools to accommodate more than 1,000 pupils?

9. How have school reform initiatives affected programming in high schools over the past two decades?

10. Many scholars believe that America's transition from an industrial society to an information-based society requires major alterations to the high school curriculum. What are some of these changes?

11. Middle schools often provide considerably more space per pupil than do elementary schools, and high schools often provide more space per pupil than do middle schools. Why?

12. Some reformers have argued that schools should provide a broader range of services to students. How does the inclusion of guidance counselors, social workers, and psychologists affect the design of an elementary school?

13. What is the difference between horizontal and vertical articulation in a school? How does each influence the building design?

REFERENCES

Alexander, W., & Kealy, R. (1969). From junior high school to middle school. *High School Journal, 53*, 151–163.

Anderson, L., & Van Dyke, L. (1963). *Secondary school administration*. Boston: Houghton Mifflin.

Bensen, M. (1988). From industrial arts to technology education. In R.S. Brandt (Ed.), *Content of the curriculum* (pp. 167–180). Alexandria, VA: Association for Supervision and Curriculum Development.

Brooks, K., Conrad, M., & Griffith, W. (1980). *From program to educational facilities*. Lexington: Center for Professional Development, College of Education, University of Kentucky.

Brubaker, C. (1988). These 21 trends will shape the future of school design. *The American School Board Journal, 175*(4), 31–33, 66.

Butts, F. (1978). *Public education in the United States: From revolution to reform*. New York: Holt, Rinehart, and Winston.

George, P.S., McEwin, C.K., & Jenkins, J.M. (2000). *The exemplary high school*. Fort Worth, TX: Harcourt College Publishers.

Hawkins, H., & Lilley, H. (1986). *Guide for school facility appraisal*. Columbus, OH: Council of Educational Facility Planners, International.

Kowalski, T.J. (1981). Organizational patterns for secondary school curriculum. *NASSP Bulletin, 65*(443), 1–8.

Kowalski, T.J. (1999). *The school superintendent: Theory, practice, and cases*. Upper Saddle River, NJ: Merrill, Prentice-Hall.

Lee, V.E., & Loeb, S. (2000). School size in Chicago elementary schools: Effects on teachers' attitudes and students' achievement. *American Educational Research Journal, 37*(1), 3–32.

National Center for Education Statistics. (2000). *In the middle: Characteristics of public schools with a focus on middle schools*. Washington, DC: U.S. Department of Education.

Nelson, N. (1972). *Performance specifications: Determining space requirements*. West Lafayette, IN: Purdue University. Unpublished paper.

Perrone, V. (1985). *Portraits of high schools*. Lawrenceville, NJ: Princeton University Press.

Roberts, A., & Cawelti, G. (1984). *Redefining general education in the American high school*. Alexandria, VA: Association for Supervision and Curriculum Development.

Sarason, S.B. (1996). *Revisiting the culture of the school and the problem of change.* New York: Teachers College Press.

Schubert, W. (1986). *Curriculum: Perspective, paradigm, and possibility.* New York: Macmillan.

Snyder, F.A., & Peterson, R.D. (1970). *Dynamics of elementary school administration.* New York: Houghton Mifflin.

Spencer, D. (1988). Implications for facility planners at the elementary and secondary level. *CEFP Journal, 26*(2), 16–17.

PART IV

Focused Issues

CHAPTER 11

Demographic Projections

Determining how many students must be served by a district or school is the single most important quantitative aspect of a needs assessment. Therefore, school administrators are expected to have a basic understanding of two demographic issues: how population patterns affect school needs and how future populations are projected. This chapter explores the latter issue with regard to general populations and school enrollment.

GENERAL POPULATION TRENDS

The content of the previous chapter emphasized that the adequacy of a school building depends on both the present and the future. For this reason, projecting demographic trends is an essential element of planning. Such projections typically address both the general population (e.g., state, regional, and city projections) and enrollment in schools and districts.

Despite their potential value, population projections are not always greeted with enthusiasm. This is especially true when the predictions are incongruous with popular beliefs. For example, some taxpayers may refuse to believe that district enrollment will decline because they are convinced (or hopeful) that the general population will grow. Taxpayers and district employees often criticize population forecasts if they are not completely accurate; therefore, administrators usually approach the task with trepidation. They know that myriad factors, many beyond their control, can affect the accuracy of their work. Even so, they are likely to be held accountable if the projections are inaccurate (Brooks, Conrad, & Griffith, 1980).

School enrollment is influenced by variables that exist within school districts and in the broader environments in which they function. Dembowski and Van Hoesen (1997) placed these variables into six categories of assumptions that are integral to enrollment forecasting.

- Fertility and birthrates
- Infant mortality rates
- Economic conditions (e.g., unemployment rates)
- District structure and school boundaries (e.g., number and size of schools)
- District policy and regulations (e.g., transportation policies)
- Natural disasters and climatic conditions (e.g., desirability of location)

The most widely used data source for studying environmental populations is the official U.S. Census. A national census is completed in the first year of each decade. Census data are especially useful for trend analysis, that is, looking back over a 20- or 30-year period to evaluate the past. Census data for states are subdivided into counties, townships, and cities or towns. They contain a number of subcategories such as gender, age groups, poverty levels, race, and so forth.

State, county, and city or town projections are also readily available to most school districts. Often these data are part of larger demographic studies conducted by state agencies (e.g., state board of health, department of education), universities, and utility companies. Local projections are less common, especially in rural counties. Some businesses or county planning commissions may complete projections of local communities. School district employees or consultants retained by the school district usually must do original projections for specific areas within school districts—areas such as neighborhoods, subdivisions, or the territory served by a specific school.

Most county planning commissions keep records for issuing single-family and multiple-family building permits that typically are recorded by townships and cities (Glass, 1987). These data are especially useful if they include specificity regarding cost and size. Approvals of lots in subdivisions also can be evaluated. These records are usually available from county or city planning commissions.

In general, two factors are most important to environmental forecasts used by schools. Migration is one of them. These data show the number of people moving in and out of a specific location; if categorized by age ranges, they are especially useful to administrators because they reveal patterns of population movement affecting school enrollments. The other factor is live births. These figures, usually maintained by states or county boards of health, provide one of the best indicators of future enrollments. More sophisticated analysis of birthrates entails cross tabulations with variables such as educational level and race. For example, Hispanic females usually have higher fertility rates than white females, and college-educated females usually have lower fertility rates than other females.

SCHOOL ENROLLMENT

When projecting student populations, the planner must be extremely careful to base projections on accurate assumptions and to analyze data frequently (Harris, Burrage, & Smith, 1986). Knowing whether a community has a stable general population, studying economic trends, and evaluating the impact of policy changes exemplify work that must be done in relation to assumptions. Since projections are not foolproof, they need to be updated periodically to adjust for changes in the environment and the school district. Annual calculations are strongly recommended.

Projections of student populations may be done on a district or school basis. Several approaches have been used to complete this task. The most sophisticated and difficult projections are designed to inject selected variables, such as migration and housing starts, into the calculations. The most common statistical procedure is regression analysis. Critics, such as Murdock and Ellis (1991) and Shaw (1984), argue that the accuracy of regression techniques is attenuated by two conditions. Because separate regression equations must be calculated for each grade level and because each calculation contains some degree of error, the errors are compounded when the total for all grades is determined. The other drawback entails the need to predict the future condition of independent variables for the period of the projections (e.g., extrapolating migration data for the next 10 years.) However, some researchers (e.g., Chan, 1993; Grip & Young, 1999) claim that regression techniques are usually more precise than other enrollment projection procedures. In the absence of compelling evidence showing that complex statistical procedures are superior, school officials have relied on less complicated techniques. Three of the most popular and straightforward are described here.

School Census Method

The school census has been used to predict kindergarten enrollment by ascertaining the number of preschool children residing within the school system (e.g., identifying the number of three- and four-year-old children residing within the district's boundaries). This technique is used far less often than it was in the past for at least three reasons.

1. Districts have become larger and more complex, making the process more cumbersome and less accurate.

2. The process is usually more expensive than other options.

3. Populations within many districts are not very stable, a condition that attenuates accuracy.

The school census technique can be reasonably accurate provided that the community population is stable and parents cooperate, so that a high percentage of census cards are returned (Leu, 1965).

Various approaches have been used to conduct a school census. The most common have been

- *Sending census cards home with children already enrolled in the district.* This approach is simple, but it obviously has a major drawback: parents having only preschool children are not included. As such, the census must estimate this segment of the population.

- *Sending census cards home with students already enrolled in the district and announcing the availability of cards widely through the media.* This approach permits parents with only preschool children to obtain census cards; thus, the outcomes tend to be slightly more accurate than the previous option. The effectiveness often depends on the availability of the media to transmit the message and the willingness of parents to cooperate. The Internet may make this option more desirable in the future, because parents could respond without having to pick up a census card.

- *Telephoning everyone in the community to determine the presence of preschool children.* This option is not very practical for larger districts. The process depends on the availability of phone numbers by school districts; this is not possible in many communities.

- *Going door to door to conduct a census of preschool children.* In small districts where it is possible to canvas all homes, this approach can be very effective. In many rural communities, for instance, school officials have been able to secure the assistance of a cadre of volunteers to complete this type of census (Stewart, 1987).

Comparison Predictions

Some demographers have used an analogy approach to predict future enrollments. This procedure requires administrators in the district making the prediction (school district A) to identify a very similar school district located in a very similar community (school district B). Conditions now prevalent in school district A are assumed to have existed in school district B in the past. By studying conditions and trends, the school district makes predictions based on what has already occurred in school district B. In essence, the process becomes a form of case study. Because school districts and communities are so unique, it is extremely difficult to meet the test of identical or near-identical conditions. As a result, comparison predictions are rarely used by school systems (Brooks et al., 1980).

Cohort–Survival Method

The cohort–survival method (also referred to as the percentage of survival technique and the grade-progression technique) is the simplest and most widely used process for estimating future enrollment. The procedure projects enrollment

Table 11–1
Actual Enrollments for a Period of Six Years

Year						Grade Level								
	K	1	2	3	4	5	6	7	8	9	10	11	12	Total
95-96	400	478	432	423	400	360	405	406	361	542	384	377	322	5,290
96-97	425	447	421	425	418	398	367	423	394	461	383	347	340	5,249
97-98	388	469	425	429	403	417	392	379	406	500	405	314	335	5,262
98-99	393	429	431	411	431	415	407	414	373	550	381	342	270	5,247
99-00	424	406	432	398	423	405	396	403	456	367	327	303	310	5,050
00-01	373	448	391	406	423	395	408	421	395	534	392	354	316	5,256

by computing the estimated size of each grade for the next immediate year from the size of the present year's next lower grade; that is, the enrollment pattern of third grade to fourth grade is used to predict future fourth grade enrollment. The technique is able to account for grade failures, dropouts, and migratory trends (Thompson, Wood, & Honeyman, 1994). In general, the process relies on the assumption that the future will be much like the past.

Because this technique is so widely used, an example of the procedure is provided here. Table 11–1 contains actual enrollment for a school district from the 1995–1996 school year to the 2000–2001 school year. Assume that a district needs to project enrollments for the next five years. The dotted lines between kindergarten and first grade and between first grade and second grade in Table 11–1 exhibit the pattern for four successive kindergarten cohorts. As an example, the 1995–1996 kindergarten class became larger when it moved to first grade the following year (from 400 to 447); but when this same cohort moved to second grade in 1997–1998, it decreased (from 447 to 425). To calculate the ratio for first grade in 1996–1997, you use the following formula.

(1996–1997 1st-grade enrollment) / (1995–1996 kindergarten enrollment) or

447/400 = 1.12

A ratio of less than 1.0 indicates a declining cohort; a ratio of more than 1.0 indicates an increasing cohort; a ratio of 1.0 indicates a static cohort. In the example above, a retention ratio of 1.12 indicates that from 1995–1996 to 1996–1997, this cohort increased by 12 percent.

Ratios must be calculated for each grade level and each year, because relying on any one single year would be precarious. The intent is to develop an average of cohort experiences. A period of six years is commonly used to calculate average ratios, because research indicates that this period provides the most effective data (Alspaugh, 1981).

Calculating kindergarten ratios presents a special challenge, because the size

Table 11–2
Survival Ratios (Grade-Level for Kindergarten: Cohort for All Other Grades)

Year							Grade						
	K	1	2	3	4	5	6	7	8	9	10	11	12
96 to 97	1.06	1.12	0.88	0.98	0.99	1.00	1.02	1.04	0.97	1.28	0.71	0.90	0.90
97 to 98	0.91	1.10	0.95	1.02	0.95	1.00	0.98	1.03	0.96	1.27	0.88	0.82	0.97
98 to 99	1.01	1.11	0.92	0.97	1.00	1.03	0.98	1.06	0.98	1.35	0.76	0.84	0.86
99 to 0 0	1.08	1.03	1.01	0.92	1.03	0.94	0.95	0.99	1.10	0.98	0.59	0.80	0.91
00 to 0 1	0.88	1.06	0.96	0.94	1.06	0.93	1.01	1.06	0.98	1.17	1.07	1.08	1.04
Means	0.99	1.08	0.94	0.97	1.01	0.98	0.99	1.04	1.00	1.21	0.80	0.89	0.94

of the cohort prior to kindergarten is often unknown. The simplest approach to dealing with this problem is to calculate the average (mean) kindergarten enrollment for the six-year period (adding the enrollments for the six years and dividing by six). The mean is then used as a constant for kindergarten enrollment in the projections. When done with data in Table 11–1, the mean is 401. Thus, if enrollment was projected for the next five years, the kindergarten enrollment would remain at 401 each year.

A slightly better approach for dealing with kindergarten projections entails calculating a grade-level ratio for each year. This ratio represents the change in the size of the kindergarten enrollment from one year to the next. Thus, it is not a cohort ratio (as used in all other grades). It is calculated using the following formula.

(enrollment in kindergarten in second year) / (enrollment in kindergarten the first year) or

$425/400 = 1.06$

When the five kindergarten grade-level ratios during the six-year period have been determined, a mean is then calculated.

Data in Table 11–2 show survival ratios for the enrollment figures in Table 11–1. The bottom row in the table contains the means for each grade. These means are the ratios used to project future enrollments. The means indicate that over the six-year period, kindergarten cohorts increased an average of 8 percent when they moved to first grade; however, during the same period, first-grade cohorts decreased an average of 6 percent when they moved to second grade. Data in Table 11–2 reveal that positive ratios existed in only four grades: 1, 4, 7, and 9. The ratio in grade 8 was exactly 1.0; all other grade levels had ratios of less than 1.0 indicating enrollment declines.

Table 11–3
Enrollment Projection for Five Years Based on Survival Ratios

Year								Grade Level					
	K	1	2	3	4	5	6	7	8	9	10	11	12	Total
01-02	369	404	423	378	409	414	390	423	421	478	428	349	331	5,217
02-03	365	400	381	409	380	400	409	405	423	509	384	381	326	5,173
03-04	361	396	377	369	412	373	396	425	405	512	409	341	356	5,130
04-05	357	391	373	365	371	403	368	410	424	490	411	363	319	5,047
05-06	354	387	369	361	367	363	398	382	410	514	393	365	340	5,004

Future enrollments are calculated by multiplying a cohort by the appropriate ratio. This produces a projected size for the cohort the following year. For example, data in Table 11–1 reveal that the first-grade enrollment in 2000–2001 was 448. Projecting the size of this cohort when it moves to the second grade in 2001–2002 is accomplished by multiplying 448 by 0.94 (the ratio for progression from first to second grade). When this is done, the projected enrollment is set at 423, or a decline of 25 pupils. This same process is repeated for each grade level for every school year in the projection. The outcome for a five-year projection is shown in Table 11–3.

The enrollment in this district is expected to decline just over 200 pupils in the next five years. This is not surprising since the majority of the grade ratios was less than 1.0. Projections based entirely on history tend to be quite accurate in the short term (i.e., for approximately two to four years). Because the projection is based on the assumption that the future will be like the past, extensions of the projections beyond a few years increase the probability of error.

Using birth data to project future kindergarten enrollment offers a slightly better approach for projections that extend beyond a few years. This process requires official birth data for either a state or a county. Since children commonly enroll in kindergarten at age five, the process requires calculating a school district's average annual draw from the birth pool. Typically, the average is based on six or more years of experience. Table 11–4 provides county birth data for the district detailed in Table 11–1. Since there are five school districts in the county, it was necessary to determine the district's average draw from county birth pools for each of the years. Once the average is determined, it can be applied to birth pools to project future kindergarten enrollments. This process is shown in Table 11–5. Once the kindergarten enrollments have been projected, they can be used in the district projections. The results are shown in Table 11–6.

The only difference between the projection in Table 11–3 and the projection in Table 11–6 is the use of birth data. The outcome, however, is quite different. The projection using birth data indicates about 355 more students in 2005 than the projection without birth data. Congruence between county birth data and school district enrollment trends should be examined when using birth data.

Table 11–4
Average Draws from a County Birth Pool

Births Year	Births	School Year	Kindergarten Enrollment	District Percentage
1990	3,494	1995-96	400	11.45%
1991	3,680	1996-97	425	11.55%
1992	3,466	1997-98	388	11.19%
1993	3,608	1998-99	393	10.89%
1994	3,714	1999-00	424	11.42%
1995	3,895	2000-01	373	9.58%
			Six-year Average	11.01%

Table 11–5
Projecting Future Kindergarten Enrollments

Birth Year	Birth Pool	District Percentage	School Year	Projected Enrollment
1996	3,902	0.1101	2001-02	430
1997	3,932	0.1101	2002-03	433
1998	3,897	0.1101	2003-04	429
1999	3,867	0.1101	2004-05	426
2000	3,967	0.1101	2005-06	437

When the two factors are symmetrical (i.e., they are both increasing or decreasing), the risk of error is lessened. If the two factors are asymmetrical (i.e., one is increasing while the other is decreasing), the risk of error increases (Lows, 1987).

Because of inclusion programs, dealing with students in special education has become less problematic with respect to enrollment projections. Demographers have exercised three basic options when dealing with this population. The first is simply to exclude them from the district's projection. If the population is relatively small and stable, this approach does not present problems. Another method is to simply take the annual average enrollment of students in self-contained classes and project that future enrollment will remain at this level. A more precise option involves placing students in the grade levels in which they would be enrolled if they were not in self-contained special education classes. In essence, the students are added to age cohorts.

Several caveats are in order with respect to conducting cohort–survival projections.

• The precision of the cohort-survival method is reduced in districts where the general population is highly unstable, because the assumption that the future will be like the past is apt to be inaccurate (Alspaugh, 1981; Grip & Young, 1999).

Table 11–6
Enrollment Projection for Five Years Based on Survival Ratios Using Birth Data

Year						Grade Level								
	K	1	2	3	4	5	6	7	8	9	10	11	12	Total
01-02	430	404	423	378	409	414	390	423	421	478	428	349	331	5,278
02-03	433	466	381	409	380	400	409	405	423	509	384	381	326	5,307
03-04	429	469	440	369	412	373	396	425	405	512	409	341	356	5,334
04-05	426	465	443	425	371	403	368	410	424	490	411	363	319	5,319
05-06	437	461	439	428	428	363	398	382	410	514	393	365	340	5,359

• The cohort–survival method assumes that grade level retentions do not change dramatically from year to year. In some school districts, this assumption is not valid. Considerable variance from the mean provides an indication if this condition exists.

• Planners often fail to identify critical events that may detract from the accuracy of a projection. For example, the closing of a major factory in a community may not be weighed properly.

• Retention ratios are most often used to do district rather than individual school projections. When the population being projected becomes smaller, the error rate generally increases; thus, projections for an individual school typically have higher error rates than do projections for entire districts (Pullum, Graham, & Herting, 1986; Schellenberg & Stephens, 1987).

Despite its potential flaws, the cohort–survival technique is still widely used, largely because of its relative simplicity and its short-term accuracy. A recent study comparing this method with the analogy approach and with a multiple-factor method showed that the cohort–survival technique produced lower error rates (Shaw, Alspaugh, & Wat-Aksorn, 1997). Generally, however, projections based on multiple inputs (e.g., cohort–survival ratios, birth data, and a school census) are likely to be more accurate than a projection based on a single input (Dembowski & Van Hoesen, 1997). For this reason, educational consultants typically use multiple approaches to projecting both general population and student population trends.

CHAPTER SUMMARY

Estimating future populations is the most essential quantitative aspect of a needs assessment. Changes in birthrates, immigration to the United States, migration among states, and policy decisions affecting enrollment have made it advisable for school districts to monitor their projections yearly (Grier & Grier, 1990). Various approaches have been used in conjunction with facility planning, and their overall effectiveness usually depends on the size and stability of a district's population. The cohort–survival method using birth data remains the most popular approach for two primary reasons. First, the process is relatively simple and thus the most understandable tool available. Second, evidence supporting the notion that more complex statistical approaches are superior remains mixed. Generally, using several techniques and comparing the results is the preferred approach.

Unfortunately, no enrollment projection is foolproof. All are likely to contain some degree of error. Nevertheless, facility planners either complete projections and/or have access to such projections before proceeding with specific plans for a facility project. Using public opinion or administrator opinion to ascertain future enrollment is a precarious practice that usually results in costly planning mistakes.

ISSUES FOR DISCUSSION

1. What are the advantages of conducting annual enrollment projections for a school district?

2. Are U.S. Census data of any value to school districts? If so, in what ways?

3. Are birth data available in your state? If so, who maintains such data?

4. Most enrollment projections assume that the future will be much like the past. In what types of districts is the assumption likely to be true and untrue?

5. Assume that a second grade has a cohort–survival ratio of less than 1.0. What could you conclude, if anything, about the increase or loss of students from first grade to second grade in this district?

6. How does the stability of a community affect the accuracy of an enrollment projection?

7. Why is it important to have enrollment projections prior to proceeding with specific plans for school construction?

REFERENCES

Alspaugh, J.W. (1981). Accuracy of school enrollment projections based upon previous enrollments. *Educational Research Quarterly, 6*, 61–67.

Brooks, K.W., Conrad, M.C., & Griffith, W. (1980). *From program to educational facilities*. Lexington: Center for Professional Development, College of Education, University of Kentucky.

Chan, T.C. (1993). How many will close? School choice and student enrollment planning. *School Business Affairs, 59*(7), 29–31.

Dembowski, F.L., & Van Hoesen, S. (1997). Predicting 21st century school enrollments: Assumptions, tools, and tips. *School Business Management, 63*(4), 19–23.

Glass, T.E. (1987). Demographic sources and data available for school district planners and architects. *CEFP Journal, 25*(2), 7–13.

Grier, E., & Grier, G. (1990). Bright ideas bringing your future into focus. *The Executive Educator, 12*(2), 11–13, 27.

Grip, R., & Young, J.W. (1999, April). *Predicting school enrollments using the modified regression technique*. Paper presented at the annual meeting of the American Educational Research Association, Montreal, Quebec, Canada.

Harris, D.E., Burrage, P.M., & Smith, W.J. (1986). Local insights keep enrollment projections on the money. *The Executive Educator, 8*(11), 20–21.

Leu, D.J. (1965). *Planning educational facilities*. New York: Center for Applied Research in Education.

Lows, R.L. (1987). Enrollment projection: A methodology for eras of growth and decline. *CEFP Journal, 25*(2), 4–7.

Murdock, S.H., & Ellis, D.R. (1991). *Applied demography*. Boulder, CO: Westview Press.

Pullum, T.W., Graham, S.N., & Herting, J.R. (1986). How to forecast public school enrollments. *American Demographics, 8*(10), 52, 54.

Schellenberg, S.J., & Stephens, C.E. (1987). *Enrollment projections: Variations on a theme*. (ERIC Document Reproduction Service No. ED 283 879)

Shaw, R.C. (1984). Enrollment forecasting: What methods work best? *NASSP Bulletin, 68*(468), 52–58.

Shaw, R.C., Alspaugh, J., & Wat-Aksorn, P. (1997). Accuracy of enrollment forecasting methods. *ERS Spectrum, 15*(4), 16–19.

Stewart, G.K. (1987). Confirming enrollment projections in rural districts. *CEFP Journal, 25*(2), 16–17.

Thompson, D.C., Wood, R.C., & Honeyman, D.S. (1994). *Fiscal leadership for schools: Concepts and practices*. New York: Longman.

CHAPTER 12

Working with Agencies

T.C. Chan

Interagency collaboration is one of the most overlooked aspects of facility planning. Often administrators enter a planning process without understanding the scope of information they must provide to other organizations and the scope of information that they may secure from other organizations. Therefore, contact with these agencies is both expedient and beneficial (Council of Educational Facility Planners, International [CEFP], 1991).

This chapter has two primary purposes. The first is to identify and discuss agencies that may be involved with facility projects; the other is to examine working relationships with these agencies. Because laws, regulations, and resources vary, the agencies discussed here may not be found in every state and every local community.

AGENCIES INVOLVED IN SCHOOL FACILITY PLANNING

There are many public and private agencies that either must or may get involved in a school facility project. The ones identified in this chapter are those most commonly involved, and they are divided into three categories: federal, state, and local.

Federal Agencies

Although the federal government continues to play only a limited role in public education, there are five federal agencies that may become involved in school facility projects. They are the U.S. Department of Education; the U.S.

Consumer Product Safety Commission; the U.S. Occupational Safety and Health Administration; the U.S. Department of Justice, Office on the Americans with Disabilities Act; and the U.S. Department of Energy.

U.S. Department of Education. The federal government's participation in funding capital outlay expenditures for public education has been limited (Burrup, Brimley, & Garfield, 1996). Aid was typically earmarked for specific purposes, such as special, vocational, and higher education. More recently the department has pursued policy initiatives that indirectly affect school facilities. Most noteworthy have been recommendations for smaller class sizes, especially in elementary schools, and a series of reports detailing problems with existing buildings. The department also provides a valuable information service via the ERIC Clearing House on Educational Facilities—a resource database on educational facility planning—that can be accessed via the Internet. In addition, the department's National Center for Education Statistics provides a range of studies that may be useful to planning activities (e.g., demographic studies).

U.S. Consumer Product Safety Commission. The U.S. Consumer Product Safety Commission sets minimum safety standards for products, and manufacturers observe these standards. Thus, school officials who are purchasing equipment for facility projects should contact the commission to obtain copies of updated standards. This information can be incorporated into bid specifications. For example, standards developed by the commission address asbestos, lead control, and playground safety (Miller, 1994).

U.S. Occupational Safety and Health Administration (OSHA). OSHA is primarily concerned with preventing hazardous work environments. The agency published regulations governing all construction work that had the potential of exposing workers to hazardous airborne lead levels. Indoor air-quality standards require employers to develop and implement a written compliance program for this potential problem. Together with the Environmental Protection Agency (EPA), OSHA implements laws to enforce environmental protection. In planning for school construction and renovation projects, administrators need to work closely with OSHA to ensure that all federal regulations are fully understood and that school districts are in compliance (Dunklee & Silberman, 1991; McKeague, 1994; Odell, 1991).

U.S. Department of Justice, Office on the Americans with Disabilities Act. The Office on the Americans with Disabilities Act in the U.S. Department of Justice is charged with the implementation of the 1990 Americans with Disabilities Act (ADA). As discussed earlier in the book, the law calls for all private and public entities to remove barriers that inhibit public access to facilities, goods, services, and jobs. To comply with the law, all school facilities must make their programs accessible, either by moving the program to an accessible location or making the program's current location accessible (Davis, 1994). School district staff and project architects should remain in constant contact with the office when conducting ADA facility audits and when developing ADA compliance plans for both new school construction and renovation projects.

U.S. Department of Energy. The U.S. Department of Energy operates the Institutional Conservation Program (ICP) that promotes energy audits and provides technical assistance for energy studies and conservation to private and public organizations. Since educational facilities are big energy consumers, a substantial amount of money can be saved by implementing a conservation program. Collaboration with the Department of Energy is voluntary, and the department offers matching grants for energy conservation efforts (Smith, 1986).

State Agencies

State agencies that may become involved in school facility planning include departments of education, departments of fire safety and protection, school building authorities, planning commissions, departments of transportation, states Boards of health, and boards of regents (for higher-education projects). In virtually all states, the first two agencies play pivotal roles in examining and approving construction initiatives. Because these agencies are housed in different branches of state government, administrators are required to work with each individually.

State Departments of Education. State departments of education usually assume both regulatory and advisory roles in relation to school construction (Arkansas State Department of Education, 1992; CEFP, 1991; Earthman, 1989; North Carolina-State Department of Public Instruction, 1998). Most departments offer two types of support services to local school districts: educational services and technical services (Georgia State Department of Education, 1996; Minnesota State Department of Children, Families, and Learning, 1999; Oklahoma State Department of Education, 1998; South Carolina Department of Education, 1983; Stenzler, 1989). Educational consultants who may or may not be full-time department employees provide the former. Services may include enrollment projections, organizational structure studies, evaluation of redistricting plans, assistance with installing pupil locator systems, assistance with developing educational specifications, and completing school facility inventories. These department-sponsored consultants may also assist with finance issues related to construction (e.g., eligibility for state funding, bond sales) (Barwick, 1990; Georgia State Department of Education, 1996; South Carolina Department of Education, 1983).

Technical services provided by some state departments of education entail architectural or engineering evaluations. Consultants in these areas review and approve construction plans, inspect school construction projects, interpret building code requirements, conduct energy conservation studies, perform structural evaluation, and provide advice relating to technical building problems (New York State Education Department, 1996). Occasionally, educational consultants, architects, and engineers collaborate on the following issues: setting minimum standards for physical environment and program requirements; evaluating and approving proposed school sites; and determining the feasibility of school renovation projects (Georgia State Department of Education, 1996; Spencer, 1989).

State Departments of Fire Safety and Protection. State departments of fire safety and protection develop and disseminate requirements and guidelines for fire safety in public buildings. These departments review proposed school plans and interpret current fire codes (NFPA 101—Life Safety Code). If local fire safety agencies do not exist, state agencies usually assume the responsibility of implementing building restrictions and fire safety regulations for local district construction. Thus, administrators need to determine conditions in the state in which they are working.

School Building Authorities. School building authorities are established in some states to assist in public school construction. These agencies typically perform two functions: they allocate state funds for school construction, and they actually construct school buildings and lease them to local districts under lease–purchase agreements (Earthman, 2000b). Small school districts, lacking sufficient in-house expertise and sufficient bonding credibility for school construction, often benefit most from collaborating with state building authorities. In several states (e.g., Ohio), state building authorities have considerable control over school building projects unless no state funding is involved. In some states (e.g., Pennsylvania), school systems are granted with the power and the authority to use public funds to enter into a contract with the state school building authorities in the construction, operation, and maintenance of school facilities.

State Planning Commissions. State planning commissions perform basic functions similar to those of the local planning commission, except they serve a larger geographical area (CEFP, 1991). They maintain updated information on land-use plans and projections on future land development that may impact future construction and site acquisition decisions. They also exercise jurisdiction over construction on flood plains, agricultural land, forest land, and park reserves. In addition, such commissions conduct comprehensive analyses of the social and economic trends shaping the development outlook of the state (Atlanta Regional Commission, 1988).

State Departments of Transportation. State departments of transportation keep detailed plans and schedules for road improvement and highway construction. Such information usually shows development trends that may impact school facility needs. Districts planning construction may need to work with transportation departments to ensure compliance with state regulation (e.g., providing adequate sidewalks near schools). Moreover, the agencies maintain updated traffic safety and parking regulations that need to be incorporated into facility planning.

State Boards of Health. State health boards maintain population records that are often useful for quantitative analyses; for example, birth data can be used to complete enrollment projections. Health boards also have or can access information about health and safety issues, such as air pollution, radon, and asbestos.

Boards of Regents. Facility projects for state colleges and universities often must be approved or funded by state boards of regents. Conditions among and within states vary, so university officials should be familiar with requirements affecting them.

Local Public Agencies

Since local public authorities typically enforce many federal and state policies and code requirements, administrators also need to work closely with these agencies. The number and nature of the agencies differ among states and among locations within states. Some of the more common agencies are identified here.

Planning and Zoning Departments. Planning and zoning departments are responsible for the comprehensive planning for either a county or a city. They engage in population forecasting and monitor growth in the area under their jurisdiction. They are the best source for property zoning and rezoning data. A school district can work closely with these departments to locate potential school sites and to develop population impact studies cogent to facility needs (Glass, 1987).

Management Information Systems Departments. Some communities have agencies that develop and maintain records and databases for geographic regions. Administrators can use basic information, such as population age, gender, race, family income, occupation, education background, religious orientation, and economic growth, in facility planning.

Environmental Control Departments. These agencies can help administrators research the history of potential school sites to ensure that the sites do not have contamination or air pollution problems. They also can determine if a proposed site is part of a flood plain. Other contributions include estimating the amount of water flow on a specific site and recommending possible locations for retention ponds.

Archaeology Departments. Where available, the agencies can contribute to school facility planning by researching the history of proposed sites to ensure that schools will not be constructed in areas designated as historically significant. These agencies also may identify the presence of cemeteries on possible school sites.

Building Departments. Local building departments typically issue building permits and maintain records on single-dwelling and multiple-dwelling residences. Such data may be very useful to administrators in relation to enrollment projections and related population studies. These agencies also may be responsible for implementing the Standard Building Code; thus, they review and approve school construction drawings, inspect school construction work, and issue school building occupancy permits.

Health Departments. Local health departments typically operate in conjunction with state health departments. In some states, local departments maintain data for births, mortality rates, fertility rates, marriages, divorces, abortions, and family-size data. Collectively, these statistics provide a snapshot of population trends that are likely to affect school enrollments (Glass, 1987). In addition, these departments have the responsibility of specifying school health standards and inspecting new school construction projects to determine if the structures comply with health codes.

Fire Departments. Local fire departments usually help to determine if projects comply with national fire safety codes. The departments conduct inspections and issue occupancy permits. In some states (e.g., Georgia), the implementation of the handicapped accessibility standards developed by the American National Standard Institute (ANSI) is also under the jurisdiction of the local fire departments.

Police Departments. Local police departments can be a valuable resource in two key areas. First, they can provide data about crime rates in designated areas—information that enhances good planning. Second, they can provide advice on student safety and vandalism prevention.

Transportation Departments. Local transportation departments can provide data on current and projected highway construction that is likely to affect housing development. These agencies keep detailed records of traffic accidents, including their locations and frequencies. Such information can be used in making site-selection decisions. In addition, transportation departments can help administrators avoid placing schools on sites requiring dangerous roads and bridges to be used for bus routes.

Engineering Departments. School buildings require utilities and other governmental services. Local engineering departments "can provide data on water and sewer connections, streets, garbage collection, lighting, and other physical aspects of the physical infrastructure associated with a school project" (CEFP, 1991, p. B9). Often, site-selection decisions are influenced by the availability of city utilities. In addition, information relating to future waterlines, sewer lines, and street extensions provide additional insights into possible changes in school enrollment.

Parks and Recreation Departments. Local parks and recreation departments are responsible for the overall planning of leisure services and facilities in their area of jurisdiction. They have a keen interest in working with school districts, especially with respect to possibly sharing facilities that serve the community (CEFP, 1991). Under appropriate circumstances, joint facility projects can produce savings in both initial construction costs and long-term operational expenses.

Utility Companies. Utility companies providing electricity, gas, and telephone services routinely complete population projection studies. In addition to providing these data, these agencies almost always get involved in facility planning because they will provide needed services to the school.

Local Private Agencies

Administrators often overlook the fact that there are private organizations in their school districts that can contribute to facility planning. Several of the common resources include local businesses, residential development organizations, and community organizations.

Local Businesses. Often local businesses and their organization, the Chamber of Commerce, maintain databases that can be used for school facility planning. Examples include market survey results, consumer profiles, economic trends, labor supply and demand studies, and long-range development studies.

Residential Development Organizations. Housing development data usually can be obtained from residential development organizations, such as builders, developers, financial institutions, real estate associations, cooperative housing societies, and tenants' groups (CEFP, 1991). Data obtained from these agencies may include housing types, density levels, market costs, rental rates, and development. Some larger subdivisions and developments have their own neighborhood associations. These organizations also may be able to provide population data.

Community Organizations. Organized parents' and citizens' groups can offer a perspective on the broad role of the school in the neighborhood, especially in the formulation of educational goals and objectives (CEFP, 1991). They can assist school districts in identifying community facility needs that could possibly be incorporated as part of the school construction projects (Cowles, 1995). Many school districts involve the community in school planning to foster public interest, concern, understanding, and support (Chan & Pool, 1999).

WORKING WITH AGENCIES

There are many reasons why school administrators decide to work or not work with other agency officials. Reluctance may be predicated on ignorance, or it may stem from previous negative experiences. In some instances, working with other agencies is simply contrary to a school district's culture. Traditional managers, who focus on efficiency, tend to view collaboration as counterproductive because such interactions breed conflict. Thus, efforts are made to minimize contact with regulatory agencies and to avoid contact with all other agencies. This type of isolationism restricts the flow of information and hampers effective planning.

Value of Working with Agencies

School facility planning is part of the comprehensive development of public services. Thus, it is most effective when communication with public and private agencies is open. Earthman (2000a) put it this way, "Unless the authorities in the school district reach out to other jurisdictions to involve them in such situations, building the new school might become an isolated event in the development of the community" (p. 5).

Benefits associated with agency collaboration are both direct and indirect. That is to say, these linkages might provide tangible data and services, and they could produce less obvious benefits such as political support and positive feelings toward education. Six of the most relevant reasons for collaborating are

- *Ensuring Compliance With Laws and Regulations.* Some agencies have direct jurisdiction over aspects of school facility planning. Therefore, their involvement is mandatory under federal, state, or local laws (or regulations). Examples of such involvement include approvals from the state fire marshal and building inspectors.
- *Producing Information and Data.* Voluntary collaboration is almost always intended to produce information and databases that can be integrated into the planning process.
- *Building Goodwill.* Working with other agencies is simply a good public relations activity. It provides administrators with an opportunity to inform the public about the district's initiatives and to get valuable community feedback.
- *Improving Overall Community Services.* By working together, agencies can improve the quality of public services. For example, districts might benefit from comprehensive land-use plans shared by all public agencies in a given community (Earthman, 2000a).
- *Maximizing Resources.* School districts never have sufficient resources to meet all of their needs. In the case of facility planning, districts can often obtain valuable services from other agencies at little or no cost.
- *Improving Planning.* Multiple inputs almost always have a positive effect on planning outcomes. Administrators commonly make the mistake of believing that they have all the information necessary to make appropriate decisions—this rarely is the case.

Potential Pitfalls

While working with other agencies produces many benefits, there are potential pitfalls. These difficulties are often related to how key figures interpret history and their respective organizational cultures. For example, some school administrators have not been prepared to work with other local agencies. They fear that collaboration will result in a loss of power or authority. Conversely, some agency managers are reluctant to help school districts because they have so many other responsibilities. The following are the more common problems:

- *Lack of Knowledge.* Some administrators simply do not know what information or assistance is available from other agencies; therefore, they are reluctant to make contacts.
- *Unwillingness to Share Information.* In some instances, agency managers are unwilling to share data. They may fear that it will be used inappropriately or that the school district may blame them if the information provided proves to be inaccurate. For ex-

ample, a utility company may not want to share its population projections because of fear that the data will be misinterpreted.

- *Poor Communication.* Collaboration requires open, two-way communication. Requests for information are not always answered in a clear and timely manner; for example, a school district's letter to the local building authority requesting housing data may go unanswered for months. Some federal and state agencies routinely take weeks to respond to data requests.

- *Bureaucracy.* All public agencies belong to a huge infrastructure of bureaucracy that consists of layers of authorities and divisions of responsibilities. School administrators do not always understand how to penetrate these layers of authority to secure the data or assistance needed (Earthman, 2000a). Conversely, some school districts are highly bureaucratic, causing delays in requests to other agencies because two or more layers of administration must approve such actions.

- *Unavailability of Data.* There are times when the data requested by school officials simply are not available or they are not available in a form that could be used by the district.

- *Lack of Trust.* In some situations, relationships between school officials and agency officials are poor; for instance, some superintendents may not trust members of the department of education to treat them fairly.

Positive Steps for Working with Agencies

Administrators should anticipate problems when working with other agencies. This is especially true if time lines for completing the planning process are narrow. While some of these barriers mentioned here are unavoidable, others can be eliminated or at least reduced substantially. The following are some positive actions that can be taken to overcome problems.

- *Know the Agencies That Can Help.* First and foremost, administrators need to develop a list of public and private agencies that have the potential of providing assistance with facility projects.

- *Know Key Agency Figures.* Often it is beneficial for administrators to have an established relationship with key agency officials prior to a facility project. Established relationships can expedite requests for information or assistance.

- *Understand What an Agency Can Do.* The agency database should include information about services and information that may be obtained.

- *Understand How an Agency Operates.* Administrators should know how to make requests for data or consultant services.

- *Know Each Agency's Strengths and Weaknesses.* Because planners can become highly reliant on agency contacts, they should have a familiarity with the agencies prior to the planning process. This is especially important with respect to knowing what each agency does well and does poorly.

- *Know the Nature of the Relationship.* Relationships with agencies vary. As an example, a district's relationship with an enforcement agency is usually very different than it is with a local civic group.

- *Recognize Contributions*. When agencies provide assistance, administrators should take steps to see that the contributions are recognized. Positive public relations will strengthen relationships and ensure future cooperation.
- *Offer to Reciprocate*. Administrators should let other agency managers know that they are willing to provide data or assistance if so requested.
- *Avoid Being Defensive*. Administrators should avoid being defensive, especially when working with regulatory agencies, provide information accurately and within the time frames that it is requested.
- *Make Requests Appropriately*. Requests for information should be made in accordance with an agency's practices. Often conflict emerges when school administrators attempt to gain access to information through informal channels (e.g., by contacting a personal friend who works in the agency).
- *Be Willing to Listen*. When contact with school officials is initiated, some agency managers use the opportunity to voice concerns. For example, when contacted for information, local businessmen or neighborhood associations may allude to problems. Collaboration is a two-way relationship. Input, even when it is negative, should not be ignored.

CHAPTER SUMMARY

Agencies at federal, state, and local levels can be assets for school facility planning. Superintendents and other administrators who have responsibility for construction and building maintenance should be familiar with these agencies, and they should know what roles these agencies must or can play in facilitating planning. It is especially important to understand the laws and policies in a given state, especially with respect to getting approvals from regulatory agencies.

Prevailing practices with respect to planning are not constant across states. In some, needs assessments and feasibility studies are done by state agencies (e.g., department of education, building authority). In other states, private consultants are retained to do much of this work. The same is true with regard to financing projects.

ISSUES FOR DISCUSSION

1. What agencies might contribute to facility planning in your state? In your local community?
2. Why is it important for district administrators to establish a relationship with agencies prior to a facility project?
3. Identify the phases of school facility planning and develop a plan of how each public agency can contribute in this planning process.
4. Discuss possible strategies for promoting a positive working relationship with the public agencies involved in school facility planning.

5. What are some reasons why administrators may shy away from collaborating with agencies?

6. Assume that your state permits you to either use consultants in the state department of education or private consultants to conduct a feasibility study. What are the possible advantages and disadvantages of each option?

7. What private agencies in your state and district might be able to provide information or assistance for facility planning?

REFERENCES

Arkansas State Department of Education. (1992). *Rules and regulations: Minimum schoolhouse construction standards.* Little Rock: Author.

Atlanta Regional Commission. (1988). *Atlanta region outlook.* Atlanta: Author.

Barwick, W.J. (1990). School facilities and the state mechanism created by "KERA" which support school construction. *Educational Facility Planner, 28*(6), 11–12.

Burrup, P.E, Brimley, V., Jr., & Garfield, R.R. (1996). *Financing education in a climate of change.* Boston: Allyn and Bacon.

Chan, T.C., & Pool, H. (1999, October). *Planning a new school building: Public participation.* A paper presented to the annual conference of the International Society for Educational Planning, Indianapolis, IN.

Council of Educational Facility Planners, International. (1991). *Guide for planning educational facilities.* Scottsdale, AZ: Author.

Cowles, R.A. (1995). *A study of shared use of school facilities between school districts and public agencies.* Unpublished doctoral dissertation, University of La Verne, CA.

Davis, L. (1994). Get your buildings ADA OK. Implementing a compliance plan. *School Business Affairs, 60*(1), 21–25.

Dunklee, D.R., & Silberman, R.M. (1991). Healthy buildings keep employees out of bed and employers out of court. *School Business Affairs, 57*(12), 19–22.

Earthman, G.I. (1989). The role of the state department of education in planning school facilities. *Educational Facility Planner, 27*(3) 4–6.

Earthman, G.I. (2000a, January 31). *Comprehensive land use and planning for school buildings.* Unpublished lecture notes at Cornell University, Ithaca, NY.

Earthman, G.I. (2000b). *Planning educational facilities for the next century.* Reston, VA: Association of School Business Officials International.

Georgia State Department of Education. (1996). *A guide for planning and construction of school facilities in Georgia.* Atlanta: Author.

Glass, T.E. (1987). Demographic sources and data available for school district planners and architects. *CEFP Journal, 25*(3), 7–12.

McKeague, K.J. (1994). Life in a regulated environment. Do you comply with environmental laws? *School Business Affairs, 60*(8), 15–18.

Miller, D. (1994). Playground safety audit protects children and your liability. *School Business Affairs, 60*(8), 31–32.

Minnesota State Department of Children, Families, and Learning. (1999). *Guide for planning school construction projects in Minnesota.* St. Paul: Author.

New York State Education Department. (1996). *Manual of planning standards for school buildings.* Albany: Author.

North Carolina State Department of Public Instruction. (1998). *Design and construction procedures for public school facilities*. Raleigh: Author.

Odell, L. (1991). Reducing lead in school drinking water: A case study. *School Business Affairs, 57*(12), 14–18.

Oklahoma State Department of Education. (1998). *The ABC's of building a school*. Oklahoma City: Author.

Smith, M.W. (1986). Invest in energy conservation with government help. *School Business Affairs, 52*(2), 26–27.

South Carolina Department of Education. (1983). *South Carolina school facilities planning and construction guide*. Columbia: Author.

Spencer, D. (1989). State education agencies facility planning services in North Carolina. *Educational Facility Planner, 27*(3), 10–12.

Stenzler, Y. (1989). State education agencies: Planning requirements. *Educational Facility Planner, 27*(3), 7–9.

CHAPTER 13

Decisions for Existing Buildings

When faced with the need to expand or improve facilities, superintendents and school boards commonly face the question, "Should we build a new school or improve the existing school?" Ideally, administrators and architects are supposed to answer this question objectively using defensible data to support their recommendation. But even when this is done, community members may line up on opposite sides of the issue for political, economic, and personal reasons.

This chapter examines three categories of decisions affecting existing facilities.

- Improvement decisions
- Expansion decisions
- Alternative-use and disposal decisions

The first two categories are associated with quantitative and qualitative space needs. The last one addresses surplus schools—that is, buildings no longer being used as schools either because they are obsolete or because the space is not needed.

IMPROVEMENT DECISIONS

Essentially, there are two reasons why a school district may want to make major improvements to an existing facility: the building is in poor condition or the building is unable to support intended or desired programs. A good example of the latter is the effects of technology circa 1980. At this time, many schools had not been designed to accommodate computers and other technologies. Administrators who wanted to place schools in their districts on the cutting edge of educational improvements had to take steps to compensate for this deficiency.

Categories of Improvement

Existing schools can be improved in two ways: modernization or remodeling. Modernization entails improvements to a facility without reshaping the spaces; some authors (e.g., Earthman, 1994) have referred to this process as rehabilitation or renovation. Examples of improvements include:

• Lowering ceilings in an older building,
• Carpeting floor surfaces,
• Painting the walls,
• Replacing windows.

Modernization improves the appearance of a building and usually extends a building's life span. However, the size and relationship of spaces within the building are not altered. Thus, a school with substandard-size classrooms that is modernized still has substandard-size classrooms after the process is completed. Accordingly, modernization usually has a limited effect on programming.

By contrast, remodeling entails extensive improvements where some or all of the spaces in a building are reconfigured to accommodate existing or anticipated instructional (and extracurricular) needs (Castaldi, 1994). This option requires educational specifications because the process is intended to improve the building's ability to accommodate programming.

There are some situations in which modernization is the best alternative. An example would be a building with a functional design that was constructed with inexpensive materials; that is, the facility accommodates programming, but many of the original features (e.g., floor surfaces, windows) need to be replaced. In general, however, remodeling is a preferred approach because administrators have an opportunity to reconsider educational needs and increase flexibility and adaptability. In this era of rapid change, these are important considerations.

Interests in Retaining Buildings

The growing interest in updating old schools as an alternative to new construction emerged with vigor in the 1970s. Several key factors were responsible. The economy was relatively unstable and inflation caused an upward spiral in construction costs, especially during the late 1970s and early 1980s (Council of Educational Facility Planners, International, 1985). Additionally, Americans were experiencing a change in philosophy about the "use-and-dispose" mentality that prevailed following World War II. The higher cost of automobiles and homes forced many citizens to consider whether it was feasible to restore costly items as an alternative to replacing them. This same form of economic scrutiny found its way into the public economy. Higher construction costs, coupled with concerns about the rising costs of governmental services, led taxpayers to look more carefully at how public funds were being expended.

Some taxpayers favor modernizing existing buildings for purely economic reasons. However, they are not driven by convictions that remodeling has a better cost–benefit ratio than building replacement; rather they believe that buildings are relatively unimportant to the educational process. For them, modernizing is a preferred approach simply because it is cheaper than either remodeling or building replacement.

Another reason why some taxpayers fight to retain existing buildings involves sentimentality or the belief that a building has historical value to the community. Persons who attended a school in a particular building may argue that their children should have the same experience. Because these arguments are largely emotional, administrators may find it difficult to respond to them. In addition, administrators may be required to mediate tensions between the community's desire to retain buildings and the state guidelines that may discourage such decisions (Johnston, 1998).

Choosing Remodeling Over Replacement

Without proper leadership from the superintendent and other administrators, decisions about remodeling may be made solely on the basis of the apparent condition of a building. With few exceptions, structures erected more than 25 years ago have some deficiencies with respect to supporting today's curriculum and instructional paradigms. This is why it is critically important to conduct both a needs assessment and a feasibility study. The needs assessment interfaces program and facility and produces a list of deficiencies; the feasibility study should determine whether remodeling can meet the district's needs and provide an objective comparison of alternative approaches to eradicating these deficiencies (Earthman, 1994).

The value of a feasibility study depends on the criteria that are selected. Carey (2000) suggested five of them: renovation costs, modification or addition costs, student enrollment, per-pupil costs for construction, and per pupil costs for operations. These five criteria were used to develop the following queries.

- What will it cost to renovate the building to ensure compliance with building and fire codes and to ensure that all building systems will perform adequately?
- Can the current building be modified and expanded to ensure that core facilities (e.g., media center, administrative complex, cafeteria) are adequate? If so, how much would these improvements cost?

- Do current or projected enrollments suggest the need for more or less space than is currently being used?
- How does the cost of renovation compare to the cost of replacement on a per-pupil basis at projected capacities?
- What is the projected cost per pupil at projected capacity for operating and maintenance costs?

All of the above queries are quantitative measures, and the fourth and fifth ones dealing with initial and life-cycle costs are the most widely used (Ginsburg, 1989). Both Castaldi (1994) and McClelland (1985) have developed formulas for calculating cost comparisons. Once such comparisons are made, some states adhere to a general guideline: *If renovation is projected to cost more than 60 percent of the projected cost of building replacement, replacement is a preferred option.*

While cost comparisons are important, they are insufficient for making an informed decision about renovations. Formulas provide a rational and objective analysis of a single criterion: cost. Decisions about school construction need to be based on more than this (Fickes, 1999). Other criteria, such as facilitating academic programs, may be even more important. This is why qualitative analysis is at least equally important (Earthman, 1994). Qualitative analysis attempts to analyze conditions specific to a district and a project within a district. Some of the criteria that can be used for this purpose were detailed in Chapter 3 (see universal criteria). They include aesthetics, proper identity, economic appropriateness (including comparisons of project costs), flexibility, adaptability, expandability, sufficient size, operational efficiency (including comparison of estimated operating costs), health and safety (including security), durability (including life span of the building), and accessibility. In addition, the building site can be both a qualitative and a quantitative criterion. With remodeling, the inability to improve site size, quality, and location may be a serious disadvantage. As an example, the current site may be too small; it may not be located centrally within the area served; or it may contain hazardous conditions.

Kennedy (1999b) contended that remodeling decisions should be based on three criteria.

- Educational needs
- The community's attachment to a facility
- The district's fiscal resources

In districts with changing demographics, location also can be especially important because of transportation problems or the need to alter attendance boundaries. A list of potential criteria for weighing renovation and replacement is shown in Table 13-1.

A comprehensive analysis that includes both accurate and objective quanti-

Table 13–1
Criteria for Comparing Building Renovation with Building Replacement

Criterion	Primary Question
Aesthetics	How do the options compare with regard to having a pleasurable and inspiring effect on users and viewers?
Proper identity	How do the options compare with regard to communicating the message that the community cares about children, youth, adults, and learning?
Economic appropriateness	How do the options compare with regard to providing solutions congruous with the community's (or state's) ability to support education?
Flexibility	How do the options compare with regard to serving changing program purposes without altering the structural system of a building?
Adaptability	How do the options compare with regard to serving varying purposes without redesigning spaces?
Expandability	How do the options compare with regard to the potential for future expansion?
Sufficient size	How do the options compare with regard to providing adequate space to accommodate programming?
Operational efficiency	How do the options compare with regard to estimated operating and maintenance costs?
Health and safety	How do the options compare with regard to meeting current health and safety standards (including security standards)?
Durability	How do the options compare with regard to the building's life span?
Accessibility	How do the options compare with regard to providing access for all potential users, including disabled individuals?
Meeting current codes	How do the options compare with regard to requiring the building to meet all current codes?
Building site	How do the options compare with regard to providing a site of appropriate size, quality, and location?
Functional adequacy	How do the options compare with regard to accommodating the entire school program?
Emotional attachment	How do the options compare with regard to community support?
Project costs	How do the options compare with regard to initial per-pupil costs? How do the options compare with regard to costs prorated over the life expectancy of the buildings?

tative comparisons and qualitative evaluations is the administrator's best tool for responding to emotions and self-interests. Quantitative comparisons should be based on broad life-cycle estimates; this includes costs related to design, research and development, investments, operations, and maintenance (Hentschke, 1986). Qualitative data should illuminate specific programming needs and the ability of options to support the total school program.

EXPANSION DECISIONS

Additions to school buildings may be completed as isolated projects or in conjunction with modernization or remodeling. Adding space to a facility is different than reconfiguring space (remodeling). It can be accomplished either by conventional construction or by placing separate structures on the school site. Both options are examined.

Reasons for Needing More Space

Most taxpayers respond to recommendations for adding space to school buildings by looking at enrollment, that is, they understand that increasing enrollment may necessitate adding space to a school. Conversely, they may question or even oppose recommendations for adding space to a school that has stable or declining enrollment.

Enrollment, however, is but one reason why additional space may be necessary. Today, additions to school buildings may be prompted by one or more of the following conditions.

- *Shifting Enrollments in a School.* As discussed in Chapter 10, many high schools are experiencing changing enrollment among departments and classes. Thus, it is possible for a high school to have an overall declining enrollment but increasing enrollment in selected areas (e.g., in science courses requiring additional lab stations).

- *Additions or Modifications to Curriculum.* Many secondary schools have broadened or changed their curricula. Examples include broader offerings in foreign languages and the transformation of industrial education into technology education.

- *Additions to Extracurricular Programs.* The effects of Title IX requiring additional athletic programs for girls is a prime example of how space needs for extracurricular programs can increase. In order to be in compliance, many secondary schools had to add an auxiliary gym.

- *Broadening the Scope of District Services.* Over the past few decades, public schools have been expected to expand the scope of programming. Three notable examples are preschool and all-day kindergarten programs in elementary schools, a wider array of social and psychological services in all schools, and broader course offerings in adult education.

- *Reduced Class Sizes.* As part of an overall reform agenda, there have been efforts to reduce class sizes, especially in the primary grades. Dropping mean enrollment in first grade from 26 to 18, for example, creates an immediate need for additional classrooms (Sylvester, 1988).

- *Introduction of New Technologies.* The infusion of technology also requires space. For example, when computers were first introduced into schools, there were no accommodations for labs, and most classrooms were too small to place four or five computers in them. Likewise, schools wanting to engage in distance learning have had to develop classrooms suited for this purpose.

- *Closing a School.* At times, additions are necessary in districts with declining enrollment. For example, an elementary school is closed and the attendance boundaries are redrawn. This may necessitate enlarging the surviving schools to accommodate the added enrollment.

Adding Space Through Conventional Construction

The customary response to the need for more space is to place an addition on an existing school by using conventional construction. This process is less complicated when a building has been designed for expansion. Additions to existing buildings may be either vertical (e.g., adding a level) or horizontal (adding a new wing); however, not all buildings can accommodate both options.

Some administrators make the mistake of not planning sufficiently for this type of construction. Any project requiring architectural services should follow the planning procedures outlined earlier in this book. In particular, administrators should not make the mistake of ignoring educational specifications. Such specifications should detail the programs and instructional processes associated with the new spaces; and, therefore, they should determine the addition's design features.

Often school officials are hesitant to recommend building additions because the duration of the factors generating the need is unknown. For instance, a school district may be experiencing an increase in elementary school enrollment, but there are differences of opinion as to whether this is an anomaly or a long-term trend. Especially in districts with fluid demographic conditions, superintendents have difficulty determining how long the enrollment increase may last. Migration patterns may be driven by relatively unstable economic conditions, such as mortgage interest rates or gasoline prices.

Congruity with the existing facility is an important consideration for conventional construction. This includes matching the exterior and making decisions about mechanical operations (e.g., heating, ventilation, and air-conditioning). Some states will not permit additions unless the entire building is brought up to current building codes. Even when this requirement is not present, administrators should consider the life span of the addition in conjunction with the life span of the remaining portions of the building.

Adding Space with Portable Classrooms

Faced with uncertainty about future enrollment, administrators may prefer to add space by purchasing or leasing temporary classrooms. These structures, referred to as portable classrooms, are typically placed on the site adjacent to the school building. Portable classrooms may have one or two single-occupancy restrooms.

The use of portable classrooms has increased markedly in this country over the past 25 years. The primary reasons have been the development of new programs requiring space and enrollment growth, particularly in warmer climate states. In Florida alone, for example, it is estimated that approximately 25,000 portable classrooms were being used in the late 1990s (Callahan, Parker, Sherwin, & Anello, 1999); in California, it is estimated that over two million students attend school in them (Ross & Walker, 1999).

Portable classrooms are used for various reasons.

- *Rapid Enrollment Growth.* Some districts are growing so fast that they are forced to use portables until additions to existing schools or new schools are constructed (Kennedy, 1999a).
- *Refusals or Inability to Fund Construction.* In some communities, administrators are forced to use portables because they are unable to pass referenda or secure construction funds from the state.
- *Management Philosophy.* Some districts have decided to use portables as a long-term solution to space problems. This decision is driven primarily by the belief that portables are less expensive than conventional construction.

Using portable classrooms for prolonged periods of time has been a controversial issue among school facility administrators and others. Some critics argue that portable classrooms do not provide the same level of health and safety found in properly designed conventional buildings. Although chemicals found in portables are similar to those found in conventional schools, a combination of tighter construction, fewer windows, and inadequate ventilation is thought to create air-quality problems (Ross & Walker, 1999). Other critics point out that although initial costs for portables are lower, long-term costs may actually be higher. Fickes (1998), for instance, argued that higher operating costs and more rapid deterioration make portable classrooms a poorer economic option when they are used for more than a few years. A third criticism is that these structures detract from a school's aesthetics qualities.

Manufacturers of portable classrooms and other proponents have responded to these criticisms by suggesting that the product provides multiple benefits. The purported advantages include

- *Cost.* They believe that portables are a low-cost option to permanent construction.
- *Size Variability.* Because portables are manufactured in different sizes, districts can select one that meets their specific needs.
- *Resale Value.* If school district officials opt for permanent construction or if added space is no longer needed, portables have a good resale value.
- *Flexibility.* The structures can be used for different instructional programs (e.g., elementary classroom, art room).
- *Low Maintenance.* Compared to traditional classrooms, portables typically require less maintenance (Sylvester, 1988).

Administrators contemplating using portable classrooms for more than four or five years should carefully consider the arguments for and against them.

Once a decision has been made to use portable classrooms, administrators should concern themselves with two other issues: deciding how the structures will be used and deciding how they will be acquired (Fleming, 1997). Before deciding what size and type of portable is needed, administrators should have a clear perspective of the programs that will be delivered in these facilities.

ALTERNATIVE USE AND DISPOSAL DECISIONS

There are two reasons why district officials may decide to stop using a building as a school: obsolescence and enrollment decline. Both issues were discussed in Chapter 2. When a building ceases to be used as a school, administrators must decide whether to keep the facility. If they decide to keep it, they must either find an alternative use for the building or "place it in mothballs" with the potential of reopening it as a school if that becomes necessary in the future. Each option has advantages and disadvantages. For example, the buildings may be expensive to insure and operate; and schools that are standing idle are especially vulnerable to vandalism.

In pondering whether to retain such a building, an administrator should be guided by the following questions.

- Is additional space needed for support services?
- Does the possibility exist that enrollment will increase in the next five to 15 years?
- What will it cost to maintain and insure the building?
- What restrictions exist regarding possible uses of the building (e.g., zoning laws)?
- What is the value of the building on the open market and what is the potential for selling it?
- How much will it cost to raze the building?
- Can the building be put to better use by some other governmental agency?

Former school buildings retained by districts have been used for a variety of purposes. Some of the more common have included

- *District Administration Building.* The effectiveness of this decision depends on operational needs and ability to convert the building as needed. Occasionally, districts move administrators into these facilities without renovations or improvements. This decision often produces a whole set of new problems.
- *Adult Education Center.* This may work quite well if the adult program is large enough and the building has sufficient parking, proper furniture, and a relatively central location.
- *Preschool Center.* There are mixed views regarding this option. Many educators believe that these programs should be located in elementary schools so that pre-schoolers get acclimated to school. Additionally, the building may not be appropriate for very young children (e.g., fixtures).
- *Area Vocational School.* This option usually requires extensive renovation.

"Mothballing" can be an expensive proposition because the buildings are often subject to vandalism. In addition, costs associated with reopening a facility after it has been idle for five or more years may be substantial.

If the school district decides not to retain the property, four basic alternatives may be possible.

- *Deeding the Property to Another Governmental Agency.* This option is attractive when the building does not appear to serve any purpose for the district and its value is relatively low. In some instances, parks and recreational departments may want to assume ownership of unused schools provided they are in reasonable condition.
- *Leasing the Property.* Retaining ownership may be advantageous when the facility in question is in excellent to good condition, and there exists a possibility that the district will once again need the space.
- *Selling the Property.* Selling the building is usually the most appealing alternative; however, this option obviously does not allow the district to retain the site for possible future use.
- *Razing the Building.* This option is most attractive when the building is obsolete but the site has value.

Any disposal of property involves legal issues. For this reason, the school board's attorney should provide direction because state statutes determine which of the options may be exercised (Baldwin, 1988).

CHAPTER SUMMARY

Making major decisions about existing buildings is an important aspect of school facility management. Improvements to existing buildings can be accomplished either by modernization or by remodeling. The former involves cosmetic improvements and parts replacement; the latter involves the same improvements plus a reconfiguration of spaces as deemed necessary. Deciding whether to improve an existing building or replace it should be predicated on both quantitative and qualitative data.

Creating additional space for schools is another important responsibility. This task can be accomplished either by conventional construction or by using portable classrooms. However, the extended use of portable classrooms, especially in rapid-growth states such as California and Florida, has come under increasing criticism. Additions are often done in conjunction with remodeling, especially when it is advantageous to bring the entire facility up to current code standards. Additions should be designed on the basis of educational specifications.

Administrators also are expected to provide leadership when decisions need to be made about buildings that are no longer to be used as schools. Obsolete structures are usually razed because they have little value. Surplus schools that are not obsolete may be converted to alternative uses in the district, leased, sold, or deeded to other governmental agencies. Placing buildings in mothballs as a hedge against potential enrollment increases is usually a risky decision because potential savings may be less than the costs associated with making the building operable at some future date.

ISSUES FOR DISCUSSION

1. Discuss the differences between remodeling and modernization.
2. Under what circumstances is modernization a preferred solution?
3. What standards could be used to determine whether remodeling is preferable to building replacement?
4. What is meant by life-cycle costs?
5. In addition to enrollment increases, what might create the need for a school to have additional space?
6. Assume that a school district was going to add a wing with 12 classrooms and a set of restrooms. Is the development of educational specifications necessary? Why or why not?
7. What is the difference between vertical and horizontal expansion? What might prevent a building from accommodating either?
8. What are the advantages and disadvantages of using portable classrooms?
9. Should portable classrooms ever be a long-term solution for space needs? Why or why not?
10. What costs might be associated with razing a building?
11. What are the laws in your state regarding the disposal of surplus property?
12. What are the advantages and disadvantages of "mothballing" a school building?
13. What problems could occur if an elementary school is converted into a district administrative office without remodeling the building?

REFERENCES

Baldwin, G. (1988). Fixed assets: Disposing of property and resulting funds. *Journal of Education Finance, 13*(3), 274–289.

Callahan, M.P., Parker, D.S., Sherwin, J.R., & Anello, M.T. (1999). *Evaluation of energy efficiency improvements to portable classrooms in Florida.* Cocoa: Florida Solar Energy Center.

Carey, K.D. (2000). Renovate or replace? *The American School Board Journal, 187*(10), 36–38.

Castaldi, B. (1994). *Educational facilities* (4th ed.). Boston: Allyn and Bacon.

Council of Educational Facility Planners, International. (1978). *Surplus school space— The problem and the possibilities.* Columbus, OH: Author.

Council of Educational Facility Planners, International. (1985). *Guide for planning educational facilities.* Columbus, OH: Author.

Earthman, G.I. (1994). *School renovation handbook: Investing in education.* Lancaster, PA: Technomic Press.

Fickes, M. (1998). Balancing permanent and portable buildings. *School Business Affairs, 64*(7), 36–37.

Fickes, M. (1999). To renovate or build? *College Planning and Management, 2*(5), 22–24.

Fleming, J.A. (1997). The saga of relocatable classrooms. *School Administrator, 54*(6), 18–21.

Ginsburg, S. (1989). Caveats and cautions. *Educational Record, 70*(1), 46–48.

Hentschke, G. (1986). *School business administration: A comparative perspective.* Berkeley, CA: McCutchan.

Johnston, R.C. (1998, October 7). Administrators joining preservationists to save schools. *Education Week, 18*(6), 16, 19.

Kennedy, M. (1999a). Bursting through: How schools are meeting the enrollment explosion. *American School and University, 71*(9), 18–20, 22, 24, 26.

Kennedy, M. (1999b). Closing doors. *American School and University, 71*(11), 16–18, 20, 22.

McClelland, J. (1985). An analysis of building replacement costs. *CEFP Journal, 23*(2), 6–9.

Ross, Z.A., & Walker, B. (1999). *Reading, writing, and risk: Air pollution inside California's portable classrooms.* Washington, DC: Environmental Working Group.

Sylvester, T. (1988). Relocatable and modular classrooms: Booming business. *School Business Affairs, 54*(1), 22–27.

CHAPTER 14

Financing Facility Projects

Planning for and managing indebtedness are two of the more challenging responsibilities assumed by school administrators. Large sums of money are involved; accountability is high; state laws for financing debt vary markedly; and many superintendents have had only limited experience with these tasks. Moreover, the effectiveness of administrative decisions is partially determined by extraneous variables, such as fluctuating interest rates, changes in tax laws, the political environments in states and local districts, and escalating construction costs.

This chapter provides a general overview of finance issues related to school construction. Included are a brief history and a discussion of funding sources. In the past, the greatest portion of funding has come from local property tax revenues; however, this is very likely to change in the future. Faced with the daunting task of repairing or replacing half of the existing school buildings in the country, policy makers are seeking ways to increase federal, state, and private funding. This chapter also covers funding strategies and other management responsibilities involving fiscal management.

HISTORICAL PERSPECTIVES

From its inception, the American public education system has been guided by a handful of values. Two of them, liberty and equality, are continuously in conflict. This is because movement toward local district independence almost always produces inequities, as wealthy districts spend more money on education. Conversely, strengthening equality of educational opportunity requires more centralized (or state) control—a condition that unavoidably lessens liberty (Swanson & King, 1997).

Although it is politically popular to allow local districts to control school construction decisions, unbridled freedom could result in economic and legal problems for state governments; for example, states may be held accountable for debt obligations if local districts default on their payments. In addition, citizens may challenge state finance systems that do not appear to provide reasonably equal access to educational opportunities across all districts. Ever since the landmark case *Serrano v. Priest I* (1971), in California, there have been repeated equity challenges to state finance systems. Such lawsuits have addressed two concepts.

- *Horizontal equity*—the equal treatment of equals based on the concept that every child in a state should receive the same amount of funding and resources
- *Vertical equity*—the unequal treatment of unequals based on the concept that there are rational reasons why some students need more state funding than others (Crampton & Whitney, 1996)

Over time, three tests have been used to determine whether resources were impartially provided for students and taxpayers.

- *Resource accessibility*—the equal availability of state funds, typically achieved when average practice or estimated needs are fully funded (Thompson, Stewart, & Honeyman, 1989)
- *Ex post fiscal neutrality*—the elimination of positive linkages between wealth and residence so that differences in pupil spending are attributed to choice rather than the adequacy of a local district's tax base; achieved when states neutralize the effect of local wealth (i.e., taxable property) on funding educational needs (Sielke, 1998)
- *Ex ante fiscal neutrality*—providing an equal yield for equal effort; achieved when districts levy uniform taxes and receive sufficient funding for average practice or estimated needs without regard for local district wealth (Sielke, 1998)

Without state intervention, the amount of money generated and spent for education is dependent on the amount of taxable property in a district and the rate at which taxes are paid in a district. More succinctly, total liberty heavily favors wealthy districts.

Historically, school construction funding has been totally or primarily dependent on property tax revenues. As a result, many states gave local district taxpayers the power to approve or prevent indebtedness resulting from construction (e.g., mandatory referenda for tax increases and remonstrance procedures). Where such power was granted, school construction decisions required two approvals at the local level: board approval and taxpayer approval. Until the early 1980s, the courts had not treated school facilities as a relevant issue in determining equal educational access; instead judges focused almost entirely on operating budgets. This practice changed in 1982 when the West Virginia Supreme Court in the case of *Pauley v. Bailey* broadened the judicial interpretation of equal educational opportunity to intentionally include facilities (Thompson, Wood, & Honeyman, 1994). Subsequently, three other state supreme courts also ruled that inequities in school facilities were relevant to determining the constitutionality of finance statutes—Tennessee: *Tennessee Small School Systems v. McWerter* (1993); Arizona: *Roosevelt Elementary School District 66 v. Bishop* (1994); and Ohio: *DeRolph v. State* (1997).

National reports identifying the need to replace or remodel approximately half of the nation's public elementary and secondary schools may have affected the decision to broaden judicial interpretations of equal educational opportunities. In addition, the courts may have been influenced by growing evidence of a nexus between district wealth and the quality of school facilities (e.g., Thompson & Camp, 1988). In any event, challenges to state finance schemes are increasingly likely to address inequities in school buildings—and this is especially true in states where most or all of the funding for school construction comes from local property tax revenues (Kowalski & Schiemlau, 2000).

While policy makers generally acknowledge that current laws for funding school construction have contributed to the sorry state of America's public school infrastructure, they disagree about a solution. Those who emphasize equality of educational opportunity prefer more centralized funding paradigms— for example, federal funding or total state funding. Those who emphasize local control believe that federal and state funding should be limited and provided without specific restrictions on local control (e.g., provided as block grants). This philosophical division is long-standing and largely responsible for vast differences that still exist among the 50 states with respect to school construction funding (Kowalski & Schmielau, 2000).

FUNDING SOURCES

Funds to support school construction come from many sources. In addition to federal, state, and local revenues, districts might obtain resources through private grants and donations. However, the vast majority of dollars come from just two sources: state aid and local property tax revenues.

Federal Funding

Historically, the federal government has played a minor role in supporting school construction. Most federal dollars designated for this purpose have been directed to state departments of education and not to local districts. State officials have then channeled the money to local districts via incentive programs designed to encourage and assist the development of special projects, such as vocational education. In 1941, for example, Congress passed the Impacted Aid Program of the Landrum Act. This legislation continues to provide assistance to local districts enrolling children of federal employees, including military personnel. Overall, however, total federal dollars used to support school construction have been minuscule.

During the 1990s, several attempts were made to provide massive federal funding, especially to large urban districts, to replace or remodel outdated school buildings. Advocates for more federal funding cite one or more of the following justifications for their position.

- There are considerable differences among the states with regard to ability to pay for school construction. Federal involvement would constitute a form of equalization that would help neutralize inequities in taxable wealth.

- The deteriorated condition of America's public schools (approximately half need to be renovated or replaced) constitutes a serious risk to the country's welfare. In the current age of information, all students need to receive a relevant education that prepares them to be productive citizens.

- Current state policies for funding school construction are contributing to rather than resolving the current facility crisis. In essence, states are unwilling to take the action necessary to repair or replace unsafe and inappropriate buildings.

- Federal support would help move construction funding away from a dependency on property tax. The tax is not a good source for funding because it is inequitable and unpopular (Guthrie, 1988; Quindry, 1979).

One difficulty inherent to any discussion of a greater role for the federal government in financing capital outlay is the realization that federal aid to education is a perennially unpopular topic among most educators and taxpayers. There is, to be sure, a mind-set that federal assistance always comes with strings attached. This condition creates an approach–avoidance situation for many superintendents and board members. They want the money, but they fear the potential of greater federal control. From political and legal perspectives, liberty-based arguments are even more disconcerting. Opponents of federal aid believe that public education, including school construction, is a state responsibility.

State Funding

The aftermath of landmark legal decisions regarding fiscal equality is a virtual smorgasbord of state school finance plans. Not surprisingly, these varying formulas include an assortment of plans for funding capital outlay. Some states have adopted plans for funding school construction that place a greater share of the burden on state revenues. Other states have maintained programs that require local districts to rely entirely on local taxes.

A 1999 study (Kowalski & Schiemlau, 2000) examining the potential of states to achieve equality for funding school construction found considerable variance. States with the potential of providing less than 35 percent of the cost share were placed in the low category; states with the potential of providing between 35 percent and 70 percent were placed in the moderate category; states with the potential of providing more than 70 percent were placed in the high category.

- *Low Potential for Achieving Equality.* There were 18 states (36 percent) in this group; seven states provided no state support (Colorado, Iowa, Louisiana, Missouri, Oklahoma, Oregon, and South Dakota).
- *Moderate Potential for Achieving Equality.* There were 12 states (24 percent) in this category.
- *High Potential for Achieving Equality.* There were 20 states (40 percent) in this category; only two states, Arizona and Hawaii, provided 100 percent state funding.

Only one state, Hawaii, was found to rank low in liberty, and this was expected because it is the only state without local districts.

Although total state funding would appear to be the ideal alternative with respect to ensuring equal educational opportunity, two considerations often reduce its attractiveness. First, full state funding can be very expensive, especially in states with rapid population growth. The state of Florida, for example, experimented with full state funding but retreated in light of costs. Second, full state funding often results in total state control over construction (e.g., determining need, priorities, architects, design).The potential loss of liberty makes the alternative politically unacceptable to many citizens (Guthrie, Garms, & Pierce, 1988).

States may make funds available to support local district construction in the following ways.

- *Low interest loans*—usually provided with interest rates below current market standards for municipal bonds
- *Flat grants*—state funds based on a common criterion (e.g., dollars per pupil)
- *Matching grants*—state funds provided through a proportional match to local contribution
- *Equalization grants*—state funds provided in an inverse relationship to district wealth (i.e., poor districts receive more aid than do wealthy districts) or through a guaranteed yield program (i.e., state guarantees an equal yield for fiscal effort)
- *Planning and categorical grants*—state funds provided to support needs assessment, feasibility studies, or specific categories of expenditures (e.g., technology grants)

In some states there is no discernible relationship between state funding and state control; that is, some states provide little or no support for school construction, yet there is a high level of state control over construction decisions. The most common examples of state controls include state health and safety codes, rules and regulations for spaces and building design, statutory limitations on indebtedness, and statutory limitations on tax rates or levies.

Superintendents and other administrators involved in making debt-management decisions need to know and understand the laws in their state pertaining to financing school construction. This is especially important because vast differences exist from state to state, and state laws, policies, and rules are constantly being modified.

Local Funding

The basic economics of generating local funds for education via the property tax is not as complicated as most believe. Two factors, property values and tax rates, determine how much revenue is generated. This is illustrated by the following formula.

$$AV \times TR = TL$$

Where:

AV = assessed valuation

TR = tax rate

TL = tax levy (amount raised)

Inequities exist when districts must raise most or all of the revenue for school construction from the local property tax. Consider the following example of two Indiana districts. Both needed to raise $500,000 per year to pay for debt on school construction. The first district had an assessed valuation of $300 million and the second had an assessed valuation of $100 million. Since Indiana calculates its tax rates in dollars and cents, not mills, the assessed valuation is divided by 100. The calculations below show that District B had to tax itself at a rate three times higher than District A. Since the assessed valuation and tax levy are known, the necessary tax rate is calculated using this formula: (AV/100) / TL = TR.

District A $500,000 / $3,000,000 = $0.1667

District B $500,000 / $1,000,000 = $0.5000

This example illustrates that because District A has three times as much assessed valuation as district B, the tax rate needed to generate the $500,000 for annual debt payments is only one-third of the tax rate needed in District B.

Even though assessed valuation determines the property tax rate necessary for debt service payments, it is inappropriate to compare district wealth using this statistic alone. Districts vary in enrollment, and, therefore, the more appropriate comparability statistic is assessed valuation per pupil. This figure is determined by dividing the assessed valuation by the district enrollment. States stipulate which enrollment statistic (e.g., average daily membership) must be used, and the quotient represents the amount of assessed valuation supporting each of the district's students. Thus, in states requiring local districts to fund all or most of the cost of capital outlay through local property tax revenues, inequities are inevitable.

Approximately 40 percent of the states still rank low in their potential to achieve equality. The cause of this problem is an intricate mix of three conditions.

1. Legislators and governors in some states have been unwilling to transfer the burden for financing school construction from local districts to state government because such a decision would probably require an increase in state taxes (largely a political fear).

2. Legislators and governors in some states have been unwilling to transfer the burden from local districts to state government because they may not be able to raise sufficient tax revenues to fund such a program (largely an economic fear).

3. Some local board members and taxpayers view fiscal ability inequities as less of a problem than increased state control.

The legal and political winds surrounding school funding are, however, shifting. Decisions for lawsuits in four states over the past two decades have established school facilities as a legitimate equity issue; and therefore, laws for financing school construction probably will be challenged in other states.

Other Revenue Sources

Some school districts have turned to fund-raising as a means of generating added revenues. This usually is accomplished by creating a tax-exempt organization (called a foundation) and soliciting donations and gifts from private citizens, businesses, and charitable trusts. Other possible sources of revenue have included user fees and fund-raisers (Pijanowski & Monk, 1996). With a few exceptions in select local districts, such actions have not had an appreciable effect on construction funding.

On occasion, school districts have used the proceeds from the sale of excess property for funding construction. For example, district officials may have purchased land in the past anticipating the need to build a school on the site. Over the years, the land has grown in value and the site is no longer considered appropriate for a school. The property is sold and the proceeds are placed in a building fund. Such transactions may not be permisssable in some states.

There also have been incidents in which a single donor has given a considerable amount of money to fund a specific project. However, these types of gifts, have been far more common for private elementary and secondary schools than they have for public schools.

FUNDING STRATEGIES

Over the years, several different school-funding strategies have emerged. They have evolved in relation to the economy, legal frameworks, and political conditions. Thus, some of them are rarely used in current practice.

Pay-As-You-Go Financing

Historically, the pay-as-you-go method of financing schools was a popular alternative during the first half of the 20th century. Advocates of this idea argued that districts should avoid debt because interest payments were an inefficient use of tax revenues. To accomplish this, districts had to accumulate the needed amount by siphoning portions of operating and reserve funds or by levying a tax for future building programs. Some states, for example, permitted local districts to levy a tax for cumulative building funds. Both the fund's principal and interest earnings could be used to pay for school construction once the assets were sufficient. The pay-as-you-go method was largely supported on the following grounds.

- The question as to whether the taxpayers could meet their obligation to pay for a building was eliminated.
- The potential for defaulting on a debt obligation was eliminated.
- No bond sale was necessary, so the district saved costs associated with that transaction.
- The option provided the best economic alternative because interest was earned rather than paid.

The pay-as-you-go method fell out of favor for several reasons.

- Some taxpayers feared that administrators and board members would misuse cumulative building funds. For example, they might raise revenues without an intention of building a school and use interest earned from the fund's assets as they wished.
- Escalating building costs made it difficult for many small and low-wealth districts to save enough money to avoid debt.

Despite these concerns, Carey (2000) argued that many school boards are showing renewed interest in this option. The key may be accumulating funds from a source other than the property tax. Georgia, for example, enacted a law in 1996, called the Educational Local Option Sales Tax, allowing local districts to levy a one-cent tax for a pay-as-you-go system of construction finance (Jacobson, 1998).

Bonding

For the majority of public school districts, long-term borrowing is the forced choice for funding school construction. Critics may be quick to attack long-term obligations as being costly; yet, the process is defended on the grounds that the debt is spread across several generations of taxpayers (Guthrie et al., 1988). This philosophy posits that those directly benefiting from a facility should share the obligation of paying for it.

The sale of tax-free bonds is the common approach to long-term borrowing used by local districts. A bond (or note) is a security whereby the issuer agrees to pay a fixed principal sum on a specified date and at a specified rate of interest. The specified date is referred to as the maturity date. Most bonds are sold through a process of competitive bidding and come under the scrutiny of underwriters and investor analysts. Bonds issued by state or local governmental agencies, including school districts, are called municipal bonds.

In some states bond banks have been established to aid in the sale of tax-exempt bonds. The underlying concept is to achieve more favorable interest rates by pooling several issues. The process also may result in a reduction of expenses, since local districts do not have to pay for bond attorneys or financial consultants. Such bond banks may be either mandatory (meaning that local districts must sell bonds through the state bank) or voluntary (meaning that local districts can choose between using the state bank or selling the bonds independently). Districts with low bond ratings obviously are more likely to benefit most from using a state bond bank, since the bond rating is assigned for the state rather than for the district.

General obligation bonds (called GO bonds) are used to finance a good portion of the school construction in this country. A GO bond is secured by a pledge of the issuer's taxing powers; and since local districts are extensions of state government, many bond buyers consider them to be solid investments. Some states have statutory limits on the amount of debt a school district can incur via GO bonds as a means of protecting state government against defaults. For example, several states limit the amount of GO bonds issued by any governmental agency to 2 percent of the agency's assessed valuation.

In a vast majority of states, school districts are required to hold a referendum prior to conducting a bond sale. Most states require a simple majority approval to go forward with the sale; however, about 25 percent of the states require more than a simple majority vote. Ever since the so-called "taxpayers revolt" in California in the 1970s, referenda have been major hurdles for school systems pursuing facility projects. In many districts less than 20 percent of the taxpayers have children enrolled in elementary and secondary schools, and this condition makes it exceedingly difficult to get political support for substantial tax increases.

Once a local district has the authority to move forward with a bond sale, a marketing strategy needs to be established. Most municipal bonds are sold on the open market in order to encourage competition. In select instances, it may be advantageous for a school district to pursue a negotiated sale (if permitted by state law). Opting for a negotiated sale over competitive bidding is a decision requiring counsel from both attorneys and financial consultants.

There are several different classifications of bonds. Among the more prevalent are the following:

- *Callable Bond.* This is a bond that can be recalled by the issuer and paid prior to maturity. The advantage is that the issuer (the school district) can take advantage of more favorable interest rates during the payback period. The process of *paying* the investors prior to maturity is commonly referred to as advanced refunding. Callable bonds create uncertainty for the bond buyer because the length of the investment and the total earnings are not guaranteed. Federal tax laws may restrict advanced refunding, therefore, legal analysis is necessary.
- *Coupon Bond.* Some bonds are sold with detachable coupons. These coupons provide evidence that interest is due. At the specified time, the coupon is detached and submitted to the issuer for payment of interest.
- *Registered Bond.* The owner is registered with the issuing agent (or its bank or trustee agent), and the bond cannot be sold or exchanged without a change of registration. Such a bond may be registered as to principal and interest or as to principal only.
- *Serial Bond.* This bond's principal is repaid in periodic installments over the life of the issue rather than in one lump sum at the end of the term.
- *Term Bond.* This bond's entire principal is paid at a specified time, even though interest payments are made periodically during the life of the bond.

Using competitive bids in an open market to sell bonds is intended to produce the most favorable interest rates possible. Interest rates may be affected either positively or negatively by five primary factors.

- *Bond rating*
- *Bond issue size* (total dollar amount)
- *Bond issue term* (duration of the debt obligation)
- *Bond issue type* (e.g., callable, term)
- *Economic conditions at the time of the sale* (e.g., inflation rates, prime interest rates)

Administrators should request that financial advisers provide an analysis of these factors in relation to the proposed timing of the bond sale. The purpose should be to maximize the probability of securing favorable interest rates.

Highly respected investment firms assign bond ratings prior to public sales. Bond ratings may affect both competition and interest rates. Bonds with high ratings, for example, generally have lower interest rates than bonds with low ratings. The two major rating firms are Moody's Investment Service and Standard & Poor's. Each firm has a rating system. Basically the ratings reflect economic and administrative qualities of the issuing school district, the community environment, current debt obligations, debt structure, wealth, the quantity and quality of industry within the school district's taxing region, debt history, and the current condition of school properties. Bond ratings and their criteria used by Moody's and Standard & Poor's are as follows:

Moody's Investment Service

Aaa   These bonds are judged to be of the best quality. They carry the smallest degree of investment risk and are generally referred to as "gilt edged." Interest payments are protected by a large or an exceptionally stable margin; principal is secure. While the various protective elements may change, such changes are most unlikely to impair the fundamentally strong position of the issues.

Aa   These bonds are judged to be of high quality by all standards. Together with the Aaa group they comprise the category of high grade bonds. They are rated lower than the best bonds because margins of protection may not be as large as in Aaa securities or fluctuation of protective elements may be of greater amplitude or there may be other elements present which make the long-term risk appear somewhat larger than the Aaa securities.

A   These bonds possess many favorable investment attributes and are considered as upper-medium-grade obligations. Factors giving security to principal and interest are considered adequate, but elements may be present which suggest a susceptibility to impairment some time in the future.

Baa   These bonds are considered as medium-grade obligations (i.e., they are neither highly protected [nor] poorly secured). Interest payments and principal security appear adequate for the present, but certain protective elements may be lacking or may be characteristically unreliable over any great length of time. Such bonds lack outstanding investment characteristics and in fact have speculative characteristics as well.

Ba   These bonds are judged to have speculative elements; their future cannot be considered as well-assured. Often the protection of interest and principal payments may be very moderate, and thereby not well safeguarded during both good and bad times over the future. Uncertainty of position characterizes bonds in this class.

B   These bonds generally lack characteristics of the desirable investment. Assurance of interest and principal payments of maintenance of other terms of the contract over any long period of time may be small.

Caa   These bonds are of poor standing. Such issues may be in default or there may be present elements of danger with respect to principal or interest.

Ca   These bonds represent obligations that are speculative in a high degree. Such issues are often in default or have other marked shortcomings.

C   These bonds are the lowest rated class of bonds, and issues so rated can be regarded as having extremely poor prospects of ever attaining any real investment standing.

Source: Moody's Bond Record (1999).

Standard & Poor's

AAA   These bonds have the highest rating assigned by Standard & Poor's. The obligor's capacity to meet its financial commitment on the obligation is extremely strong.

AA   These bonds differ from the highest-rated obligations only in small degree. The obligor's capacity to meet its financial commitment on the obligation is very strong.

A   These bonds are somewhat more susceptible to the adverse effects of changes in circumstances and economic conditions than obligations in higher-rated categories. However, the obligor's capacity to meet its financial commitment on the obligation is still strong.

BBB   These bonds exhibit adequate protection parameters. However, adverse economic conditions or changing circumstances are more likely to lead to a weakened capacity of the obligor to meet its financial commitment on the obligation.

    Obligations rated below BBB are regarded as having significant speculative characteristics. These ratings range from BB to D. In addition, a plus (+) or minus (−) may be added to any rating to show relative standing within the major rating categories.

Source: http://www.standardandpoors.com/ratings/publicfinance/index.htm.

Investors are attracted to school bonds because they are usually exempt from taxation. The Tax Reform Act of 1986, which replaced the Internal Revenue Code of 1954, established new parameters for tax-free bonds. The 1986 act is more stringent with regard to arbitrage, that is, benefiting from the interest rate differential between the rate on a municipal bond and the yield made with the investment of the bond proceeds. If criteria established in the 1986 act are not met, a district's bonds could become taxable retroactively.

All information pertaining to the bond sale is presented in a prospectus. This document is designed to inform and attract potential buyers. A financial consultant familiar with the needs and interests of potential bond buyers usually prepares it. Administrators typically supply information for the prospectus and check the document's accuracy before it is made available to the public.

Lease-Purchase Agreements

As mentioned earlier, some states impose limitations on debt obligations for school districts. The concept of lease–purchase emerged as a means to circumventing such limitations. The process basically entails a school being erected (or remodeled) by a legal entity other than the school district. The school district then pays the owner rental payments that are equal to the annual debt obligation; the rental payments are also purchase payments (Demers, 1989). At the end of the payment period, the school district assumes complete ownership of the building.

States permitting lease–purchase agreements stipulate whether such agreements can be executed with both public and private holding corporations (or holding authorities). With a public holding corporation (i.e., a not-for-profit organization), a bond sale must be executed to generate necessary funds. This is because the corporation is formed solely for the purpose of building a school; thus, the corporation has no assets. When a public holding corporation and a district sell bonds, the bond attorney's opinion on the lease agreement is critically important because the opinion addresses the tax-exempt status of the bonds. If a private holding corporation (i.e., a for-profit organization) is used, no bond sale is necessary because the corporation uses its assets to pay for construction. There are differing opinions as to which alternative is more efficient and economical for local districts. Whereas private corporations save costs associated with bond sales, public corporations typically produce lower interest rates. Again, careful analysis involving a bond attorney and a financial consultant is warranted before choosing between private and public holding corporations.

OTHER MANAGEMENT RESPONSIBILITIES

Regardless of whether a school district sells bonds or enters into a lease–purchase arrangement, administrators must have a plan to retire the debt. It should be based on sources of revenue and determined debt retirement parameters. With regard to acquiring local property tax revenues, the school district usually establishes a sinking fund or debt-service fund—an account that includes moneys accumulated for the specific purpose of making debt payments.

Business managers must know how much will be required to make semiannual or annual debt payments. This information is found in an amortization schedule—a document showing the amount of principal and interest to be paid each year for the debt obligation's duration. If a district has more than one outstanding debt, the required tax levy for the debt-service fund is determined by adding the separate amounts from the amortization schedules for each debt obligation. An example of an amortization schedule is presented in Table 14–1, showing how interest payments decline and principal payments increase throughout the life of a bond issue. Yet, the annual total debt payments remain relatively stable. Data in Figure 14–1 further illustrate what the cost associated with interest payments can be (in this example, interest payback is about 250 percent of the principal).

In addition to projected tax revenues, a debt-management plan also should contain the following information.

- Other sources of revenue (e.g., loans, state aid)
- Dates on which financial transactions must occur
- Amortization schedules for any loans other than the bond issue (e.g., state loans)
- A list of agencies and officials involved (e.g., paying agent, insurance agent)

Table 14–1
Sample Bond Amortization Schedule

Amount: $9,995,000.00
Term: 25 years, 9 months
Interest Rate: 8.5%

Bond year Ending Jan.1	Principal balance (000)	Principal payment (000)	Interest payment (000)	Total payment (000)
1998	$9,995		$ 618,441	$ 618,441
1999	9,995		824,588	824,588
2000	9,820	$ 175	824,588	999,588
2001	9,635	185	810,150	995,150
2002	9,435	200	794,888	994,888
2003	9,225	210	778,387	988,387
2004	9,000	225	761,063	986,063
2005	8,760	240	742,500	982,500
2006	8,505	255	722,700	977,700
.	.	.	.	.
.	.	.	.	.
.	.	.	.	.
2021	1,580	715	189,337	904,337
2022	815	765	130,350	895,350
2023		815	67,238	882,238
Totals		$9,995	$14,313,853	$24,308,853

Because a debt may be repaid over many years, the plan should be written so that changes in personnel will not affect its execution. This requires the planners to provide clarity and completeness of information.

While some districts direct the architect to specify all equipment and furniture, other districts delegate this task to the administrator. If the latter option is chosen, the administrator must specify the items, develop a process for their purchase, and build a budget for this purpose. In larger projects, this can be quite time-consuming.

Budgeting adequately for operations is another fiscal responsibility associated with school construction. While new or renovated buildings are often more cost-efficient per square foot, they almost always increase the number of square feet. Thus, the overall utility costs for a school are likely to increase. Not estimating utility costs and budgeting appropriately can result in a serious revenue shortfall. One district, for example, replaced its existing high school with a building that was 45 percent larger. In addition, the new building used only electricity, whereas the old building burned fuel oil. The budget for utilities was only increased by 4 percent to account for inflation. When the new high school opened, the higher utility costs resulted in a $1.5 million deficit in the first year of operation.

Risk management is another task related to managing debt. Schools should be protected against loss due to fire, tornadoes, and the like. Coverage also is needed for the contents of the school. Most administrators readily realize that property insurance is standard. Less obvious are special insurance policies related to construction, construction contracts, and debt financing. In concert with the architect and other professional resource personnel, a comprehensive insurance document should be completed for a facility project. This document details all the insurance policies obtained for various phases of the project.

CHAPTER SUMMARY

Replacing or improving half of America's elementary and secondary schools requires massive funding efforts. Historically, local districts have had to rely heavily or entirely on local property tax revenues to cover these costs. At the same time, states have commonly given taxpayers considerable authority with regard to approving tax increases. Collectively, these policies have contributed to serious inequities among local districts. Over the past 15 years, there are growing indications that the courts are likely to view schoolhouses as relevant to determining whether state financial schemes provide reasonably equal access to educational opportunities.

This chapter also examined potential sources of funding for school construction; financing options and debt management issues were discussed. Because laws vary considerably across the states, administrators need to be aware of current policies for financing capital outlay, and they must work closely with attorneys and financial consultants to structure and manage debt obligations.

ISSUES FOR DISCUSSION

1. What are the advantages and disadvantages of having a full state funding program for capital outlay?

2. Why are liberty and equality almost always in conflict with each other?

3. What are the advantages and disadvantages of the pay-as-you-go method for financing school construction?

4. What are the arguments for and against federal support for school construction?

5. Why do callable bonds usually have a higher interest rate than [noncallable] bonds?

6. Does your state permit lease–purchase agreements? If so, may such agreements be executed with both public and private holding corporations?

7. What is a general obligation (GO) bond? Why do many states place limits on the amount of indebtedness local districts can incur using GO bonds?

8. What is a bond rating? Who issues a bond rating? Why is it important?

9. What are the primary variables that may affect bond interest rates?

10. Define the concept of arbitrage. Are districts in your state permitted to engage in arbitrage?

11. List the advantages and disadvantages of incorporating all equipment and furniture into the total cost of a project (thus including these items in the bidding process for the project).

12. What is an amortization schedule? What purpose does it serve?

13. How does total or near-total local funding contribute to inequities in school facilities?

REFERENCES

Carey, K.D. (2000). Pay as you go: A better way of funding school construction. *The American School Board Journal, 187*(6), 44–46.

Crampton, F., & Whitney, T. (1996). The search for equity in school funding. *NCSL Education Partners Project*. Denver, CO: National Conference of State Legislatures.

Demers, D. (1989). Lease/purchase: A viable alternative for financing schools. *School Business Affairs, 55*(1), 21–27.

DeRolph v. State, 78 Ohio St. 3d 193 (Oh. 1997).

Guthrie, J. (1988). Educational finance: The lower schools. In N. Boyan (Ed.), *Handbook of Research on Educational Administration* (pp. 373–389). New York: Longman.

Guthrie, J., Garms, W., & Pierce, L. (1988). *School finance and education policy* (2nd ed.). Englewood Cliffs, NJ: Prentice-Hall.

Jacobson, L. (1998). Georgia schools tap new source for construction. *Education Week, 17*(38) 13–14.

Kowalski, T.J., & Schmielau, R. (2000, April). *Potential for achieving liberty and equality in funding school construction: Analysis of state laws and policies for financing capital outlay*. Paper presented at the annual conference of the American Educational Research Association, New Orleans, LA.

Moody's Investment Service. (1999). *Moody's bond record*. New York: Author.

Pauley v. Bailey, 324 S.E. 2d 128 (W.V. 1984).

Pijanowski, J.C., & Monk, D.H. (1996). Alternative school revenue sources: There are many fish in the sea. *School Business Affairs, 62*(7), 4–6, 8–10.

Quindry, K. (1979). The state–local tax picture. *Journal of Education Finance, 5*(1), 19–35.

Roosevelt Elementary School District 66 v. Bishop, 179 Ariz. 233, 877 P. 2d 806 (Ariz. 1994).

Serrano v. Priest, I. 487 P. 2d 1241 (Calif. 1971).

Sielke, C.C. (1998). Michigan school facilities, equity, issues, and voter response to bond issues following finance reform. *Journal of Education Finance, 23*, 309–322.

Standard & Poors. (2000). Standard & Poors bond ratings. [On-line]. Available: http://www.standardandpoors.com/ratings/publicfinance/index.htm.

Swanson, A.D., & King, R.A. (1997). *School finance: Its economics and politics* (2nd ed.). New York: Longman.

Tennessee Small School Systems v. McWerter, 851 S.W. 2d 139 (Tenn. 1993).

Thompson, D., & Camp, W. (1988). Analysis of equity in capital outlay funding mechanisms in Kansas. *Journal of Education Finance, 13*(3), 253–263.

Thompson, D.C., Stewart, G.K., & Honeyman, D.S. (1989). *Achievement of equity in capital outlay financing: A policy analysis for the states*. Charleston, WV: ERIC

Clearinghouse on Rural and Small Schools. (ERIC Document Reproduction Service No. ED 314 224)

Thompson, D.C., Wood, R.C., & Honeyman, D.S. (1994). *Fiscal leadership for schools: Concepts and practices*. New York: Longman.

CHAPTER 15

Maintaining School Facilities

Superintendents, other central office administrators, and principals spend far more time managing school facilities than they do planning for their construction. Ensuring that multimillion dollar investments are properly maintained and safe is no simple task, even in very small districts, and this challenge has become increasingly difficult because approximately one-third of schoolhouses in use have already exceeded their life expectancy. Today, maintenance specialists and even building custodians are expected to have many diverse skills so that they can meet the increasingly technical dimensions of their jobs. Just consider how much time administrators must devote to employing, training, supervising, and evaluating these employees.

This chapter addresses major contemporary tasks associated with facility management. Clearly the most evident and time-consuming are general maintenance and custodial services. In addition to discussing these functions, the concept of outsourcing and a principal's responsibility for building management are discussed.

MAINTENANCE SERVICES

Maintenance is generally defined as those actions intended to keep a building in relatively good condition and functioning properly. Often the term is used generically to include both custodial and maintenance services; however, these functions are treated here as separate topics.

Types of Maintenance

The term "maintenance" is used in varying contexts. Some writers distinguish between long-term and short-term maintenance; others differentiate between planned and unplanned maintenance. Four maintenance terms are widely used in conjunction with educational facilities.

- *Preventive maintenance*—a proactive concept that utilizes scheduled inspections and interventions (e.g., cleaning, parts replacement) intended to keep the facility operational according to design and manufacturer specifications.
- *Repair maintenance*—the unplanned repair or adjustment of equipment or components made necessary by obsolescence, malfunctions, or damage.
- *Deferred maintenance*—necessary care and improvements that are not completed, usually because of insufficient resources or inadequate management.
- *Valet maintenance*—a term used to describe improvements done by request of school officials (e.g., repainting classrooms, installing new carpeting in the principal's office).

Preventive maintenance is the ideal; however, it has not been implemented in many districts. The failure to provide preventive maintenance inevitably leads to problems. The three primary negative outcomes are

- *Disruption to School Operations*. When schools must be closed because of mechanical failures, instructional time is lost and students suffer.
- *Costly Emergency Repairs*. When a building's systems are not serviced regularly, they are much more likely to be taxed beyond their tolerance limits. When mechanical systems and equipment break, repairs are expensive. The district must secure parts or replacement equipment immediately; thus, competitive bidding or other cost-effective procurement methods cannot be used. In addition, emergency repairs usually require employees to work overtime resulting in added personnel costs.
- *Deferred Maintenance*. Districts typically do not use preventive maintenance because administrators decide they do not have sufficient resources. Such a decision almost ensures that needed repairs will be deferred—an action that has a cumulative negative effect on a district's infrastructure.

Given these possibilities, more enlightened administrators and school board members are treating preventive maintenance as an investment. More precisely, they are abandoning the practice of viewing maintenance costs solely in the context of annual operating budgets. Instead, they are concentrating on life-cycle costs. In this context preventive maintenance costs are more defensible.

Although inadequate funding is the primary reason given by administrators for not engaging in preventive maintenance, two equally important reasons for this deficiency exist. First, some administrators do not understand the concept; and second, some are incapable of calculating necessary data (Morris, 1981). In an effort to rectify this situation, various strategies have been developed for implementing preventive maintenance. Simko (1987), for instance, described a relatively simple proactive approach. He broke the task into four stages.

- *Stage 1*. Develop a strategic plan covering the next two decades and use life-cycle inventories to set realistic goals and priorities.
- *Stage 2*. Assess existing facilities and identify deferred maintenance; calculate the remaining useful life of key components.
- *Stage 3*. Create an effective action plan and budget for funding priority work on an annual basis by integrating anticipated life-cycle data and the actual assessment data.
- *Stage 4*. Obtain approval for the budget and execute the work.

Over the past few decades, the computer has facilitated preventive maintenance. Using this tool, maintenance personnel are able to create extensive databases that allow them to do complex calculations and precisely monitor mechanical operations (Borowski, 1984). Such inventories are now maintained for individual schools in a growing number of districts (Stronge, 1987).

Maintenance Staff Responsibilities

Typically maintenance personnel have district-wide rather than individual school responsibilities because they have trade skills usually not needed continuously in one school. In small districts, superintendents usually employ one or two mechanics, that is, individuals who have basic skills to do a variety of tasks. In larger districts, however, individuals might be employed in the following trades.

- Painters
- Masons
- Plumbers
- Electricians
- Mechanical systems specialists
- Millwrights
- Carpenters

In some districts, maintenance personnel also provide training for custodial staff in areas such as emergency electrical repairs or mechanical systems maintenance.

Typically, maintenance personnel are paid higher salaries than custodians because they have more specialized skills and usually are in greater demand in most labor markets. Because they have district-wide responsibilities, these individuals must be properly licensed to drive district-owned vehicles.

Table 15–1
Key Maintenance Staffing Questions

Question	Implications
What types of components must be maintained?	This query produces an inventory of the types of components and materials found in the buildings.
How should the components be maintained?	This query produces a database showing manufacturer specifications for preferred care and maintenance.
What skills are necessary to provide maintenance?	This query produces a database listing all skills needed.
What is the frequency of preferred maintenance?	This query produces a database listing the amount of work that needs to be produced within each skill category.
What financial resources are available for staffing?	This query produces funding parameters that help determine how many full-time and part-time personnel can be employed.
What jobs will be contracted to outside providers?	This query helps administrators determine if outsourcing is a preferred action for certain low-incidence tasks.
Can skills be combined?	This query helps administrators determine if they need to employ individuals who have skills in several trades.

Maintenance Staffing Decisions

Smaller districts obviously are unable to employ maintenance specialists in all of the trades. Districts with approximately 1,000 pupils often employ just one or two persons with diversified skills. These districts often must rely on outside contractors to do complex maintenance and repairs. Contracting for maintenance and custodial services is discussed in greater detail later in this chapter.

Determining how many and what types of employees are needed is predicated on a series of essential questions about the buildings to be serviced. Table 15-1 identifies the more relevant questions and their implications. Districts should have a staffing plan for district-wide maintenance services (Shaw, 1998). It should include the following components.

- *Mission Statement.* This statement details the goals and functions of the maintenance department. It is especially important to differentiate between maintenance and custodial services and to identify work assignments that will be done by external contractors.

- *Organizational Chart.* The chart details line and staff relationships for department personnel. In addition, the expected relationship between maintenance personnel and building-level administrators and custodians should be explained.

- *Staffing Grid.* This grid identifies the number of personnel needed and their specific assignments by trades.

- *Job Descriptions*. These documents should be completed for every position. They should include qualifications, employment conditions, job responsibilities, and supervisor–subordinate relationships. Criteria in job descriptions should be used in conjunction with performance evaluations.

- *Employment Practices*. This section of the plan details how vacancies are announced and filled, including relevant district policies and rules. It is especially important to identify the person(s) responsible for making employment recommendations to the superintendent.

- *Program Evaluation*. The evaluation component specifies the frequency and methodologies for examining the staffing plan. Such an evaluation should be conducted at least every two years.

The district's school board should approve the staffing plan, and copies should be provided subsequently to all district administrators.

CUSTODIAL SERVICES

In some districts, custodial services are taken for granted because administrators mistakenly see the function as nothing more than sweeping floors and collecting trash. Consequently, neither the district nor individual schools have comprehensive programs detailing what is to be accomplished. In addition, custodial positions are likely to be first affected when budget cuts are necessary (Milshtein, 1998).

Nature of Custodial Work

The school custodian's job has become more demanding and essential as buildings and their equipment have become more sophisticated (Stewart, Owens, & McKernan, 1998). For example, many districts expect these employees to use instruction and maintenance manuals—a job condition that requires both reading skills and sufficient intelligence to make the necessary interpretations. Most custodians are expected to process work orders, purchase orders, and conduct inventories. In newer facilities, they also may be expected to be computer literate in order to operate sophisticated mechanical and communication systems. The overall responsibilities of custodians are summarized in the following five goals.

- Protecting the facility and its equipment
- Maintaining a healthful and safe environment
- Keeping the building functional for instructional purposes
- Ensuring that public perceptions of the building are positive
- Maintaining a clean environment (Jordan, McKeown, Salmon, & Webb, 1985)

Despite the influence of technology, custodial services remain highly labor-intensive. Approximately 80 percent to 90 percent of custodial operation costs are attributable to personnel; the remaining 10 percent is attributable to supplies and equipment. Tasks most commonly performed by custodial staff include

- cleaning floor surfaces,
- removing trash,
- cleaning windows, mirrors, and wall surfaces,
- cleaning light fixtures,
- sanitizing appropriate areas,
- monitoring equipment and reporting malfunctions,
- keeping fixtures operational (e.g., filling soap dispensers, replacing toilet paper, cleaning drains),
- regulating climate control,
- maintaining the site (e.g., mowing),
- inventorying custodial supplies and equipment,
- contributing to building security (e.g., locking doors),
- assisting with accidents (e.g., mopping up spills in the cafeteria).

In addition, some custodians may be assigned to do light maintenance work such as minor electrical repairs, minor carpentry tasks, light painting, minor plumbing repairs, and replacing broken windows. Divisions of labor between maintenance and custodial staff depend on management philosophy, staffing patterns, and policies (including those that may be developed in conjunction with union contracts).

Custodial teaming is a concept that has gained some popularity in recent years. Based on the bureaucratic notion of divisions of labor, an assembly-line approach is used to clean schools. Instead of the product moving down the assembly line, the assembly line moves through the school. Cleaning tasks typically are grouped into four distinct functions.

- Light-duty cleaning (e.g., dusting, emptying trash, spot cleaning)
- Vacuuming carpets and hard floors
- Cleaning, sanitizing, and restocking restrooms
- Utility cleaning (e.g., glass, mopping and scrubbing floors) (David, 1999)

The purpose of team cleaning is technical efficiency. By having employees concentrate on a limited number of tasks, the assumption is that they can be trained to do the work at a high level of efficiency. The team method also is considered advantageous for identifying cleaning problems because administrators can identify the work that was not done or not done properly. This concept, however, does not work well if employees reject the idea. Routine work can be very boring and in some cases even demeaning.

Custodial Staffing Decisions

Custodial staffing and employment practices certainly are not consistent across districts. Some smaller school systems, for example, have neither a plan nor a formula for making these decisions. Various guidelines have been developed to determine the level of staffing needed. Some rely on enrollment ratios (e.g., one custodian for a given number of students), some rely on space ratios (e.g., one custodian for a given number of square feet), and still others rely on room ratios (e.g., one custodian for a given number of rooms). For example, Greenhalgh (1978) suggested that one custodian should be employed for every 15,000 sq. ft. of space, for every 11 classrooms, for every eight teachers, and for every 250 pupils.

Another quantitative approach involves making staffing decisions on the basis of time estimates. Kerry Leider, director of facilities and risk management for the Duluth, Minnesota, public schools, provides a good formula for this approach. He breaks the custodial task into three components.

* *Time in Relation to Materials.* Different materials require different levels of cleaning. For each type of material, an average time per square foot should be calculated.
* *Amount of Space to Be Cleaned.* Because areas in a school are not uniform, each must be measured to determine the total square footage of the material to be cleaned.
* *Frequency of Cleaning.* Materials also differ with regard to how often they must be cleaned. For each type of material, a preferred frequency needs to be established.

Once these three factors have been determined, the following formula is used to estimate cleaning time: (time needed p/square foot) $\times$ (number of square feet) $\times$ (frequency) (Milshtein, 1998).

Today, administrators are likely to combine qualitative and quantitative data to make staffing decisions. The following criteria often provide qualitative inputs.

* Age of the building
* Quality of original construction
* Current condition of the building and equipment
* Division of labor between custodial and maintenance staff
* Site development (e.g., number of athletic fields, playgrounds)
* Frequency and types of building used by community groups

In addition, technology and automation for mechanical and other systems affects staffing needs (Rondeau, 1989). While quantitative inputs such as ratios and time estimates contribute to effective decision making, they should always be used in conjunction with qualitative criteria.

OUTSOURCING OPTIONS

During the mid-1980s, Myron Lieberman wrote a thought-provoking book entitled *Beyond Public Education* (1986) urging public school districts to contract for services with outside agencies. At the core of his argument was the belief that union contracts had steadily eroded the power and resources of local boards. Today, the idea of using private contractors is commonly referred to as "outsourcing" or "contracting out."

Many private organizations embraced outsourcing over the last 20 years as a way to reduce operating costs. In the case of school districts, the concept has been most popular in four areas of operation: transportation, food services, maintenance, and custodial services. Some districts have attempted to consolidate all of these services into one contract with a single provider (Haertsch, 1999).

Arguments favoring outsourcing include

- *Reductions in Operating Costs*. This advantage is presumed to result from better management decisions and tighter staffing (Miller, 1993).
- *Lessening of Political Effects*. In many communities, maintenance and custodial personnel are long-time community residents who have political ties to school board members and other influential individuals. This advantage is lost when an outside company employs the personnel.
- *Reduction in Administrative Problems*. Because management is provided by the contractor, principals and central office personnel supposedly do not have to spend as much time supervising and evaluating personnel. In addition, they do not have to negotiate with an employee union or manage a union contract.
- *Flexibility*. Outsourcing allows administrators to make budgetary decisions more easily because reduction-in-force decisions can be avoided (provided that the contract with the external provider does not include restrictions in this area).
- *Improved Operations*. Contractors often claim that they can employ more highly skilled individuals, especially in the trades.

Critics, however, charge that these claims are supported only by anecdotal evidence produced from atypical districts. They point out the following weaknesses.

- *Loss of Control Over Operations*. Administrators are at the mercy of the companies with whom they have contracts. If the companies have financial problems or they experience an employee strike, the schools suffer.
- *Loss of Control Over Personnel*. Administrators may have little or no power to employ, discipline, or dismiss the contractor's employees.
- *Negative Effect on Employee Moral*. Partial outsourcing can create concerns among employees who begin to wonder if their job is the next position to be eliminated.

• *Political Problems.* Public schools always have been and continue to be political institutions. Maintenance and custodial personnel are usually district residents, and when outsourcing displaces them, serious political problems may result (Saks, 1995).

To outsource or not to outsource is another issue that most appropriately is decided on a district-by-district basis. The following questions should be answered if this option is being considered:

• Does the political environment of the district support outsourcing?
• Will the school board and district employees support the concept?
• What goals will be served by outsourcing? How will these goals be measured?
• What are the specific advantages and disadvantages for this district?
• Are contractors with established reputations for success available to the district?
• How much control must be sacrificed?

Administrators should also consider what resources would be needed if the outsourcing does not work. For example, vehicles that were used by maintenance personnel may be sold as a result of outsourcing, and sometime in the future when the district decides to return to its traditional in-house program, new vehicles will have to be purchased. There is a tendency to emphasize initial savings without giving equal consideration to possible expenses if the contract for services proves to be unsatisfactory.

PRINCIPAL'S MANAGEMENT RESPONSIBILITIES

Basically, a principal has two primary responsibilities in the area of facility management. The first is to ensure that programming (i.e., curriculum and instructional practices) is directing facility decisions and not vice versa. This responsibility includes keeping equipment operational, keeping the building clean, and making proper utilization decisions. Second, he or she is held accountable for security, health, and safety. Central to both of these tasks is a principal's relationship to the custodial staff.

The degree of responsibility for custodial personnel delegated to principals varies among districts. Often district size is a major factor. Larger districts are more likely to have directors of facilities, district master plans for facility maintenance, and uniform policies and rules for custodial operations. Thus, larger districts are more likely to minimize the principal's role. Proponents of centralized management approaches (i.e., control of custodial services within the district's facilities department) argue that uniform practices contribute to efficiency and reduce employee problems. Opponents counter by arguing that custodians are detached from principals and see themselves as not being part of the school's staff. No matter how large the school system, excluding the principal totally from critical activities (such as employment interviews and decisions, staff development, and performance evaluation) contributes to a perception that custodians are not an integral part of a school's staff.

Selecting Custodial Staff

Even though custodians are part of the overall district maintenance program, a school principal or assistant principal typically supervises them, partially or totally. In addition, superintendents in many districts either delegate the authority to employ custodians to building principals or they involve principals in the employment decisions (e.g., having them interview candidates). Accordingly, building-level administrators should have an understanding of custodial work and the qualifications for the position. More important, they should be able to apply this knowledge to contextual variables that represent the real needs and existing practices of a particular school because needs and operations are not standard across all schools.

Employment decisions for custodians should be guided by job-related criteria. For example, whether or not applicants are expected to have basic carpentry skills depends on the scope of job responsibilities as defined by the district and individual school. Some superintendents allow principals to tailor job descriptions and vacancy notices to their schools; more often, however, union contracts and administrative procedures result in generic documents. Even when job descriptions do not address human relations, principals should be cognizant of this criterion. Custodians should exhibit a sense of cooperation, an ability to work with others, and a respect for teachers and students. Either the personnel department or the superintendent should approve custodial job specifications before they are used for employment purposes. A district-wide maintenance plan is helpful in this regard, because it usually contains this information.

Historically, some board members have treated custodial positions as patronage jobs. This practice, needless to say, is precarious for legal, political, and practical reasons. A custodian protected by a relative or close friend on the school board is often a less-than-effective employee. Administrators are best able to avoid political employment decisions when they are armed with defensible job requirements. Thankfully, many school systems now have nepotism policies that reduce the frequency of unfair employment practices.

Determining the Work Schedule

Unless custodians report directly to someone outside of the school (e.g., reporting to the district's director of facilities), principals need to do two things to ensure effective practice. First, they should meet with custodians to review job expectations (Hughes & Ubben, 1984); second, they should maintain work schedules for custodial staff that detail work assignments and time schedules for completing those assignments.

Most schools now have both daytime and nighttime custodians. This scheduling arrangement is designed to minimize disruptions to the school's regular programs. Evening custodians can complete work that is difficult or impossible to do during school hours. They also provide necessary services for evening functions, and their presence in the building deters vandalism.

An example of a daily schedule for a custodian working from 4:00 P.M. to 12:00 A.M. is detailed here.

4:00	Check messages and/or instructions provided by supervisor
4:10	Start cleaning classrooms in assigned area of the building (empty trash, sweep floors, clean chalkboards, arrange desks, clean walls if necessary)
5:45	Coffee break
6:00	Clean restrooms in assigned area of the building (empty trash; clean lavatories and other fixtures, mop floors; clean walls if necessary; check if all systems are functional)
7:15	Dinner
8:00	Clean corridors in assigned area of the building
9:00	Clean teachers' lounge
9:30	Clean media center (sweep floors, empty trash, dust tables and cabinets, clean window surfaces)
10:30	Coffee break
10:45	Check areas after evening use and clean up if necessary
11:30	Check alarm systems, heating/ventilation systems, turn off lights in area, put away materials, lock doors where appropriate

Principals in larger schools may delegate the responsibility for establishing work schedules to the head custodian or to an assistant principal. Even when this is done, the principal should periodically monitor work assignments to ensure that they are effective. Several organizations sell guides that can facilitate the development of work schedules. Two examples are: *Good School Maintenance: A Manual of Programs and Procedures for Buildings, Grounds, and Equipment* (1996) available from the Illinois Association of School Boards and *School Facilities Maintenance and Operations Manual* (1988) available from the Association of School Business Officials International.

Enhancing the Value of Custodians

School climate is a concept that conveys feelings about the physical environment (ecology), social relationships, organizational structure, and shared values and beliefs (Kowalski, 1999). In some schools, custodians are respected and valued and in others they are not. Clearly, the principal is a key figure in determining this outcome. Principals reinforce attitudes about custodians in a number of ways.

- *Emphasizing the Value of Good Custodial Services.* When principals remind staff and students why it is important to have a clean and safe school, they are illustrating the value of having good custodians.
- *Recognizing Custodial Achievements.* Complimenting custodial staff to the school personnel and to the community is one way to do this. Providing special recognitions and awards for service also contributes to this goal.
- *Treating Custodial Staff With Respect.* Involving custodians in decisions that affect their work, addressing them appropriately in public, and inviting them to staff functions are ways this can be accomplished.
- *Resolving Conflict Fairly and Objectively.* Tension between custodians and other employees is inevitable. Principals should neither let these situations linger nor should they treat custodians as second-class citizens. Being impartial reinforces the belief that custodians are important personnel.

Perhaps the most direct way to enhance attitudes about the importance of custodial staff is to improve the performance of these employees. Both staff development and performance evaluation are essential in this regard. Regrettably, some districts totally exclude principals from participating in these activities. Thus, principals—the administrators who work with these personnel on a day-to-day basis—are deprived of opportunities to help these employees improve themselves. When this occurs, training activities are not building-specific and thus are less likely to have an immediate effect on operations (Griffin, 1998).

CHAPTER SUMMARY

Keeping existing facilities safe, clean, and operational is a critical management responsibility. This overall task is shared between maintenance and custodial services. Maintenance personnel usually are specialists possessing one or more trade skills. They provide services on a district-wide basis as needed. Such services may either be preventive or repair-oriented. Districts often defer necessary maintenance because of resource shortages—a condition that has contributed substantially to the current facility crisis in this country.

Custodians provide services in individual schools; therefore, principals are usually involved in employing and evaluating these employees. Although different quantitative formulas are available to help determine staffing needs, a combination of quantitative and qualitative standards is likely to produce the most effective outcome. This is because schoolhouses differ dramatically in their condition and quality.

Custodial costs are primarily attributable to personnel. Thus, cost savings are most likely when the number of personnel is reduced or the quantity of work performed by current employees is increased. Two cost-cutting approaches discussed in this chapter are outsourcing and team cleaning. While each can contribute to budget reductions, they are not without potential pitfalls.

No matter how large a school system, totally excluding a principal from being involved in custodian selection, staff development, and evaluation is a precarious decision. All of these functions should be related to contextual variables that frame the specific needs of a building. The principal is in the best position to provide information about programming and existing facility problems.

ISSUES FOR DISCUSSION

1. What is deferred maintenance? What conditions cause it?
2. What is preventive maintenance? Why is preventive maintenance considered advantageous?
3. What are the advantages of having a district-wide maintenance plan?
4. How might master contracts with unions affect the division of labor between maintenance and custodial personnel?
5. In many schools, custodial personnel are considered relatively unimportant. What might contribute to such feelings?
6. What are the arguments for and against having principals provide direct supervision of custodians?
7. What are some qualitative factors that should be considered when determining the appropriate number of custodians for a school?
8. Why do most schools have daytime and evening custodians?
9. Make a list of criteria you would use to employ school custodians.
10. What are some ways a principal can enhance the importance of custodial personnel?

REFERENCES

Association of School Business Officials International. (1988). *School facilities maintenance and operations manual*. Reston, VA: Author.

Borowski, P. (1984). Maintaining a computerized building file. *CEFP Journal, 22*(5), 18.

David, F. (1999). Team work. *American School and University, 71*(8), 46, 48, 50.

Greenhalgh, J. (1978). *Practitioner's guide to school business management*. Boston: Allyn and Bacon.

Griffin, W.R. (1998). Training your custodians. *School Planning and Management, 37*(11), 43–44.

Haertsch, T. (1999). To outsource or not to outsource. *School Planning and Management, 38*(8), 29–30.

Hughes, L., & Ubben, G. (1984). *The elementary principal's handbook* (2nd ed.). Boston: Allyn and Bacon.

Illinois Association of School Boards. (1996). *Good School Maintenance: A Manual of Programs and Procedures for Buildings, Grounds, and Equipment* (3rd ed.). Springfield: Author.

Jordan, K., McKeown, M., Salmon, R., & Webb, L. (1985). *School business management*. Beverly Hills, CA: Sage.

Kowalski, T.J. (1999). *The school superintendent: Theory, practice, and cases*. Upper Saddle River, NJ: Merrill, Prentice-Hall.

Lieberman, M. (1986). *Beyond public education*. New York: Praeger.

Miller, G. (1993). Maintenance and custodial services: Getting the most for the money. *School Business Affairs, 59*(7), 18–21.

Milshtein, A. (1998). Setting the cleaning standard. *School Planning and Management, 37*(5), 29–31.

Morris, J. (1981). Developing a small-scale preventive maintenance program. *American School and University, 53*(8), 15.

Rondeau, E. (1989). The future of facility management. *CEFP Journal, 27*(1), 9–14.

Saks, J.B. (1995). Exercising your options. *The American School Board Journal, 182*(10), 38–40.

Shaw, R. (1998). Building a staffing plan. *American School and University, 70*(6), 54.

Simko, E. (1987). Proactive maintenance saves money. *American School and University, 59*(7), 31–38.

Stewart, K., Owens, L., & McKernan, P. (1998). Working with custodial staff. *High School Magazine, 5*(5), 44–45.

Stronge, J. (1987). The school building principal and inventory control: A case for computerization. *CEFP Journal, 25*(6), 4–6.

CHAPTER 16

Pervasive Maintenance Concerns

In addition to routine building care, several problems present special challenges to administrators responsible for overall facility management. Although many of them are not new, others have only been recognized as serious problems in the past few decades; asbestos and radon gas are examples. This chapter identifies pervasive problems and provides insights into managing them.

INDOOR AIR-QUALITY PROBLEMS

School buildings, especially if they are not designed and maintained properly, are susceptible to indoor air pollution. The concentration of pollutants can be two to five times greater indoors than outdoors according to the Environmental Protection Agency (EPA) (Woolums, 2000). According to the American Association of School Administrators (AASA; 2000), schools have four times the number of occupants per square foot as office buildings, and the performance of ventilation systems in many buildings has been diminished either by a lack of proper maintenance or by renovations. Administrators should be concerned about indoor air pollution for two important reasons. First, "sick" buildings clearly present a health hazard; and second, they often lead to legal problems (Hays, 2000).

Sources of the Problem

One of the causes of indoor air pollution is biological contaminants. Biological factors such as bacteria, mold, parasites, viruses, and other similar agents are not due entirely to unclean conditions as some would surmise. Schools often contain animal, plant, and microbiological specimens that require proper storage and ventilation designs (Rowe, 1987). In other words, biological contaminants are more likely to present a serious danger in schools that otherwise have poor air quality.

A rather recent addition to the list of concerns regarding interior air quality is radon. This chemically inert, radioactive gaseous element is produced by the disintegration of radium. Since 1986, radon has become a well publicized health hazard. Radon problems are more likely to occur in schools erected on concrete slabs. Administrators should be familiar with environmental standards and guidelines, and they should know how to identify mitigation strategies.

Virtually all secondary schools (and many elementary schools as well) contain chemicals that are used for science instruction. These elements may produce gases and odors that negatively affect the air, especially if they are stored improperly or if they are stored in areas not properly ventilated. The classic syndrome for a sick building is improper ventilation in a tightly sealed building containing airborne pollutants (Reecer, 1988). Some common causes of poor ventilation in schools are

- selecting a poorly designed ventilation system,
- installing a ventilation system improperly,
- reducing the operation of a ventilation system below its recommended level in order to conserve energy,
- occupying the building at a level that exceeds design capacity,
- executing operations that were not anticipated when the building was designed and constructed (e.g., using chemicals for experiments in an elementary-school classroom),
- failing to maintain the ventilation system properly (Reecer, 1988).

Dust and fibers also contribute to poor air quality. Dust is generated primarily from chalk, but other sources may include dirt, pollen, and pet dander. One of the most dangerous fibers found in some schools is asbestos. This material was used in older schools as insulation and as a fire and corrosion inhibitor. This harmful substance may be found in flooring tiles, ceiling tiles, plaster, corrugated pipe insulation, spray-on acoustical soundproofing, spray-on thermal insulation and fireproofing, fire doors, stage light wiring, and roofing and siding shingles. Asbestos is a mineral that has been demonstrated to be a carcinogen and linked to lung cancer and other pulmonary diseases (Rublin, 1985). Asbestos dust, the primary concern, is created when material containing asbestos crumbles and enters the air freely (referred to as the "friable" nature of asbestos).

Other substances that may contribute to indoor air pollution include

- *Fiberglass*. This material has been used in thermal insulation and duct linings, and it becomes airborne when disturbed (Woolums, 2000).

- *Emissions*. Internally, harmful emissions may be produced by office machines, lab materials, and cleaning materials. Externally, vehicles operating near the building may generate them.

- *Sewer Gas*. This problem is usually associated with dry traps allowing the gas to pass into the building.

- *Lead*. This metal may be found in deteriorating paint and dust, air, drinking water, food, and contaminated soil and it can become airborne (Grubb & Diamantes, 1998).

- *Pesticides*. These chemicals may be used on the site or even in the building; if not applied properly, they constitute a hazard.

- *Formaldehyde*. This is a colorless, strong-smelling gas that is used in products such as adhesives and pressed wood.

Managing Indoor Air Pollution

Managing indoor air quality is both a policy issue and a technical challenge. Quraishi and Kapfer (1999) proposed that districts should, at a minimum, set the following goals.

- Monitor and ensure proper maintenance for heating, ventilation, and air-conditioning systems
- Improve building cleaning procedures and equipment
- Minimize exposure to volatile organic compounds
- Control water entering the building
- Provide appropriate training for all maintenance and custodial personnel (p. 46)

Air-quality problems are often difficult to manage because they can occur suddenly as a result of some undetected change in the school's environment (e.g., a malfunction in the ventilation system). In addition, symptoms may disappear when students and teachers leave at the end of the school day (Gembala, 1999). Generally, management solutions either entail removing or controlling the pollutants or using improved ventilation to offset the possible negative effects of potential pollutants.

The following actions facilitate finding and correcting air-quality problems.

- Develop a checklist for potential problems and have school employees fill them out periodically.
- Have maintenance personnel or consultants conduct periodic inspections.
- Investigate all air-quality complaints.
- Make all repairs to structural, mechanical, and plumbing systems as soon as possible.

An audit of air quality is highly recommended for all public buildings. School officials can consult with local health department or state health department officials regarding the availability of consultants to conduct such audits. The recent concerns surrounding the possible presence of asbestos and radon have heightened public awareness regarding the need for periodic testing of air quality.

Dealing with asbestos problems is a more challenging task. A 1987 law classified any material with more than 1 percent by volume of asbestos as an asbestos material (McGovern, 1989). The measures school administrators need to pursue include

- designating an in-house asbestos manager,
- securing a competent consultant,
- involving the school district attorney in actions that may be necessary (Simoter, 1988).

If removal is deemed necessary, districts retain asbestos removal firms. Toll (1988) offers nine suggestions with regard to doing this.

- Check the qualifications of any firm you might consider.
- Make sure a firm is properly licensed.
- Request competitive bids.
- Check a firm's experience and quality standards (work standards and practices).
- Make sure a firm will provide proper on-site supervision.
- Inquire if a firm has an employee safety training program that complies with local, state, and federal agency specifications.
- Check to see if the firm uses subcontractors for any of its work; and if so, investigate the subcontractors.
- Insist on obtaining information regarding a firm's bonding and insurance.
- Investigate a firm's history with regard to maintaining documentation of work completed (e.g., job-site logs, air-sampling records, personnel-monitoring reports).

Districts should have a policy statement on asbestos, and the district's maintenance plan should detail a strategy for dealing with this hazard.

ENERGY CONSERVATION

Prior to 1970, energy conservation was not a major issue in school-facility design. Energy costs were so low that it was considered unnecessary to use higher-priced, energy-efficient construction components. As an example, many buildings were designed with single-pane windows and without vestibules at entrances. Rising energy costs over the past three decades, however, have created a different perspective about operational efficiency.

Building design is clearly the most important variable contributing to energy efficiency. In all likelihood 80 percent of the decisions that affect energy conservation are made in the first 10 percent of the design process (Lawrence, 1984). Yet, energy conservation does not relate entirely to design. Maintenance and operation also play critical roles in determining usage levels in schools. The U.S. Department of Energy estimates that $6 billion is spent annually by districts on energy consumption, and as much as 25 percent of those costs could be reduced (Reicher, 2000). The cost figure increased markedly in 2001 as the cost of oil and other energy sources rose sharply. The three most effective actions associated with energy cost reductions are

- improved building design,
- the use of energy technologies,
- improved operations and maintenance (AASA, 2000).

The first step in determining whether a school district has a consumption problem is conducting an energy audit. Districts commonly retain consultants for this purpose. Energy audits entail analyzing the amount, cost, and sources of energy consumption. Energy expenditures can be calculated in two ways: cost per square foot of space and cost per occupant. Averages should be calculated using at least a three-year base in order to avoid distortions caused by unusual circumstances in any given year (e.g., an unusually warm winter). Once determined, district cost figures are compared to average costs for schools in the same geographic area. Such comparisons provide a relative indicator of consumption.

Energy consumption studies usually reveal that districts face unique problems requiring individualized conservation plans. Worner (1981) summed it up this way.

In general, each school district has its own characteristic energy problem. Structures are made of different building materials. Numerous types of heating, cooling, and ventilation systems are used with varying degrees of automatic and manual control. Operating efficiency varies from poor to excellent. Use patterns, programs offered, and climatic conditions differ over a wide range. Therefore, each district must develop its own unique approach to addressing local energy problems. (pp. 306–307)

After problems are identified, administrators need to develop alternative solutions and select an appropriate course of action. Typically actions to reduce consumption fall into one of three categories.

- Solutions requiring alterations in operations
- Solutions requiring alterations in maintenance (especially preventive maintenance schedules)
- Solutions requiring design changes (major renovation)

Many districts have turned to energy service companies (referred to as ESCOs) for assistance. ESCOs engage in performance contracting; that is, they upgrade equipment for a district, implement energy savings practices, and recoup their investments and a fee through cost savings. Basically, this is done in the following manner.

- The district purchases a package of services that includes the design, purchase, installation, maintenance, and operation of the equipment.
- The ESCO finances capital outlay costs associated with the contract.
- The district's costs are guaranteed to be less than the amortized capital outlay costs.
- Management and maintenance resources are included.

Essentially, any risk associated with energy savings performance is transferred from the district to the ESCO. Advocates of ESCOs stress the following possible benefits associated with this service.

- Single-point accountability is achieved by working with one contractor.
- The design of HVAC equipment, control systems, operations and maintenance procedures, and project quality are optimized—a condition that improves long-term equipment performance.
- Cost savings can be used to support educational programs.
- Many efficiency decisions also have a positive effect on indoor air quality (Birr, 1999).

    Since ESCOs have a great deal at stake, including profit margins, they carefully monitor and review energy use throughout the life of a contract (Mahoney & Thompson, 1998). Some even provide a full-time project coordinator who remains on site to ensure that equipment remains in working order and energy conservation steps are being followed.

ROOF MAINTENANCE

    A school board member once asked an architect, "Why can't you design a roof for a school that won't leak?" "I can," responded the architect, "but I don't think you can afford it." There is more truth in this answer than most school administrators realize. Roofs are a constant headache for facility administrators. They consume a major portion of the maintenance budget, and they have been the leading source of litigation between school districts and architects/engineers (Nimtz, 1988). Often roof problems stem from pressures to accept low bids in original construction. The problems also may stem from faulty design or improper installation.

    Since the early 1970s, the single-membrane roofing industry has evolved as the major supplier for schools. Prior to that time, built-up roof systems were rather standard for schools. Basically, there are three types of single membrane systems.

- Modified bitumen or rubberized asphalt
- EPDM (ethylene propylene diene monomer)—a rubber polymer compound
- PVC (polyvinyl chloride) (Mullin, 1985).

The roof material that has grown in popularity is the standing-seam metal roof. Nimtz (1988) described the system as follows:

The concealed fastening system is the key weather tight feature of the standing seam roof. The metal panels are attached to the building structural members—called purlins— with a series of movable clips inside the panel's raised seam. The seam stands two to three inches above the roof plane in a typical system. With fewer exposed fasteners than in the traditional through-fastened metal roof or conventional roofing systems, the areas for potential leaks are reduced. (p. 51)

Advocates of the standing-seam metal roof argue that the product is the most cost-effective alternative when data are produced from life-span comparisons.

Young (1987) advised using a three-step approach to roof management.

- Establishing roofing information files (e.g., design, installation, warranty, and inspection information)
- Developing a roof inspection program
- Developing a maintenance schedule

The information file is essentially a database and may already be available in school districts with comprehensive information systems. Periodic assessments are designed to identify potential malfunctions prior to actual emergencies. Waldron (1988) suggested the following components for such a survey.

- Readings to determine subsurface moisture (e.g., nucleur scan, capacitance meter readings)
- Visual observations of the general appearance, surface conditions, and membrane conditions
- Visual observations of edge conditions and around equipment (e.g., flashing, caulking)
- Visual observations of pitch pans, vents, drains, and other roof penetrations
- Interviews with custodial and maintenance staff to determine if problems occurred and the nature of problems

Galvanic moisture probing and roof cores also provide valuable data, but these techniques should not be used if the roof is still under warranty. Finally, a critical element of roofing maintenance is a schedule for performing necessary work. Preferably, this schedule should be integrated into the overall preventive maintenance program.

Most schools are designed with flat (or relatively flat roofs); therefore pooling water is a common problem, especially if the roof does not have adequate drains or drains that are not functioning properly. The primary factor in roof design is slope. Roofs can be designed on a continuum from flat with minimal pitch to a ski-slope pitch. The amount of roof pitch is measured in inches of rise per foot of run.

When roof problems occur, administrators are likely to be asked why school buildings continue to have relatively flat roofs. Part of the answer is related to compromises that are made between roof maintenance and projected energy costs. While most administrators recognize that roofs with higher pitches reduce or even eliminate problems with standing water, they may not realize that roof pitch affects the interior volume of a building. As the pitch of a roof is increased, the interior volume of the room below is increased. And if the added interior space is to be heated and cooled, the higher pitch results in higher energy costs. Thus, architects often recommend an acceptable compromise between roof pitch and the building's interior volume.

Faced with roofing problems, the maintenance department must make a choice between repair and replacement. Accordingly, it is advisable to have an architect or a qualified engineer examine the roof and recommend a course of action. Repair should be justified in terms of being cost-effective in relation to the remaining life span of the building and the roof. When considering roof design and maintenance, the following principles may prove helpful.

- Select an architect or engineer who has a proven track record in working with roofs.
- Study the specifications of roof materials being recommended; be sure that they are appropriate for the climate in which the school is located.
- Insist that the top surface of a roof is sun- and fire-resistant.
- Do not take proper surface drainage for granted; insist on seeing a detailed analysis of drainage specifications.
- Do not assume that a roof will be installed properly; insist on having installation inspections.
- Use life-cycle costs to do comparisons—both for selecting a type of roof and for making decisions regarding replacement versus repair.

Preventive maintenance is an important factor in reducing roof repair or replacement costs. The normal life expectancy of a roof is estimated to be in the range of 20 to 25 years. Kallinger (1998) provides the following formula for determining the useful service life of a school roof.

$$USL = D + M + A + E + Mc$$

Where:

USL = useful service

D = design

M = roofing materials

A = application at installation

E = exposure (abuse, climate)

Mc = maintenance.

Once schools are operational, the only variable administrators can manage is maintenance.

CONTROLLING VANDALISM

Some critics charge that vandalism is not a maintenance problem but rather an administrative problem. In truth, it is both. Exposure to vandalism may be associated with several of the following variables.

- *District Economic Conditions.* Schools in lower economic neighborhoods are usually more susceptible than are other schools.
- *District Location.* Urban districts almost always have higher incident rates than do rural schools.
- *District Size.* The larger the district, the greater the susceptibility; districts with over 5,000 students tend to be more vulnerable than are smaller districts (Lindbloom & Summerhays, 1988).
- *Building Condition.* Schools that are well maintained are less likely to incur vandalism than are schools that are poorly maintained.
- *Security Provisions.* Schools with proper security designs (e.g., outdoor lighting, alarm systems) are less susceptible than are schools with poor security designs.
- *Maintenance Programs.* Districts that repair damage quickly are less susceptible than are districts that do not.

However, all school buildings have some risk of incurring vandalism.

Research indicates that vandalism may be caused by a myriad of factors (Cooze, 1995). They broadly fall into three categories.

- Those associated with other criminal acts (e.g., breaking windows or doors during a burglary)
- Those constituting acts of retribution (e.g., angry students retaliating against the school because of some grievance)
- Those constituting senseless destructive behavior (e.g., individuals who simply obtain gratification from destroying another person's property).

Regardless of causes, vandalism can be reduced by positive administrative and maintenance actions. They include

- developing policies and regulations,
- installing security lighting and fencing on the site,
- repairing damage to building and site as soon possible,
- keeping the building, and especially areas susceptible to vandalism, clean at all times,
- installing proper bathroom fixtures and exercising preventive maintenance (Kennedy, 2000),
- installing alarm systems (Stover, 1990),
- installing effective communication systems (e.g., telephone access in all classrooms),
- installing door security systems (Steward & Knapp, 1997),
- installing video cameras (Lebowitz, 1997).

No school district can totally eradicate vandalism, but positive steps, including an effective maintenance program, can reduce incidences. Overall building security, an issue discussed earlier in this book, is the most effective tool for doing this.

PLAYGROUND SAFETY

School playgrounds, including outdoor athletic facilities, can be a source of serious problems. These areas are almost always used during and after school; thus, some of the use occurs when no adult supervision is provided. It is estimated that approximately 170,000 children are injured each year in playground accidents in this country (Thompson, 1991). Most accidents are caused by poor maintenance, antiquated design, or layout problems (Miller, 1994). Administrators and maintenance personnel are responsible for ensuring that playgrounds comply with government standards, such as the Americans with Disabilities Act (Goltsman, 1997) and state and local safety codes.

An analysis of student accidents on playgrounds has resulted in a number of guidelines for playgrounds. They include the following:

- *Choose Appropriate Equipment.* Playground equipment should be selected based on the age groups that will use it. For this reason, most elementary schools have two playgrounds—one for the primary grades and one for the intermediate grades (Thompson, 1996).
- *Provide Adequate Fall Zones.* Areas under and between playground equipment should be covered with a minimum of 12 inches of protective, resilient material extending six feet in all directions.
- *Provide Adequate Space Between Playground Equipment.* A minimum of 12 feet should be provided between play structures.
- *Provide Guardrails for Elevated Surfaces.* Elevated surfaces such as platforms, ramps, and bridge ways should have guardrails.

- *Eliminate Dangerous Protrusions.* Protruding objects such as nails, screws, bolts, pipe ends, and hooks should be eliminated.
- *Eliminate Entrapment Areas.* Young children may get their heads caught in areas such as ladder rungs. For this reason, openings on playground equipment should measure less than three inches or more than nine inches.
- *Avoid Using Hard or Bulky Swing Seats.* Wooden or metal swing seats can cause injuries to children walking past them.
- *Avoid Equipment With Moving Parts.* Equipment such as suspension bridges, merry-go-rounds, swinging gates, and seesaws (teeter-totters) may have moving parts that can cause injuries (e.g., pinching or crushing fingers or other body parts) (Hendricks, 1993).
- *Provide Regular Safety Inspections.* Someone should be assigned the responsibility of conducting periodic inspections. They should be completed at least three times each year.
- *Provide Regular Maintenance.* Equipment that is maintained on a regular basis is less likely to cause accidents.

The key to a safe playground is developing it properly. This includes decisions about surfaces and landscaping (Sipes, 2000).

When selecting new playground equipment, Christoph (1999) recommends the following:

- Be sure that the Independent Play Equipment Manufacturers Association has certified the equipment.
- Try to purchase equipment from well-known, insured manufacturers that have been in business under the same name for several years.
- Document warranty information.

Administrators also should develop and follow an equipment replacement plan. Most playground equipment will need to be replaced approximately every 15 years. Most litigation brought against school districts with regard to playgrounds and outdoor accidents focuses on the responsibility to properly maintain equipment and conditions or negligence in supervision. The courts usually apply the "duty-to-warn" standard. In essence, the person filing suit against a school district must show the following in court.

- That a duty to warn existed.
- That no warning was given or the warnings were inadequate.
- A failure to warn or an inadequate warning caused the injury (Davis, 1988).

Improper maintenance of the site also may be a litigation focal point. Cracked sidewalks, dangerous conditions such as uncovered holes on the site, and protrusions from equipment may cause expensive lawsuits.

In addition to carefully reviewing the maintenance program for playgrounds, administrators should pay careful attention to adequate insurance. Specifically, superintendents and principals need to know what liabilities exist; they should pursue corrective actions where possible to eliminate or reduce risk; and they should seek risk transfer (insurance) when possible.

CHAPTER SUMMARY

This chapter examined five issues that are especially cogent to maintaining schools. The first, indoor air pollution, is often caused by inadequate ventilation in large buildings. Energy conservation, the second issue discussed, has resurfaced as world oil prices have once again increased significantly. Many schoolhouses still in use were designed during periods of relatively low energy costs.

Roofs, the third focused issue, are a perennial headache for most administrators. Potential problems occur both during planning and during maintenance. Actions recommended include demanding proper roof design, selecting good materials, ensuring proper installation of the materials, and engaging in preventive maintenance.

The final two issues were vandalism and playground safety. Although proper security measures are a primary deterrent to vandalism, effective policy and maintenance practices also are critical. Playgrounds present a challenge because of the high probability of accidents and injury. Administrators can reduce risk exposure by ensuring proper design, equipment purchases, and maintenance.

ISSUES FOR DISCUSSION

1. Identify substances and materials commonly found in schools that may contribute to indoor air pollution.

2. Why is ventilation critical to controlling indoor air quality?

3. How can schools be made more energy-efficient?

4. What are the potential benefits of executing a performance contract for energy management?

5. What are the causes of vandalism?

6. How can effective maintenance contribute to reducing vandalism?

7. What may cause a roof on a school to fail?

8. Are school roofs an inevitable problem? Why or why not?

9. How can administrators reduce risk on playgrounds?

10. What site features might contribute to playground accidents? What equipment features might contribute to playground accidents?

11. How can roof designs affect energy consumption?

REFERENCES

American Association of School Administrators. (2000). *In focus: Clean air, efficient energy use.* Arlington, VA: Author.

Birr, D. (1999, November). School solutions. Special report: IAQ and energy. *Energy Decisions,* 32–36.

Christoph, N.J. (1999). Playgrounds with maximum safety and minimal risk. *School Planning and Management, 38*(2), 58, 60–63.

Cooze, J. (1995). Curbing the cost of school vandalism: Theoretical causes and preventive measures. *Education Canada, 35*(3), 38–41.

Davis, J. (1988). Playground safety. *American School and University, 61*(2), 43–44.

Gembala, W.W. (1999). An air of concern. *American School and University, 71*(8), 40, 42, 44.

Goltsman, S. (1997). Designing playgrounds for children of all abilities. *School Planning and Management, 36*(10), 26–29.

Grubb, D., & Diamantes, T. (1998). Is your school sick? Five threats to healthy schools. *Clearing House, 71*(4), 202–207.

Hays, L. (2000). Lawsuits in the air. *American School and University, 72*(10), 35–36.

Hendricks, C.M. (1993). *Safer playgrounds for young children.* (ERIC Document Reproduction Service No. ED 355 206)

Kallinger, P. (1998). The benefits of preventive roof maintence. *School Planning and Management, 37*(6) 44–47.

Kennedy, M. (2000). An eye on prevention. *American School and University, 72*(9), 65–66.

Lawrence, J. (1984). Energy-conscious design. *American School and University, 56*(12), 43, 46, 49–50.

Lebowitz, M. (1997). Smile, vandals: You're on candid camera. *School Planning and Management, 36*(12), 28–29.

Lindbloom, K., & Summerhays, J. (1988). School security. *American School and University, 61*(1), 50–55.

Mahoney, J., & Thompson, L. (1998). Upgrade your facilities without a bond issue. *School Planning and Management, 37*(2), 56–60.

McGovern, M. (1989). Asbestos, the law. *CEFP Journal, 27*(1), 18–21.

Miller, D. (1994). Playground safety audit protects children and your liability. *School Business Affairs, 60*(8), 31–32.

Mullin, P. (1985). Outlook on roofing systems. *American School and University, 58*(4), 42, 44.

Nimtz, P. (1988). Metal roofs: Cost effective alternative. *School Business Affairs, 54*(12), 50–55.

Quraishi, A., & Kapfer, T. (1999). A blueprint for IAQ. *American School and University, 72*(1), 46–49.

Reecer, M. (1988). When students say school makes them sick, sometimes they're right. *American School Board Journal, 175*(8), 17–21.

Reicher, D. (2000). Nature's design rules. *Learning By Design 9,* 16–18.

Rowe, D. (1987). Healthful school living: Environmental health in the school. *Journal of School Health, 57*(10), 426–431.

Rublin, L. (1985, February 11). Asbestos fallout: It can be hazardous to a company's financial health. *Barron's,* 6–7, 22, 24.

260   Focused Issues

Simoter, D. (1988). Limiting asbestos liability. *American School and University, 61*(3), 225–227.

Sipes, J.L. (2000). Playground safety. *Landscape Architecture, 90*(2), 38, 40, 42.

Steward, G.K., & Knapp, M.J. (1997). How to modify your facilities to minimize violence and vandalism. *School Business Affairs, 63*(4), 43–46.

Stover, D. (1990). How to be safe and secure against school vandalism. *The Executive Educator, 12*(11), 20–22, 30.

Thompson, D. (1996). Ten ways to keep playtime safe. *School Planning and Management, 35*(8), 28–29.

Thompson, T. (1991). People make the difference in school playground safety. *The Executive Educator, 13*(8), 28–29.

Toll, M. (1988). Choosing an asbestos abatement contractor. *American School and University, 61*(3), 219–220, 225.

Waldron, L. (1988). The map to cost effective roofing. *School Business Affairs, 55*(12), 57–58.

Woolums, J. (2000). *Managing indoor air quality in schools*. Washington, DC: National Clearinghouse for Educational Facilities.

Worner, W. (1981). Small school districts and the high cost of energy. *Journal of Education Finance, 6*(3), 297–309.

Young, D. (1987). Roof management program: Three steps to success. *CEFP Journal, 25*(4), 14–15.

Glossary

AASA   American Association of School Administrators

acoustics   the science that deals with the production, control, transmission, reception, and effects of sound

ADA   acronym used for the Americans with Disabilities Act

AIA   acronym for the American Institute of Architects—the professional association for architects

alcove   a recess or small opening off a larger room; in schools, a nook for study or counseling

alternate bid   a proposal to use a different method, material, or quantity than is specified in the bidding documents (e.g., bidding a tile floor when carpeting is specified)

amortization schedule   a schedule of payments needed to retire an outstanding debt (both principal and interest)

arbitrage   district investing proceeds from a bond sale at a higher interest rate than is being paid on the bonds

architect basic services   duties commonly included in an architect's standard contract; includes (a) schematic design phase, (b) design development phase, (c) construction document phase, (d) bidding and negotiating phase, and (e) construction phase

architectural drawing   a line drawing containing plan and elevation views of a proposed building for the purpose of exhibiting the overall appearance of the building

asbestos	soft, fibrous, incombustible material formerly used in many building materials; considered to be a health hazard if not properly contained
ASBO	Association of School Business Officials
backfill	earth used to fill in the cavity created during the construction of exterior foundation walls
backup heating system	secondary source of producing heat for a building in case the primary system cannot function (e.g., using fuel oil as a backup system for natural gas)
barrier-free environment	with relation to schools, a facility that is free of barriers that would prevent normal and customary usage by the handicapped
baseboard	the finish board covering the plaster (or other wall material) where it meets the floor
base molding	molding used to trim the upper edge of interior baseboards
bid	amount offered or proposed to complete specified works
bid bond	a surety submitted by a bidder that assures that the bidder will meet obligations stated in the bid
bid form	standard form given to potential bidders specifying the information and signatures required for submitting a legitimate bid
bid opening	an open or closed session in which submitted bids are opened, certified as being in compliance with predetermined standards, and tabulated
bid price	the amount stipulated on a bid
bidder prequalification	a process of determining which contractors are qualified to submit bids; judgments are usually based on criteria such as competence, integrity, dependability, responsiveness, bonding rate, bonding capacity, work on hand, and overall reputation
bidding documents	packet of materials provided to potential bidders; typically including an invitation to submit a bid, bidding instructions, a bid form, proposed contract documents, and information regarding bid submission (e.g., time and date deadlines)
bond	written promise, generally under seal, to pay a specified sum of money (called a face value) at a fixed time in the future (called the maturity date) and carrying a specified rate of interest

bond attorney	attorney who specializes in rendering opinions regarding bond issues; in relation to schools, an attorney who certifies that the bonds qualify as tax-exempt investments
Bond Buyer	newspaper with wide circulation advertising the sale of bonds
bond election	referendum asking voter approval for the sale of bonds
bond rating	judgment made by a rating agency identifying the relative level of risk involved with purchasing specific bonds
breach of contract	when one or both parties to a contract fail to meet stated obligations
BTU	acronym for British thermal unit, which is a unit of heat used in measurements
building code	legal requirements established by government agencies that prescribe minimum acceptable requirements for all types of construction
building permit	written document issued by an appropriate governmental authority permitting construction of a specific project as detailed in approved drawings and specifications
cafetorium	room in a school that is designed to serve the dual purpose of cafeteria and auditorium
callable bond	bond that may be redeemed by the owner prior to maturity
capital outlay	expenditure that results in the acquisition of fixed assets or additions to fixed assets that are presumed to have benefits for more than one year; an expenditure for land or buildings
casement	glass frame that is made to open by turning on hinges affixed to its vertical edges
casing	metal or wooden member around door and window openings to give a finished appearance
catch basin	cast-iron, cement, or wooden receptacle into which the water from a roof, a floor, and so on will drain; it is connected to the sewer or drain tile
CEFPI	Council of Educational Facility Planners International
ceramic tile	clay product with an impervious, glazed surface designed for easy maintenance
change order	an order issued by the architect on approval of the owner directing a change (in materials, methods, or quantity) in the building contracts (e.g., deciding to increase the number of rooms that are to be carpeted after contracts are awarded)

circuit   path over which electrical current may pass

clerk-of-the-works   individual representing the owner who completes clerical and supervisory tasks during the construction phase of a project in addition to those assigned to the architect

column   round vertical shaft or pillar that can be either load bearing or non-load bearing

commons area   area in a building designed as a gathering place (e.g., a place where students could socialize after lunch)

construction costs   that portion of a project's costs related to construction; typically includes labor, material, equipment, services, contractor overhead and profit, and other direct construction costs; does not include soft costs; often referred to as "hard costs"

construction documents   drawings, specifications, and addenda for a specific construction project

construction management   involves various services ranging from structuring bidding documents to serving as the owner's representative during construction

construction manager   person or firm employed by the owner to provide construction management

construction reports   written documents that may be issued daily or at other intervals providing evidence of activities at the construction site; such documents provide historical records that may be used to settle legal disputes and general information to parties who do not have regular contact with the construction site

contingency fund   specific amount set aside in a project budget to pay for unanticipated costs (e.g., emergencies or change orders)

contractor   person offering to do work for a specified amount of money (e.g., an electrical contractor)

contract overrun   difference between original contract amount and the final amount paid if the latter is greater (e.g., due to change orders); contract underrun is used when the former is greater

contract payment bond   written form of security from a surety company submitted to the owner on behalf of a contractor or subcontractor, guaranteeing payment to all persons providing labor, materials, equipment, or services in accordance with the contract

contractor's option   written contract provision allowing the contractor to select specified materials, methods, or systems without altering the amount of compensation stated in the contract

convector	heat transfer surface designed to emit its heat to surrounding air largely or entirely by convection currents
cornice	part of the roof that projects from the wall
cost-plus-fee contract	service provider (e.g., architect or contractor) is reimbursed for direct and indirect costs plus a predetermined services fee (either a percent or a dollar amount)
CPM	acronym for critical path method; a scheduling program requiring a listing of tasks, sequencing of tasks, and estimated times for completing tasks
critical path	term used to designate activities that must be completed as scheduled to ensure completion of the entire project by a designated date
curb cuts	used in relation to barrier-free environments; a gentle slope in curbs allowing persons in wheelchairs to cross the curb
damper	movable plate that regulates the draft of a stove, a fireplace, or a furnace
debt-service fund	fund used to finance and account for payment of interest and principal on debts (e.g., retirement of bond obligations)
design architect	architect(s) actually doing the design work for a project
design development	typically, the phase following schematic development in which the architect(s) prepares drawings and other presentation documents to fix and describe the size and character of the entire project
double-hung window	window designed with two sashes, one made to raise and the other to lower
drain	means for carrying off wastewater; a sewer or other pipe used to convey ground, surface, or water; a conveyor of wastewater
drawings	term used to represent that portion of contract documents that graphically illustrate the design, location, and dimensions of the components and elements contained in a specific project
dry well	pit located on porous ground walled up with rock allowing water to seep through the pit; used for disposal of rainwater or effluent from a septic tank
eave	part of the roof that extends beyond the wall line
educational consultant	planning specialist who identifies educational needs for a school-facility project; usually a professor specializing in school-facility planning

educational specifications	document containing information about the intended uses of a school building (e.g., how instruction will occur, the scope of the curriculum, and so on); used by architects to design the school; also called educational-program statement
egress	the act, place, or means of exiting
elevation drawings	drawings of the front, sides, and rear faces of a building
eminent domain	right of a governmental agency to obtain private property either by a negotiated sale or by court action
enamel	paint comprised of a considerable portion of varnish; produces a hard, glossy surface
enrollment projection	mathematical estimate of future school enrollment; used to produce quantitative data used in facility planning
erosion	gradual wearing away of a substance such as soil by water
excavation	pit or hole formed by digging
expansion joints	designed break in walls, floors, or ceilings that permits expansions and contractions to occur without unduly damaging the structural integrity of the facility
face brick	brick used on the exterior of a building
fascia	vertical board nailed on the ends of rafters; part of a cornice
fenestration	arrangement, design, and proportioning of windows and doors within a building
field order	written order for a minor change or clarification in work not affecting the compensation or time provisions of a contract
final acceptance	action of the owner accepting the work from the contractor after the owner deems the work completed in accordance with the contract requirements and making final payments to the contractor
final inspection	final review of the project made by the contractor(s), architect, and owner (or owner's authorized representative) prior to issuing final certificates for payment
financial consultant	specialist who assists school districts in creating a plan to finance a long-term debt and assists in the sale of bonds; usually a professor specializing in school finance or a certified public accountant
fire door	door that is designed to remain intact in fires
fixed fee	set contract amount for all labor, materials, equipment, and services

fixture	receptacle attached to a plumbing system in which water and other waste may be collected until it is discharged into the plumbing system
flashing	sheet-metal work over windows and doors, installed to prevent water from seeping into the structure
floor plan	horizontal cut through a building showing rooms, partitions, windows, doors, and stairs
foot candle	a measurement of light equal to that emitted by a candle at a distance of one foot; a common reference point for lighting standards and codes
footings	that part of the building that is placed on soil of sufficient quality to bear the weight of the building
foundation	the base or lowest part of a structure
foyer	entrance hallway or lobby
friable	easily crumbled; used in relation to asbestos
GO bond	(general obligation bond) a bond secured by a pledge of the issuer's taxing power
grade	the level of the ground around the building
graphics	pictures, drawings, or other designs usually placed on interior walls in schools
HVAC	acronym used for heating, ventilation, and air-conditioning
IDEA	Individuals with Disabilities Act
inspection list	list prepared by the owner or owner's representative of work requiring immediate corrective or completion action by the contractor; also referred to as a punch list
invoice	statement sent from a vendor to a purchaser identifying items or services purchased and the amount of payment required
load-bearing walls	walls that are part of a building's structural system
locker bays	alcoves created to place student lockers in a specified area as opposed to dispersing them along hallway walls
lump-sum bid	bid containing one amount covering labor, equipment, materials, services, and overhead and profit
masonry	material such as brick, stone, or concrete block used in construction
multipurpose room	area in a school that serves multiple functions (e.g., an area in an elementary school that serves as a cafeteria and a gym)

natatorium	swimming pool
non-collusion affidavit	sworn statement indicating that a bidder has not conspired with other bidders to fix prices
nosing	rounded edge of a stair tread
open-space concept	term used to describe a school that does not have walls between classrooms
OSHA	acronym used to refer to the Occupational Safety and Health Act of 1970
outdoor learning lab	outdoor area used for teaching (e.g., wooded area used to teach science units)
panic bars	mechanisms placed on doors that release the hatch when pushed
PCCR	Pre-construction Coordination and Constructibility Review
penalty clause	contractual provision stipulating a penalty if conditions of the contract are not met (e.g., financial penalty incurred by a contractor for not completing work on time)
percolation tests	tests that determine the soil's ability to absorb liquids
performance bond	written form of insurance issued by a bonding company on behalf of a contractor guaranteeing payment in the event the contractor fails to perform contractual responsibilities
phased construction	building project completed in distinct phases; often used in renovation projects requiring that portions of a school building remain operational
progress payment	payment to a contractor based on the difference between the completed work and materials stored and a predetermined schedule of values or unit costs
project cost	all costs for a specific project including hard and soft costs
proposal	written statement from a bidder to provide specified services and/or materials for quoted prices
purchase order	written statement from a buyer to a seller specifying materials, services, equipment, or supplies to be purchased
radon	heavy radioactive gaseous element of the group of inert gases formed by disintegrating radium
reimbursables	expenses or costs that are to be reimbursed by the owner as stipulated by the terms of a contract with a contractor
resident architect	an architect assigned to provide ongoing supervision for a project; also referred to as the project architect

RFP   acronym used for request for proposal

safety glass   glass with plastic or wire laminated within to prevent splintering when damaged

safety report   a report issued after a scheduled safety inspection to be in compliance with OSHA

satellite food service   program where food is prepared at one site and delivered to and served at another site

schematics   preliminary drawing showing the general concepts, scale, and elevations proposed by the architect

site survey   geographic survey of a parcel of land designed to determine (a) the property's boundaries, (b) the existing gradients of the various slopes, and (c) possible obstructions

soft costs   costs not directly attributable to construction; examples include legal fees, insurance, land acquisition, and interest payments during construction

soil tests   borings and geotechnical laboratory tests of soil from a designated building site conducted to determine land suitability for structural designs

solar heat   heat transferring devise that relies on sunlight as an energy source

sq. ft. per pupil   term used to designate either a building's square feet divided by its design capacity or a building's square feet divided by its actual enrollment

stipulated sum agreement   same as lump-sum agreement

structural systems   load-bearing assembly of beams and columns on a foundation

subcontract   written agreement between a prime contractor and another contractor stipulating that the subcontractor will provide services and/or materials as set forth in the agreement

substructure   refers to the supporting part of a structure or a building's foundation

terrazzo   durable floor surface commonly found in schools (especially hallways) composed of marble chips and cement that is ground and polished

timely completion   term used to designate completing work on or before the scheduled date

topography   distinctive features of land

UBC   acronym used for the Uniform Building Code

visual contact	refers to the ability of a person in one area to see into another area
wainscot	lower part of a wall when finished with a material different from the remainder of the wall
working drawings	drawings that include plan and section views, dimensions, details, and notes allowing contractors to complete their work without instructions but subject to architect clarifications
work order	written order issued by the owner (or representative) of a contractual status requiring performance by a contractor and not subject to negotiation
zoned heating	system allowing heating to be controlled in a specific area of a building
zoning	restrictions placed on land within specific geographical areas that stipulate conditions for allowable building size, character, and uses; established by governmental agencies (e.g., zoning boards)

Author Index

Subject Index

About the Author and Contributor

THEODORE J. KOWALSKI is Kuntz Professor of Educational Administration at the University of Dayton.

T. C. CHAN is Associate Professor of Educational Leadership at Georgia Southern University.